Forensic Accounting and Fraud Investigation for Non-Experts

SECOND EDITION

Howard Silverstone
Michael Sheetz

WILEY
John Wiley & Sons, Inc.

For general information on our other products and services, or technical support, please contact our Customer Care Department within the United States at 800-762-2974, outside the United States at 317-572-3993 or fax 317-572-4002.

Wiley also publishes its books in a variety of electronic formats. Some content that appears in print may not be available in electronic books.

For more information about Wiley products, visit our Web site at www.wiley.com.

Library of Congress Cataloging-in-Publication Data:

Silverstone, Howard.
    Forensic accounting and fraud investigation for non-experts / Howard Silverstone, Michael Sheetz.—2nd ed.
        p.   cm.
    Includes bibliographical references and index.
    ISBN-13: 978-0-471-78487-6 (cloth)
    ISBN-10: 0-471-78487-7 (cloth)
        1. Fraud investigation.   2. Forensic accounting.   3. Fraud—Prevention.   I. Sheetz, Michael.   II. Title.
HV8079.F7S55 2007
363.25'963—dc22

                                                                                2006015452

Printed in the United States of America

10   9   8   7   6   5   4   3   2

This book is dedicated to my family for putting up with so many Sunday afternoons and late nights that I was enmeshed in the world of forensic accounting.

—Howard Silverstone

This book is dedicated to Susan Sheetz, my wife, whose tireless patience, endless encouragement, and unyielding optimism has made my life immeasurably better.

—Michael Sheetz

CONTENTS

ACKNOWLEDGMENTS

I would like to thank my long-time colleagues and friends for their support, especially Jim and Marie Stavros for helping me to realize the American dream! Thanks also to Kip Hamilton, Steve Butler and others for their insight and case examples. Extra special thanks to my wife Debbie, and my children, Jonathan, Alec, and Emma, for their support. Thanks also to my mother, Coba, for taking a 3,000-mile journey into the twenty-first century, and to my father, Nat, whose spirit is still so strong.

—Howard Silverstone

I would like to thank Dr. Grace Telesco, who provided invaluable editorial and organizational assistance during the preparation of this edition. Additionally, I would like to thank my colleagues in academia, law enforcement, and the court system, without whose comments, suggestions, and encouragement I would not have been able to complete this work. In particular, I owe Gladys Perez and Captain Richard Facchine an especially heartfelt thanks for all their support and encouragement.

—Michael Sheetz

PART I

FRAUD AND FORENSIC ACCOUNTING OVERVIEW

1

FRAUD IN SOCIETY

*"Yes! Finally captured Martha Stewart. You know, with all the massive
and almost completely unpunished fraud perpetrated on the American
public by such companies as Enron, Global Crossing, Tyco and Adelphia,
we finally got the ringleader. Maybe now we can lower the nation's
terror alert to periwinkle."*[1]

WHAT IS FRAUD?

Fraud is an activity that takes place in a social setting and has severe consequences for the economy, corporations, and individuals. It is an opportunis-
tic infection that bursts forth when greed meets the possibility of deception.
The fraud investigator is like the attending physician looking and listening for
the signs and symptoms that reveal an outbreak.

The Association of Certified Fraud Examiners defines occupational fraud
as: "The use of one's occupation for personal enrichment through the deliberate misuse or misapplication of the employing organization's resources or
assets."[2]

Before dealing with the accounting details and the investigation itself, we
introduce some attempts by the courts, law enforcement, and regulatory authorities to define fraud. Since the subject of this book is workplace fraud, we
then outline the nature of workplace fraud through a look at the accounting
cycle. We complete the tour with a look at the motives of fraudsters and the
consequences of their acts.

The modern definition of fraud is derived primarily from case and statute
law, but many of the ancient elements remain. Those roots can be traced to
fraus, a Latin noun carrying a wide range of meanings clustered around the

notions of harm, wrongdoing, and deceit. The modern definition derived from case law focuses on the intent of the fraudster(s) to separate the trusting victim from property or a legal right through deception for his or her own benefit. This deception involves any false or misleading words or actions or omissions or concealment of facts that will cause legal injury. Criminal prosecution of fraud must prove beyond a reasonable doubt that an act meeting the relevant legal definition of fraud has been committed by the accused. In civil cases, liability must be demonstrated on a balance of probabilities.

White-collar crime should be viewed as a subclass of fraud. Fraud includes confidence schemes, art forgery, falsified scientific research data, lying on a resume, and so on. White-collar crime, however, is committed by individuals embezzling, manipulating accounts, taking bribes, and so on at their place of business. What they all have in common, however, is the intent to deceive. This book limits its discussion to the field of white-collar crimes committed against businesses and their accounting systems and will not discuss consumer and other types of fraud. The forensic accounting techniques discussed below are central to the discovery of fraud in the business environment.

U.S. Supreme Court Definition of Civil Fraud

Fraud takes many forms, and the courts and other institutions have had a hard time finding a definition broad, yet specific, enough to give anything beyond a working definition. While there may not be one definitive all-encompassing definition, it is clear that the public and those not involved every day in its detection have a better understanding than perhaps even five years ago.

The U.S. Supreme Court in 1888 provided a definition of civil fraud as:

First: That the defendant has made a representation in regard to a material fact;

Second: That such a representation is false;

Third: That such representation was not actually believed by the defendant, on reasonable grounds, to be true;

Fourth: That it was made with intent that it should be acted on;

Fifth: That it was acted on by complainant to his damage; and

Sixth: That in so acting on it the complainant was ignorant of its falsity, and reasonably believed it to be true. The first of the foregoing requisites excludes such statements as consist merely in an expression of opinion of judgment, honestly entertained; and again excepting in peculiar cases, it excludes statements by the owner and vendor of property in respect of its value.[3]

FBI Definition of Fraud

The Federal Bureau of Investigation (FBI) offers a broad but useful definition of fraud that incorporates the elements recognized over the centuries:

> White-collar crimes are characterized by deceit, concealment, or violation of trust and are not dependent upon the application or threat of physical force or violence. Such acts are committed by individuals and organizations to obtain money, property, or services; to avoid the payment or loss of money or services; or to secure a personal or business advantage.[4]

Financial fraud, the subject of this book, is criminal fraud of the white-collar type. It is committed against businesses by both employees and outsiders such as vendors and contractors. Sadly, this type of crime has also gone beyond the typical "business" or commercial organization. Case in point is highlighted in a recent article entitled "Stealing from the Collection Plate," where it was noted, "Churches and religious groups are at greater risk for financial misconduct because of the nature of their missions and management structures."[5]

SEC Definition of Fraud

The U.S. Securities and Exchange Commission (SEC) has its own definition of fraud as it applies to transactions involving securities. Although the law governs securities, the principles invoked reiterate the constellation of ideas central to definitions of fraud with broader application. The Securities Exchange Act of 1934, Section 10b-5, states:

> It shall be unlawful for any person, directly or indirectly, by the use of any means or instrumentality of interstate commerce, or the mails, or of any facility of any national securities exchange,
>
> a) to employ any device, scheme, or artifice to defraud,
> b) to make any untrue statement of a material fact or to omit to state a material fact necessary in order to make the statements made, in the light of the circumstances under which they were made, not misleading, or

c) to engage in any act, practice, or course of business which operates or would operate as a fraud or deceit upon any person, in connection with the purchase or sale of any security.

TYPES OF FRAUD

White-collar fraud involves an intentional deception by employees, management, vendors, and customers to obtain money or other assets or services from a business. Some frauds are perpetrated by individuals and some in collusion across the management–employee social boundaries or between insiders and outsiders. The most useful way to classify the activity of the fraudster is to discuss briefly the five typical accounting cycles of any business where it will likely leave some kind of audit trail. The five cycles follow:

1. Sales and Collections
2. Purchases and Payments
3. Payroll and Personnel
4. Inventory and Warehousing
5. Capital Acquisition and Repayment

Sales and Collections Cycle

The sales and collections cycle bills clients for sales of goods and services and collects the money. This is the most cash-intensive of the five cycles. The most common frauds in this cycle are:

- Outright cash thefts
- Theft of other assets
- Kickbacks to customers
- Front-end frauds

Outright Cash Thefts Cash thefts are the easiest and most common type of fraud to perpetrate in this cycle and are usually carried out through unrecorded sales, underringing of sales, lapping schemes, and overbilling, among others.

Theft of Other Assets Assets can be stolen by ordering and shipping goods to an address other than that of the business.

Kickbacks to Customers In customer kickback schemes, the fraudster underbills the customer for merchandise and they split the difference or receivables are written off as uncollectible for a fee.

Front-End Frauds Front-end frauds are committed by the fraudster directing customers to take their business elsewhere or misappropriating a rebate.

Purchases and Payments Cycle

This cycle includes non-capital procurements and payments for goods, equipment, and services used in company operations. The buyer may act alone by setting up shell companies to receive goods misdirected from his company by false invoices. These schemes are often extremely complex and involve bank accounts, mail drops, and even corporate filings for the dummy entities. Procurement fraud is frequently a collusive employee–vendor fraud. The vendor will typically provide a bribe or kickback in return for business or, in the case of tendered contracts, for the employee to rig the bidding in favor of the fraudulent vendor. In another scheme, which may or may not be related to the original procurement scheme, once the vendor has been awarded the contract, the cost of the bribe may be recovered and profits increased by substituting products inferior to contract specifications, billing for work not done, shipping less than ordered, padding overhead expenses, and so on. Collusive fraud is the most common form of acquisition-and-payment fraud.

Payroll and Personnel Cycle

This cycle deals with hiring and termination, salaries, timekeeping, expense account reimbursements, and health and other types of employee insurance coverage. Common forms of fraud in this cycle are paying ghost employees, overstating hours worked, overstating expenses, and filing false medical claims. Employee and management fraud can overlap in this cycle, especially in the area of false expense account reports. An important but often overlooked area of personnel fraud is the improper vetting of job applicants. Collusion between a personnel department employee and a fraudster applicant could install a fraudster within the company with untold consequences.

Inventory and Warehousing Cycle

This cycle controls the purchase and storage of goods for later processing and sale or just for sale. The most common frauds in this cycle are ordering unneeded inventory and then stealing it for personal use; committing outright theft; and charging embezzlements occurring elsewhere in the company to inventory losses. These schemes can often become extremely complex and involve loading-dock workers, inventory accounting personnel, truck drivers, and receivers of stolen goods in other parts of the state or country.

Capital Acquisition and Repayment Cycle

This cycle accounts for debt and equity financing, interest, and dividend payments. The results of these transactions are reflected on the financial statements of the company. Because these accounts are developed at the executive level, this type of fraud is committed almost exclusively by management. The usual frauds are borrowing company money for personal use, misuse of interest income, and misuse of proceeds from financings.

Other Types of Financial Fraud

Some frauds that affect business often occur outside the typical accounting cycle. Customer fraud, for example, can severely affect insurance companies through filing of false applications and fraudulent claims, especially those for personal injury. Banks and other financial institutions suffer customer fraud through submission of false financial information on loan applications.

Management fraud deserves special mention in these days of corporate scandals. In addition to theft through the capital acquisition and repayment cycle, management can commit fraud through the manipulation of earnings reported on the financial statements prepared for shareholders and creditors. This type of fraud can affect the stock price, management bonuses, and the availability and terms of debt financing. Enron, WorldCom, Global Crossing, and many others are particularly egregious examples of management manipulation of the financial statements that enriched a few but caused the collapse of company pension plans, enormous losses to innocent shareholders, and unemployment for thousands of staff. These frauds have also contributed to the downfall of a major accounting firm (Arthur Andersen), a spate of suits against others, and the decline in the public's confidence in the accounting profession.

As we discuss later in this book, fraudsters often rationalize their deeds by claiming "I wasn't hurting anyone"—clearly, this is far from reality.

Recent Corporate Fraud in Perspective It is sometimes suggested that the size and complexity of the Enron, WorldCom, Global Crossing, and other cases mean we are living in a new era of fraud. What should we make of this suggestion? Is this a new phenomenon, or is it because we are in the age of "real-time" reporting (news hits us instantly, rather than when it isn't "new" anymore)? Instant news means instant reaction—the media searches for instant answers, perhaps before even those of us considered experts have had a chance to digest, reflect, and then comment.

Perhaps, rather than being trend-setting events, these scandals are merely the latest in a history of revelations that have always followed market excesses since the Dutch Tulip Mania of the 1630s.[6] The dot-com bubble of the late 1990s was no exception. The English polymath Walter Bagehot captured all the elements of excess in the following passage from *Lombard Street*, his 1873 critique of the English banking system:

> The mercantile community will have been unusually fortunate if during the period of rising prices it has not made great mistakes. Such a period naturally excites the sanguine and the ardent; they fancy that the prosperity they see will last always, that it is only the beginning of a greater prosperity. They altogether overestimate the demand for the article they deal in, or the work they do. They all in their degree—and the ablest and the cleverest the most—work much more than they should and trade far above their means. Every great crisis reveals the excessive speculations of many houses which no one before suspected, and which commonly indeed had not begun or had not carried very far those speculations, till they were tempted by the daily rising price and the surrounding fever.[7]

A Bit of Background The great bull markets of the twentieth century were all followed by revelations of malfeasance that only came to light after equity values had declined from heights unjustified by earnings growth rates and historical price-earnings multiples. When the Jazz Age ended in October 1929, the reputation of business executives was in just as much trouble as it is today. The shenanigans of the bigger players were ultimately exposed when the investigations of the Senate Committee on Banking and Currency in 1933–

1934 revealed the true behavior and ethics of the bankers and brokers in the previous decade. The practices of the great financiers of the day as presented in 12,000 pages of testimony were so shocking that the government felt it necessary to establish the Securities and Exchange Commission in 1934 to regulate the financial industry.

Richard Whitney, head of his own investment firm and five times president of the New York Stock Exchange, proved to be an exceptionally poor businessman. He borrowed $30 million from his friends, relatives, and accounts in his trust and owed $6.5 million at the time he declared bankruptcy. He served three years and four months of a five- to ten-year sentence for misusing funds from his father-in-law's estate.

The More Things Change . . . We may have short memories, but let's just go back to the bull market of the mid-1980s, which was a time of merger mania and the heyday of the junk bond market. The *crime du jour* was insider trading. The investment banker Drexel Burnham Lambert collapsed, and Denis Levine, Ivan Boesky, Michael Milken, and others went to jail.

Perhaps we can learn from previous experience to avoid overlooking possibilities of fraud into the future. Look no further than www.theprosand thecons.com, a speakers' bureau that employs experts and ex-cons to help companies avoid and detect fraud. Fraudster-turned-consultant Frank Abagnale has spent the past 30 years working with the FBI and lecturing on fraudtechniques. Abagnale was the subject of the 2002 movie *Catch Me If You Can*. Comments director Steven Spielberg, "I did not make this film about Frank Abagnale because of what he did . . . but because of what he has done with his life the past 30 years."[8]

Sarbanes-Oxley The purpose of the Sarbanes-Oxley Act of 2002 was to provide investors with greater confidence in American corporations and allow them to rely on financial statements as an accurate representation of the financial condition of the companies in which they are stakeholders. The Act was a response to the revelations of lax auditing practices and conflicts of interest between auditors and their clients.

This book will not discuss Sarbanes-Oxley in great detail, as much has been written about it elsewhere. However, what is key is to look at the Act's effect and how its effectiveness is perceived.

In its "2005 Oversight Systems Report on Corporate Fraud," Oversight Systems[9] surveyed certified fraud examiners "to report the trends, risks and major concerns that businesses face today." Oversight noted that while most examiners saw Sarbanes-Oxley as an effective tool, "few think it will change the culture of business leaders." That is a very telling comment. Whether we discuss the Dutch Tulip Mania, the heady days of insider trading, or recent corporate scandals, what we need to realize is that perhaps we cannot stop fraud from happening, but we can limit the vehicles that allow it. We discuss later in this book Business as a Vehicle; most worrying is that similar to automobiles, when one model becomes obsolete, another is sure to follow. Just because certain types of business scandals are behind us, this does not mean new methods will not ensue.

WHAT THE NUMBERS TELL US ABOUT FRAUD

Comprehensive concrete and official fraud statistics are hard to come by because government agencies and industry groups tend to keep records only of those frauds that affect their area(s) of interest.

We must also remember that all fraud statistics are based on known frauds. What is most unnerving is the fact that the numbers quoted are considered to be only the tip of the iceberg. Aside from the many undetected frauds are those frauds not reported by the harmed organization for fear of embarrassment. Many organizations would rather complete an investigation and move on, than bring to public light the full extent of a fraud perpetrated against them.

Notwithstanding the uncertainty of the true extent of financial fraud, there are studies that shed light on the enormous impact.

Study: Association of Certified Fraud Examiners

For purposes of this book, the best overview of financial fraud comes from studies done by the Association of Certified Fraud Examiners (ACFE). In 1996, the ACFE published *Report to the Nation on Occupational Fraud and Abuse* based on occupational fraud cases reported by its members. In its 2004 *Report to the Nation on Occupational Fraud and Abuse*, the results were based on a study of 508 cases reported by the Certified Fraud Examiners (CFE) who investigated them.[10] These reported cases resulted in over $761 million of losses. The ACFE estimates that applied to the Gross Domestic Product, this translates to approximately $660 billion in total losses. This is a significant increase over the $400 million estimated to have been lost in 1996 when the first report was written.

Small-Business Fraud

According to the ACFE study, "small businesses suffer disproportionately large losses due to occupational fraud and abuse." The median loss for these businesses was $98,000, which was higher than for all but the very largest companies.

Frauds committed by owners and executives caused a median loss of $900,000, six times higher than losses caused by managers and 14 times higher than losses caused by employees. However, the study added that companies are less likely to take legal action against owners than against employees.

Additionally, only 12 percent of fraudsters in the study had previous convictions for a fraud-related offense. To reiterate what we said earlier, one should keep in mind that, although the billion-dollar scandals at Enron, World-Com, and other corporations have splashed onto the front pages in recent times, it is the slow, steady drip, drip, drip of fraudulent activity at small businesses that is larger in aggregate and potentially does the greater damage to the economy over the long run. Also, while you may make one vehicle obsolete, newer generations of fraudsters will create new models to perpetrate their crimes.

Categories of Occupational Fraud

The ACFE divides occupational fraud into three broad categories:[11]

1. Asset misappropriation
2. Corruption
3. Fraudulent statements

Asset Misappropriation Asset misappropriations are the theft or misuse of assets and account for 90 percent of all occupational fraud in the study. It is pointed out in the study that these schemes have the lowest median loss ($93,000), while fraudulent statements, the subject of much news surrounding WorldCom et al., only occurred in 7.9 percent of the reported frauds, but had the highest median loss at $1 million.

Cash thefts usually occur in three different ways:

1. Fraudulent disbursements
2. Skimming
3. Cash larceny

FRAUDULENT DISBURSEMENTS Fraudulent disbursements use some device such as false invoices or timecards to create a false payment obligation for a company. It is the most common type of cash fraud, accounting for 74.1 percent of the studied cases and creating a mean loss of $125,000.

Fraudulent disbursements break down into five principal types:

1. *Billing:* Fraudulent billing schemes accounted for 52.1 percent of fraudulent disbursements and created a median loss of $140,000.
2. *Check tampering:* Check tampering made up 31.3 percent, with a median loss of $155,000.
3. *Expense reimbursement:* Expense reimbursements comprised 22.1 percent of schemes and caused a median loss of $92,000.
4. *Payroll:* Payroll schemes represented 19.6 percent of cases studied, and the median loss was $90,000.
5. *Register disbursement:* Register disbursements made up only 4.3 percent, with the smallest median loss of the group at $18,000.

SKIMMING Skimming is the theft of cash during its collection but *before* it is recorded on the company books. Skimming occurred in 28.2 percent of the cash frauds and showed an $85,000 mean loss.

CASH LARCENY Cash larceny is the theft of cash *after* it has been recorded. This form of fraud accounted for 23.9 percent of the cases, with a mean loss of $80,000.

Drawing Conclusions

Returning to the Oversight Systems survey, 52 percent of those surveyed believed Sarbanes-Oxley has been effective in helping identify instances of financial statement fraud. Remember, Sarbanes-Oxley relates solely to public companies. However, the survey also revealed that 67 percent of those surveyed believed institutional fraud is more prevalent today than five years ago. Put this fact together with our previously noted fact from the ACFE study that frauds committed by owners and executives are six times higher than losses caused by managers and 14 times higher than losses caused by employees, and the conclusion is still worrying.

As noted in the Oversight Systems study, by Dana Hermanson of Kennesaw State University, "the risk of financial statement fraud is real and not going away." Sadly, the risk of financial fraud by any method is real and not going away.

Society's Perception of Fraud

Until recent years, and the full realizable impact of WorldCom, et al., through the loss of jobs and life savings, and the impact on at least one major accounting firm and countless others, fraud was often perceived as a victimless crime. Governments and businesses were seen as so wealthy that the money taken by fraud wouldn't be missed. "They can afford it," is the classic rationalization heard in confessions. Fraud is also viewed as an easy way to get money without running the risk of severe punishment. Dismissal is certainly a possibility, but many employers will, in fact, try to hush up news that they have been defrauded for fear of adverse publicity with their customers, vendors, bankers, and insurers.

In a recent PricewaterhouseCoopers (PwC) survey, the number of companies reporting fraud globally has increased from 37 percent to 45 percent in the past two years.[12] Said one PwC representative, "Deterrents aren't sufficiently strong because too many white collar crimes seldom result in conviction." Despite the public outrage caused by Enron and others, it would seem many of these crimes are still under the radar and escaping the light of day.

If, as noted earlier, $660 billion in revenues is diverted annually by fraudsters, then $660 billion will never work its way through to shareholders' equity and increase the wealth of the national industrial base. Since most fraud occurs at small, and thus more vulnerable, businesses, the risk is greater that it can cause bankruptcy with its consequent costs to vendors and lenders and unemployment for company staff. A lifetime of building respect in business, in the community, and with the family can be destroyed when a trusted employee who felt protected by a reputation for honesty is exposed as a fraudster.

Fraud is far from benign. As fraudsters take advantage of technology, fraud becomes more sophisticated. It can no longer be characterized solely as employee theft for personal benefit. It is international. An American businessman who was the victim of a Nigerian letter scam went to Lagos to check on his "investment" and was murdered for his troubles.[13] The line between individuals stealing for themselves and fraud as part of organized crime is getting harder and harder to draw. Ruthless Russian gangs have been discovered behind corporations boasting respectable boards of directors that are actually set up to launder money and create stock frauds. As regulators close the traditional charities and other fronts used to raise money, terrorists are turning to identity, mortgage, and other types of fraud to raise the money needed to attack U.S. interests. Today the occupational fraud uncovered at a small company could be part of something much larger.

Who Commits Fraud?—Profile of the Typical Fraudster

Despite enormous scandals such as Watergate, the Iran-Contra Affair, the Savings and Loan debacle, the Wall Street insider trading exposé, the collapse of the Bank of Credit and Commerce International (BCCI), and Barings Bank, white-collar crime has not been subjected to as much research as other types of crime.[14] The lack of research on crimes of this type has resulted in a paucity of research on the criminals. The small number of prosecutions and subsequent convictions further hampers such research. In this respect, corporations work against their own best interests when they refuse to prosecute employees because of a fear of adverse publicity. The result is a lack of the raw material for academic study that could lead to a better understanding of the white-collar criminal and development of better hiring and prevention policies.

Despite the deficiencies in gathering evidence and developing theory, several studies have been done that show some consistency. For those of us who write and speak regularly on the subject of financial fraud, in general terms we typically describe the perpetrator as someone who has experience, is placed in a position of trust, and who will have to be in a position of having the opportunity to commit the crime.

The 2004 ACFE study shows that 67.8 percent of the perpetrators were employees, 34 percent were managers, and 12.4 owner/executives. The findings of Weisburd et al. showed that men in the 40–50 age group with high school or less education and working alone committed most frauds. The largest amounts, however, were stolen by university-educated older men with no criminal records who were in positions of financial responsibility and perpetrating the frauds in collusion. Dishonest managers and executives working alone caused median losses of $250,000, or about 4.2 times the $60,000 stolen by lower-level employees operating by themselves. When executives and managers colluded with employees, however, the median loss jumped to $500,000, or double what executives and managers stole on their own and 8.3 times what employees stole on *their* own. Since management is responsible for the application of controls to detect fraud, the involvement of management makes detection more difficult and the fraud potentially more devastating for the company.

Women commit just about as many frauds as men, but the median amount is smaller. Fraud, too, has its "glass ceiling"! Most executive and managerial positions are still held by men, and their opportunities to steal large sums are greater. Fraudulent acts by women seem to increase as one descends the occupational hierarchy. The activity of women is especially marked at the clerical levels of the financial industry.[15] One can reasonably expect that the admission of greater numbers of women to positions of power will result in a more equitable balance in the gender statistics.[16]

Men over 60 also stole more than 27 times the median $18,000 taken by persons under 26 years of age, despite the fact that the older group accounted for only 2.5 percent of the cases studied, while the younger group accounted for 6.0 percent. In fact, one can conclude from this study that the median amounts taken vary directly with age.

Frauds by persons with university education are less frequent but involve larger median amounts than those committed by persons with only high school or below. Once again, this reflects the fact that educated people tend to rise to higher levels of responsibility and thus control larger amounts of money.

Perhaps the most disturbing statistic in the ACFE study is the one showing that only 12 percent of fraudsters had previous convictions for a fraud-related offense, which means 88 percent of the frauds were committed by persons who had never been charged with or convicted of any previous crime. This is consistent with Romney et al. and Weisburd et al., who discovered no sociopathic behavior patterns in the fraudsters studied in their research.

Crisis Responders and Opportunity Takers

What, then, makes a person commit that one act that turns a respectable citizen into a criminal? How does a person who does not have the statistical profile of the common criminal form the intent to break the law? Weisburd and Waring identify two broad classes of offender: crisis responders and opportunity takers. The crimes of the crisis responders "seem to be situational responses to real stress or crisis in their professional or personal lives." The crimes of the opportunity takers seem to be "linked strongly to some unusual or special set of opportunities that suddenly materialize for the offender."[17]

The crisis responders were people in positions of trust who saw a criminal act as the way out of a perceived financial crisis. These events were anomalies in their social histories. The women acted to pay family bills, and the men stepped over the line for a variety of reasons, such as financial troubles at the company they owned or to reduce their income taxes payable.

The opportunity takers were not driven to commit a crime by financial pressures; they were drawn in by the temptation created by an unusual opportunity. Many of these events were isolated wrong choices. This group, however, also includes those recruited into conspiracies operating in permissive environments. Once involved, these offenders become socialized into criminal activity that can last for years or even decades. The offense for which they suffered their one arrest was, in fact, often one long, systematic criminal activity.

The commission of a crime requires a place that connects opportunity and victim. The most harm is done by officers and managers colluding with others in ways that exploit an organization for which they work. This is the quintessential middle-class crime. Owners and sole proprietors may be from a higher social class, but the businesses they control are usually too small to permit the magnitude of the thefts possible from large corporations. Others of high social status, such as doctors and lawyers, rarely commit large complex crimes. Exceptions are those doctors who open clinics to exploit Medicaid.

It is the officers and managers who hold their positions in large companies through education and hard work rather than birth who have the opportunities to commit the big frauds. This is because they command the accounting systems as well as the controls that should safeguard those same systems. These crimes are most frequently collusive because their commission requires an assembly of skills capable of exploiting the complexity of the corporate structure.

Detection

In the ACFE's 2004 survey, approximately 40 percent of cases are initially detected by tip, approximately 24 percent by internal audit, 21 percent by accident, 18 percent by internal controls, 11 percent by external audit, and 1 percent notified by police.

Since the victims of white-collar crime rarely know anything has happened at the time the action occurred, often a long lag develops between the commission of a crime and its discovery and report. The ACFE notes that the majority of tips came from employees (almost 60 percent), along with tips from customers (20 percent), vendors (16 percent), and anonymous tips (13 percent).

In the recent PwC study noted earlier, internal audit was disclosed as the most successful of all processes in the management of fraud. Matching this study with the ACFE, which showed internal audit accounting for 24 percent of initial detection, should give us a pretty good clue as to where resources should perhaps be spent in organizations. However, for every point in the world of fraud detection, there is a counterpoint, and many smaller business owners will tell you their organization is too small for an internal audit department and they cannot afford such a luxury. Perhaps this then ties in with the fact that companies with fewer than 100 employees accounted for almost 46 percent of cases in the ACFE study, the largest group in the study. Companies with over 10,000 employees accounted for just over 13 percent, the smallest group in the survey.

Motivations for Fraud

In a 2001 article, "The Psychology of Fraud,"[18] the authors noted that fraud, "like other crime, can best be explained by three factors: a supply of motivated offenders, the availability of suitable targets and the absence of capable guardians—control systems or someone to mind the store."

Financial motivators obviously have a big impact on the cause of financial crime. These can range from an employee with an inability to pay her domestic bills to a senior executive under financial strain because he knows that market factors have adversely affected the business and analysts will be watching the latest results with eagerness. In this case, the strain may go beyond pure financial impact, but also to stature and reputation. Take the recent case of Computer Associates and its former CEO, Sanjay Kumar, and two other company executives. The government's indictment noted, "Computer Associates prematurely recognized $2.2 billion in revenue in FY 2000 and FY 2001 and more than $1.1 billion in premature revenue in prior quarters." The government also noted that "the SEC alleges that from 1998 to 2000, Computer Associates routinely kept its books open to record revenue from contracts executed after the quarter ended in order to meet Wall Street quarterly earnings estimates."[19] Computer Associates agreed to settlements with the SEC and the Justice Department to the tune of $225 million and agreed to reform its financial accounting controls.

Some theorists have taken a big-picture approach and argued that white-collar crime is the inevitable outcome of the competitive ethic of capitalism. According to this theory, competition is the field on which egotism and recklessness can have full play.[20] We are constantly bombarded by images of the wealth and success that can be achieved through winning in the great experiment in social Darwinism in which we live. The inevitable result of such competition is the recognition of the economic inequality of winners and losers, which can be internalized as the constant fear of failing. This discontent may be sufficient to make a person see white-collar crime as the great equalizing act. The drive for money and the trappings of success are, therefore, the motivators of the act.[21]

Recent theorizing has shifted the focus to the situation in which the crime is committed. This newer thinking does not dismiss the role of personal history, which is so important in the creation of the street criminal, but questions its explanatory power. It raises the question of why certain people commit certain crimes in certain situations. This is a useful line of theorizing since it allows the criminal act to be conceptually distinguished from the criminal's life story and explained as the pursuit of short-term gratification and not the culmination of a long history of personal disadvantage.

The situation in which the potential white-collar offender finds him- or herself plays a most significant role in determining whether a crime will be committed. The corporate culture lived daily at the workplace can often create enormous pressures to commit criminal acts. Examples are common in the famous cases of price-fixing, bribery, and manufacture of dangerous products that occurred throughout the last century.[22] A corrupt corporate culture can lead to the inversion of all values. The comfort of conformity then becomes the Achilles' heel of the middle-class person under pressure to "go along to get along." Loyalty can easily slip into complicity. Criminal behavior becomes normal. Team-playing becomes conspiracy. Fear of dismissal, ostracism, or losing the favor of superiors can be compelling forces in the world of a department or small company. In such an atmosphere, one learns criminal behavior "in association with those who define such behavior favorably," as Sutherland contended.[23]

These acts cannot be explained by a personal history of instability and deviance since stability and conformity are the principal characteristics of these criminals' lives. Even while committing the crimes, white-collar offenders are able to lead their conventional lives, which are, indeed, their camouflage. Their conventionality and stability are the foundation of the trustworthiness that gives them the opportunity to commit the crime in the first place. It is this life of conventionality that gives the criminal act the character of an aberration.

It is, however, the white-collar criminals' power of rationalization that is one of the most amazing aspects of their behavior. They are able to behave normally and aberrantly at the same time without feeling conflict. This behavior is possible through the use of techniques of "neutralization."[24] These are acts of mental deftness that allow persons to violate behavioral norms without simultaneously seeing themselves as deviant or criminal. Such self-exculpating explanations can occur both before and after the commission of a criminal act.

The most common rationalization noted several times already in this chapter is that financial crimes do not hurt other people. Embezzlers commonly tell themselves they are merely "borrowing" the money and intend to return it later without anyone else being affected. Many embezzlers justify it because they had to do it to pay mounting family bills. "Everybody's doing it" is frequently heard as an argument for systematic wrongful company behavior. Corporate offenders often consider laws as an unjust or unnecessary form of government interference disrupting free market forces. They may even argue that breaking the law was necessary for the survival of the company.

Employees frequently offer a moral justification for their thefts with the argument that their employer "owed" them the money. Fraud simply expressed their grievance. For example, they feel exploited and underpaid or hurt after receiving a smaller-than-expected bonus. Many feel justified after being passed over for promotion; others feel they can do the job just as well as, if not better than, the person with the higher education. Personal antipathies, anger after a reprimand from the boss, and the like can all be self-serving explanations for fraud. Such a sense of being wronged, whether justified or not, can fester for years before developing into a plan to defraud.

In rare cases, mental illness can drive a person to commit fraud through a wish to damage the company. Others can be motivated by pure egotism; they commit fraud just to show how smart they are. Yet others are driven by anti-capitalist ideologies and think they are destroying the system from within.

Summary

It would appear from everything said thus far that the white-collar criminal is more like Mr. and Ms. Average than like the common street criminal. It remains a mystery why these outwardly normal and respectable people commit white-collar crimes. We still cannot answer the question why the bank clerk with too much personal debt decides to embezzle instead of seeking credit counseling. No one can say why the opportunity takers decide to commit and rationalize a crime when they have never before sought out criminal opportunities to better themselves. What tips these people in the one direction rather than the other? No one knows.

THE SOCIAL CONSEQUENCES OF ECONOMIC CRIME

Economic crime is an enormous social problem whose consequences are often not fully realized by the public at large. The *2004 Report to the Nation on Occupational Fraud and Abuse* of the Association of Certified Fraud Examiners estimated that fraud would cost the American economy $660 billion, or 6 percent of gross domestic production (GDP). These amounts represent only the known amounts stolen directly by the fraudsters and do not measure the ripple effect that can engulf whole companies, employees, vendors, suppliers, and banks. The trickle-down effect of Enron, WorldCom, and others has become familiar to us all.

At the ACFE's 15th Annual Conference in Las Vegas, NV, July 2004, Bernard Katz, CFE, CPA, noted that "the WorldCom scandal has taught the world many things. It's also a classic study of what not to do in the corporate world when it comes to financial records and how to avoid disaster."[25]

In a recent *Washington Post* survey, a variety of experts (accountants, chief executives, and others) completed a corporate governance report card. Their conclusion was that "the ingredients for a similar financial disaster remain."[26] According to former SEC Chairman, Harvey Pitt, "many shareholders may have been led to believe that [reforms] have cured all the problems and we're home free. Unfortunately, that's a prescription for disaster." The article also noted the U.S. Chamber of Commerce and others complaining that boards and accountants spend too much time meeting meaningless criteria rather than getting to the root of the more insidious problems."

The previously noted Oversight Systems survey seems to echo this sentiment. "The findings of this survey foreshadow a real need for continued vigilance among executives toward institutional fraud" according to Patrick Taylor, CEO of Oversight Systems. As we said earlier in this chapter, the more things change . . .

SUGGESTED READINGS

www.ftc.gov/reports/Fraud/execsum.htm.

www.bizstats.com/numberbizs.htm.

Bagehot, Walter. *Lombard Street*. New York: Scribner, Armstrong & Co., 1873. New ed., London: Smith Elder & Co., 1915. Rpt., New York: Arno Press, 1978.

Brooks, John. *The Go-Go Years*. New York: Weybright & Talley, 1973.

Coalition Against Insurance Fraud., www.insurancefraud.org/news/study021303_set.html.

Coleman, James William. *The Criminal Elite*. New York: St. Martin's Press, 1989.

Croall, Hazel. *Understanding White Collar Crime*. Philadelphia: Open University Press, 2001.

Galbraith, J.K. *The Great Crash of 1919*. Boston: Houghton Mifflin, 1979.

Levi, M. *The Prevention of Fraud*. Crime Prevention Unit, Paper 17. London: HMSO. In Hazel Croall, *Understanding White Collar Crime*. Philadelphia: Open University Press, 2001.

Pecora, Ferdinand. *Wall Street under Oath*. New York: Simon & Schuster, 1939.

Romney, Marshall B., W. Steve Albrecht, and David J. Cherrington. "Red-Flagging the White-Collar Criminal." *Management Accounting* (March 1980): 51–57.

Rosenmerkel, Sean P. "Wrongfulness and Harmfulness as Components of Seriousness of White-Collar Offenses." *Journal of Contemporary Criminal Justice*, 17, no. 4 (November 2001): 308–327.

Shlegel, Kip, and David Weisburd. *White-Collar Crime Reconsidered*. Boston: Northeastern University Press, 1992.

Shover, Neal, and John Paul Wright, eds. *Crimes of Privilege: Readings in White-Collar Crime*. New York: Oxford University Press, 2001.

Sutherland, Edwin H. *White Collar Crime*. New York: Holt, Rinehart & Winston, 1949.

Sutherland, Edwin H. "White-Collar Criminality." *American Sociological Review*, 4, no. 1 (February 1949): 1–12. Rpt. in Neal Shover and John Paul Wright, eds., *Crimes of Privilege: Readings in White-Collar Crime*. New York: Oxford University Press, 2001, pp. 4–11.

Sykes, Gresham M., and David Matza. "Techniques of Neutralization: A Theory of Delinquency." *American Sociological Review*, 22 (December 1957): 667–670.

2002 Report to the Nation: Occupational Fraud and Abuse.

www.cfenet.com/pdfs/2002RttN.pdf.

2004 Report to the Nation on Occupational Fraud and Abuse.

www.cfenet.com.

Weisburd, David, and Elin Waring with Ellen F. Chayet. *White-Collar Crime and Criminal Careers*. Cambridge: Cambridge University Press, 2001.

Weisburd, David, Stantton Wheeler, Elin Waring, and Nancy Bode. *Crimes of the Middle Classes: White-Collar Offenders in the Federal Courts*. New Haven, CT: Yale University Press, 1991.

Wheeler, Stanton. "The Problem of White-Collar Crime Motivation." In Kip Shlegel and David Weisburd, *White-Colar Crime Reconsidered.* Boston: Northeastern University Press, 1992, pp. 108–123.

White Collar Crime: A Report to the Public. U.S. Department of Justice, Federal Bureau of Investigation. Washington, DC: U.S. Government Printing Office, 1989, p. 3. Cited in Cynthia Barnett, *The Measurement of White-Collar Crime Using Uniform Crime Reporting (UCR) Data.* www.fbi.gov/ucr/whitecollarforweb.pdf.

NOTES

1. Jon Stewart, comedian and actor, http://en.thinkexist.com/quotations/fraud/.
2. *2004 Report to the Nation on Occupational Fraud and Abuse.* www.cfenet.com.
3. *Southern Development Co. v. Silva,* 125 U.S. 247, 8 S. C. Rep. 881, 31 L. Ed. (1888).
4. Federal Bureau of Investigation: *Facts and Figures 2003,* http://www.fbi.gov/libref/factsfigure/wcc.htm.
5. Herbert Snyder, Ph.D, CFE; and James Clifton, MA, CPA, CFE, *Fraud* magazine, December 2005, published by the Association of Certified Fraud Examiners.
6. The prices of tulips and the practice of tulip speculation became so extreme that the States of Holland passed a statute in 1637 curbing this activity!
7. Walter Bagehot, *Lombard Street* (New York: Scribner, Armstrong & Co., 1873; new ed., London: Smith Elder & Co., 1915; rpt., New York: Arno Press, 1978).
8. www.abagnale.com/index2.asp.
9. www.oversightsystems.com.
10. www.cfenet.com/.
11. www.cfenet.com/.
12. www.eaststandard.net/print/news.php?articleid=35927.
13. The intended victim of this scam typically receives a letter purporting to be from a Nigerian official who needs to use the victim's bank account to move millions of dollars out of Nigeria. The letter requests the victim's address and bank account numbers on the promise of a share usually between 15 and 30 percent of the amount.
14. Hazel Croall, *Understanding White Collar Crime* (Philadelphia: Open University Press, 2001), p. 5.
15. Ibid., p. 55.
16. Ibid., p. 56.
17. Weisburd and Waring, *White-Collar Crime and Criminal Careers*, p. 58.
18. Grace Duffield and Peter Grabosky, *Psychology of Fraud*, Australian Institute of Criminology, www.aic.gov.au/publications/tandi/ti199.pdf.
19. www.sec.gov/news/press/2004-134.htm.
20. James William Coleman, *The Criminal Elite* (New York: St. Martin's Press, 1989), p 211 ff.

21. For an interesting attempt to combine microeconomics, psychology, and risk analysis into a motivational theory, see: Stanton Wheeler, "The Problem of White-Collar Crime Motivation," in Kip Shlegel and David Weisburd, *White-Collar Crime Reconsidered* (Boston: Northeastern University Press, 1992), pp. 108–123.

22. Coleman, *The Criminal Elite*, passim.

23. Sutherland, *White Collar Crime*, p. 234.

24. Gresham M. Sykes and David Matza, "Techniques of Neutralization: A Theory of Delinquency," *American Sociological Review*, 22 (December 1957): 667–670, cited in Coleman, *The Criminal Elite*, p. 211.

25. Bernard Katz, CFE, CPA, "Preventing and Detecting Financial Statement Fraud."

26. http://seattletimes.nwsource.com/html/businesstechnology/2002800032_corpfraud12.html.

2

UNDERSTANDING THE BASICS
OF FINANCIAL ACCOUNTING

INTRODUCTION

*The company accountant is shy and retiring. He's shy a quarter
of a million dollars. That's why he's retiring.*[1]

Clearly we have seen in Chapter 1 that despite its increased exposure, better
corporate governance, and general increased awareness, financial fraud is not
going away. While financial fraud includes the increasing problem of identity theft and other nontraditional crimes, our focus here remains on the use
of accounting systems and circumventing controls to achieve financial
gain.

No forensic investigation can be undertaken without some knowledge of
accounting principles. So much of the media coverage of the recent events involving Enron, WorldCom, Computer Associates, and others has focused on
manipulation of financial results. The financial crimes perpetrated on smaller
companies, as evidenced by the ACFE survey, included fraudulent disbursements, where funds are disbursed through false invoices or forging company
checks; skimming, where cash is stolen before it ever gets recorded; and cash
larceny, where cash is stolen after it is recorded. Even if you are not examining a company's books and records yourself, you may well be talking to the
people who are and need to know how an accounting system works in order
to understand their language. The purpose of this chapter is to introduce you

to some fundamental concepts that will show you how money moves through a corporation and how business transactions should be recorded.

Accounting is a method of tracking business activities in a particular time period (whether it be a week, a month, or a year). Such tracking is needed internally for owners and decision makers to have timely information on the performance of their business. Although most savvy business owners may have day-to-day control over their business, as companies grow larger and their business becomes more complex, the need for more detailed information increases. However, as recent events have shown, people on the outside of a business also need financial information. Their need for information results from the relationship they have with the particular company. An investor will want to know about results and the company's financial stability. Similarly, a creditor will want to know if his debt is likely to be paid, and a potential investor or vendor will need information on the company before moving forward in a financial relationship.

As we will see throughout this book, many corporate frauds are described as crimes committed within the accounting system of various companies. The accounting system comprises the methods by which companies record transactions and financial activities. It tracks the business activity of an entity and is usually categorized as recording data (i.e., the initial entry into the company's records), classifying information into related items, and then summarizing the data for the end user to readily understand.

Although internal fraud has historically centered on manipulation of accounting entries, recent events have been focused more directly on financial statements and the manipulation of the underlying data. From an early age, accountants are taught that the financial statements are a "snapshot," one point in time to capture the profitability (or unprofitability) and financial position of an entity. The balance sheet should convey the financial position of the business at one point in time (e.g., at the company's year-end), listing the company's assets and liabilities, together with the company's equity.

The concept of the balance sheet comprises what is known as the accounting equation—the fact that assets always equal liabilities plus equity. The father of double-entry bookkeeping, Luca Pacioli, who developed the accounting process in the late fifteenth century, believed that one should not sleep until the debits equaled the credits. The facts alone from Chapter 1 clearly should cause us to lose sleep over the propriety of what is underlying those debits and credits!

THE FIVE ACCOUNTING CYCLES

To understand how fraud occurs within businesses is to understand how the cycles work within an accounting system. Specifically, the cycles are defined as:

1. Sales and Accounts Receivable
2. Payments/Expenses and Accounts Payable
3. Human Resources and Payroll
4. Inventory and Storage/Warehousing
5. Capital Expenditures

Sales and Accounts Receivable

The fundamental concept of any business involves getting business from customers, billing for those goods or services, and then making sure the accounts receivable are collected. In terms of the accounting equation and accounting cycle, the revenues from sales appear on a company's income statement, and the respective accounts receivable appear on the balance sheet. Cash sales would directly affect the cash balance, which is also a balance sheet item.

Within this part of the cycle are steps that a business must undertake to minimize its financial risk. These steps include approval potential for credit before entering into a business relationship; having a system for receiving orders from the customers and then invoicing them; and then collecting the amounts owed from the customers, along with the appropriate system for making adjustments to the account for returns, write-offs, and so on.

Fundamental within this accounting cycle are the safeguards put in place by a company—the internal controls to minimize the opportunity for theft or misappropriation. While no different than other aspects of the accounting cycle, it is relevant to note them here. At the same time, the concept behind these controls is similar for all cycles. Specifically:

- *Separation of duties.* This is a fundamental concept of accounting and one through which companies can prevent a lot of frauds by properly segregating the functions of custody, authorization, and recordkeeping. For the sales and accounts receivable cycle, this would apply to separating the credit function and sales function (thereby minimizing the chances of granting credit to an unsuitable potential customer in order to force a sale). Similarly, sales recording and receipt of cash should also be separated.

- *Physical safeguards of assets.* On the most basic level, this should involve restriction of access to computers by specific password, physical locks, and the use of, for example, lock boxes for customers to mail checks, instead of check and cash handling by company employees.

- *Audit trail* (i.e., adequate and proper documentation of transactions). As with other cycles, the need for adequate documentation in an accounting system is fundamental. At a minimum, this should include prenumbered documents for sales orders, shipping documents, sales invoices, credit memos, and remittance advices (or a computer system that assigns numbers as printed, but with sufficient controls over access limited by specific passwords for users).

- *Approval process.* This process extends to credit approval, write-off approval, and the shipment of products.

- *Independent checks on the system* (whether by an internal audit function or an outside source). While many companies have an internal audit function, others do not consider themselves large enough for such a system. In both cases, the organization needs to have adequate awareness that there is some kind of independent monitoring. This should, at a minimum, include independent preparation of bank and other account reconciliations, supervision, and perhaps the use of an outside accountant as an additional monitor.

Case Study: Accounts Receivable Fraud

The bookkeeper of a small but growing bread company prepared bills to be sent to customers and was responsible for collecting payments. Sales were growing through the acquisition of new customers and increasing sales to existing ones. A surprise internal audit revealed, however, that bank deposits were not as large as would have been expected considering the rate of sales growth. An examination of customer copies of sales invoices revealed that the amounts being billed were higher than the amounts being recorded in the cash receipts journal (see below for a discussion of journals) for the same transaction. Office copies of the invoices had been altered to reflect the falsified journal entry. The bookkeeper had stolen more than $15,000 over a period of a year before the fraud was discovered. The bookkeeper was dismissed and agreed to repay the money in order to avoid having the matter brought to the attention of the police.

Payments and Accounts Payable

In order to manufacture and/or supply goods and services, a business must obviously procure and pay for the goods and services that underlie their sales. In terms of the accounting equation and accounting cycle, the expenses appear on a company's income statement, and the respective accounts payable appear on the balance sheet. Similar to cash sales, cash purchases would directly affect the cash balance, which is also a balance sheet item.

As previously discussed for the Sales and Accounts Receivable cycle, the steps and controls for safeguarding a company's assets are of a similar ilk. These steps include approving vendors and ensuring they actually exist and are legitimate businesses; proper processing of purchase orders; proper handling in the receipt and recording of goods and services; recording of liabilities; and processing of cash for payment.

This is one of the accounting cycles that is susceptible to breakdowns in controls, for it involves the flow of funds out from an entity. The safeguarding of a company's assets thus proves just as important, if no more so, in this cycle.

In terms of the accounts that companies typically have in their "chart of accounts" (i.e., their roadmap through their financial statements), this cycle can affect many different balance sheet and income statement accounts. Specifically, the payments and accounts payable cycle can affect balance sheet accounts, including cash, inventory, prepaid expenses, accounts payable (collectively "current assets"), equipment, land and buildings, depreciation ("fixed assets"), and other, perhaps longer-term assets and liabilities.

Similarly, in the income statement, just about every account is affected by this cycle, from cost of good sold (which typically when deducted from sales results in a company's gross profit) to all of the entity's expenses, such as administration, travel, advertising, professional fees, and taxes, among many others.

Within the same guidelines as for the Sales and Accounts Receivable cycle, fundamental controls are essential, especially over the reconciliation of accounts, including the entity's bank accounts. Without a regular (usually monthly) independent reconciliation of the company's bank accounts, the true financial position cannot be known. Similarly, the propriety of transactions and completeness of information cannot be known. At its simplest level, the person who generates checks, the person who signs checks, the person who mails checks, and the person who reconciles the bank account (or accounts) cannot be one and the same. This is a fundamental principle of accounting, which, while it may not exactly date back to Luca Pacioli, still harks back to Pacioli's quote. Once again: "He who does business without knowing all about it, sees his money go like flies."

Along with the reconciliation process, the concepts of budgeting and tendering and vendor knowledge are also key. These processes also include the segregation of duties, proper approvals, and audit trail through proper documentation. Similar to the other accounting cycles, proper documentation includes prenumbered purchase requisitions, purchase orders, receiving reports, and checks. With the advent of sophisticated computer software, many systems now print this information as documents are generated. This therefore puts the onus on a business to safeguard entry to the accounting system and be in a position to identify who enters the system and when. Limiting access at key points therefore makes it more difficult for one person to compromise the system without collusion.

At the entry level of this cycle, acceptance of a vendor, system controls must include background checks on the vendor in order to ensure that the business exists and is legitimate. Adherence to credit limits is another fundamental control in the safeguarding of the company's assets. Companies should also have bid and procurement policies to ensure competitive bidding and to minimize the opportunity for purchasing managers to compromise their position.

Case Study: Accounts Payable Fraud

The administrator of the school board in a small city had ultimate authority for all items payable from the board's annual budget. As an administrator, he traveled frequently to education conventions and meetings of administrators in the state capitol and across the country. Although he was an excellent CPA and the day-to-day affairs of the board ran smoothly, his prickly personality did not endear him to the board and made his attempts to get approval for his proposals difficult. Frustrated and increasingly embittered, he saw a way to get back at the board by using his signing authority to approve personal expenditures and write checks to himself. He submitted mileage expenses while using a car leased for him by the board, and he used the board credit card to put gas in his own car. Other bills submitted and approved by himself were for meals and entertainment on weekends and repairs to his car. After his secretary blew the whistle on him, forensic investigators found that invoices for many transactions did not exist. The administrator was dismissed from his job, but no charges were ever laid.

Human Resources and Payroll

By definition, this aspect of the cycle includes recruitment, disengagement, and remuneration of employees and the related underlying data of time records, expense reports, and other related matters.

From an accounting cycle perspective, there are many accounts affected by this function, specifically, cash and taxes payable on the balance sheet and salaries/payroll, tax, travel and entertainment, and others in the income statement.

The safeguards for this cycle are necessary for the prevention of nonexistent (also known as "ghost") employees, falsified hours and overtime, false expense reports, and false medical claims.

Again, the underlying fundamental concepts are similar to those for all other accounting cycles, with the need for proper documentation (i.e., timecards, time sheets, timely entry into a computerized timekeeping system, etc.); proper approval (related to hiring, firing, overtime, travel, etc.), and separation of duties. In terms of the last-named, this would include separating the functions of processing and distributing paychecks and approval and payment of expenses, among others.

Case Study: Payroll Fraud

A suburban construction company employed several hundred laborers at any given time. With a lean operation, the home office included a one-person accounting department, with a long-serving bookkeeper/controller who coordinated the weekly payroll, printed the payroll checks, placed the owner's mechanical signature on the checks, hand-delivered the checks to the job sites, and reconciled the company's bank account.

It came as no surprise then that, after several years, it was discovered that the bookkeeper had perpetrated a scheme whereby at any point in time, she kept several laborers on the payroll after they had left the company ("ghost employees"). She would endorse the back of their checks and deposit them in her own bank account. At the same time, she paid the withholding taxes, union dues, and other deductions! It was only an alert bank teller who eventually noticed the scheme, after several years and over $600,000 had been taken. The company received $500,000 from its fidelity bond carrier, got back much of the tax and union dues, and reached a settlement with the bank for its lack of oversight.

Inventory and Storage/Warehousing

This part of the cycle encompasses the purchasing function as it relates to the company's inventory, but it also includes the warehousing of product for both manufacture and then resale. Physical control is therefore as important as the other system controls within the other accounting cycles.

The processes for this cycle, from an accounting standpoint, include processing requisitions for purchases, receipt of raw materials and finished goods, storage of raw materials and finished goods, and shipment of goods, among others.

From an accounting cycle perspective, this function affects the inventories on the balance sheet and cost of goods sold in the income statement. Important in this process is the maintenance of an audit trail—specifically, receiving reports, perpetual inventory records, control over requisitions, shipping documents, among others.

As well as the audit trail, proper segregation of duties is also essential to this accounting cycle—for example, separation of warehouse custody and purchase authorization. In addition, those with custody over the warehouse should not conduct, or be the lead in conducting, the physical count of inventory. It also goes without saying that physical security is critical for this particular cycle.

Case Study: Inventory Fraud

Auditors doing their annual review of the books of a gold refiner were unable to reconcile the inventory value of the gold carried on the company's balance sheet with the assessed value. In an attempt to show he was trying to solve the problem, the vice president of finance hired forensic investigators to review the inventory. The discovery of a brass bar of exactly the same weight as a gold bar on the inventory list raised a question in the minds of the investigators. An interview with a smelter worker revealed that brass scrap had been melted down, cast into bars, and added to the inventory. There was no record of brass bars on the inventory lists. Forty-five brass bars had been valued at $8 million on the balance sheet. Another $5 million was classified as gold bars "in transit." The fraud had been going on for about five years when discovered. It had not been perpetrated for the direct personal gain of the VP of finance and his colluding CEO, but as an attempt to hide the operating losses that would have precipitated a fall in the company's stock if made public in the annual report. The VP of finance and CEO were both charged with fraud, convicted, and served terms in prison.

Capital Expenditures

This part of the accounting cycle is also known as the capital acquisition and repayment cycle or the financing cycle. It includes the borrowing of funds, the debt of a company, and so on. Several transactions surround this part of the cycle, specifically, recording of debt and interest, payment of interest and dividends, and equity financing, among others.

From an accounting cycle perspective, this function affects cash, liabilities (such as mortgages), capital and retained earnings on the balance sheet, and interest paid and received, among other items on the income statement.

An audit trail will once again assist in the safeguarding of the company's assets through, for example, control over bank deposits and authorizations for loans. An entity must ensure proper documentation of loans, journal entries, stock certificates, and the like. In addition, duties should be segregated, such as stock issuance and handling of cash, as well as separating accounting from handling of cash.

Case Study: Capital Expenditures

A government agency responsible for overseeing mortgage brokers was concerned that many brokers were borrowing and lending money as if they were licensed as banks or trust companies. The agency made a random selection of brokers and hired forensic investigators to examine their books.

Under government regulations, the brokers' activities were limited to finding specific mortgages and investors to invest in them. In a typical case, an investor would give the broker $50,000 to be put out in a particular mortgage at the prevailing rate per annum to be paid monthly. The investigators soon discovered that one broker had exceeded his authority by issuing so-called corporate notes secured by the company's guarantee rather than by a mortgage. The money was being used instead to purchase property for the broker, who then reduced his risk by selling partial interests to family members or other relatives. By the time the investigators arrived, more than $5 million had been taken in through the issuance of corporate notes and pooled instead of being directed to specific mortgages.

What should have been securely backed mortgages on the balance sheet turned out to be high-risk investments in other ventures that were not paying the rates of return required to service the corporate notes. The broker was meeting his monthly obligations to his investors through borrowings on a bank line of credit and was rapidly getting overextended. In the end, the government agency revoked the broker's license and closed his operations with the help of several banks that took over the mortgages to protect the investors.

JOURNALS

As we have previously discussed, the activities, and hence transactions of a business that underlie the entity's financial statements are known as the accounting cycle. Many of us are familiar with the term *month-end closing*, which signifies a company closing its books on a particular month of transactions and reconciling its various accounts, to ensure everything is in balance as well as the propriety of the underlying data. This is therefore known as a monthly cycle. The accounting cycle can be weekly, monthly, quarterly, yearly, or otherwise, but is always known as a particular cycle.

General Journal

So what is a journal? Typically, a journal is described as a chronological listing of transactions or business activities. It has also been defined as an accounting book of original entry where transactions are initially recorded.[2] The journal essentially shows each transaction and the corresponding debit and credit entries and identifies which accounts they affect within the chart of accounts.

These debit and credit entries form the basis from which amounts are transferred to their respective accounts in the ledger. Hence, the controls and audit trail, which we discussed within the various aspects of the accounting cycles, are critical to the ability to trace individual transactions and the documents that support them.

This procedure requires the recording of individual transactions through entries in the general journal, followed by a posting from the general journal to the appropriate ledger account. However, in the practicality of business today, the volume of transactions necessitates the grouping of like transactions and the use of a special journal.

Special Journal

Most transactions fall into one of four categories: sales journal, purchases journal, cash receipts journal, and cash payments journal.

Sales Journal Exhibit 2.1 contains an example of a sales journal.

Exhibit 2.1 presents an extract from a company's sales journal showing entries made on a particular day to certain customers. The check in the "posted" column indicates the entry was made in the subsidiary ledger, or the ledger, which lists the specific accounts receivable. Thus, the total of $5,200 is posted and shown as the sales for that day, and the individual amounts ultimately are shown in the individual customer accounts. A subsidiary ledger supports the general ledger but is also controlled by the general ledger.

Purchases Journal Similar to the sales journal, the purchases journal handles purchase transactions in the same way as the sales journal handles sales transactions. In a similar vein, the individual invoices from the customer would be posted to a subsidiary ledger, which reflects the company's accounts payable.

Cash Receipts Journal It may go without saying, but it is nonetheless true, that all cash transactions involving receipts are recorded in the cash receipts journal. Where cash is received from customers, the amounts are posted to the respective customer's account in the accounts receivable subsidiary ledger. The total cash received is posted to the cash account in the general ledger.

Cash Payments Journal Similar to cash receipts, all cash payments must go through the cash payments journal. Items include payment of accounts payable to creditors, payment of expenses, and other cash payments. Similar to cash receipts, entries are typically posted daily; and then on a monthly basis

Date	Account	Invoice Number	Posted	Amount
1/2/2006	Henry Silk	1001	✔	$1,200.00
1/2/2006	Persie Vans	1002	✔	$2,425.00
1/2/2006	Spurs Scrap	1003	✔	$1,575.00
				$5,200.00

EXHIBIT 2.1   Sample Sales Journal

a business will post cash, accounts payable, purchases, and any other accounts to the respective accounts in the general ledger.

TYING THE THREAD

*Never call an accountant a credit to his profession; a good
accountant is a debit to his profession.*[3]

At the beginning of this section, we spoke of how Luca Pacioli believed that a person should not go to sleep at night until the debits equaled the credits. At the end of a designated accounting period (for example, monthly), an entity will prepare a trial balance—a listing of all account balances in the general ledger. Each subsidiary ledger must also agree to its control account. For example, a listing is prepared of all accounts receivable balances from the subsidiary ledger, which should then be reconciled to the accounts receivable balance in the general ledger.

The simplified explanation of the accounting cycles and the journal system illustrates how relatively simple Pacioli's double-entry system of bookkeeping vision was. However, the complexity of the human mind and the deviation from accepted behavior require business to drill down beneath the surface of simple bookkeeping and maintain control over every transaction and the manner in which transactions are recorded.

Without the controls and checks and balances, the system will be undermined, and the integrity of data will also be compromised.

SUGGESTED READINGS

CPA's Handbook of Fraud and Commercial Crime Prevention. American Institute of Certified Public Accountants, 2000.
Luca Pacioli: Unsung Hero of the Renaissance. Paul Jackson, with David Tinius, Ph.D., and William Weis, Ph.D. Cincinnati: OH: South-Western Publishing, 1990.
Macve, Richard H. "Pacioli's Legacy." In *New Works in Accounting History*, edited by T.A. Lee, A. Bishop, and R. H. Parker. New York and London: Garland Publishing, 1996.
Pacioli, Luca. *Summa de Arithmetica.* Toscalano: Paganino de Paganini, 1523.
Taylor, R. *No Royal Road: Luca Pacioli and His Times.* Chapel Hill: University of North Carolina Press, 1942.

NOTES

1. Milton Berle, comedian and actor, 1908–2002; www.brainyquote.com/quotes/
quotes/m/miltonberl145991.html.
2. InvestorWords.com.
3. Charles Lyell, British geologist, 1797–1875; www.brainyquote.com/quotes/
quotes/c/charleslye188407.html.

3

THE ENTITIES

When discussing the role that business plays in crime, it is important to first understand the various business structures the investigator may encounter. There are essentially three main types of business entities that are recognized in most common law countries: the sole proprietorship, the partnership, and the corporation.

In the United States, the regulation of business entities and the forms under which they may legally transact business are entirely within the purview of the individual states. Because of this, each individual state has crafted its own rules and regulations dealing with each type of business entity. While there are similarities among each, it is advisable that you check your local jurisdiction to determine any particular nuances unique to your own state.

Consider this comment from the Organization for Economic Co-Operation and Development (OECD):

> Almost every economic crime involves the misuse of corporate entities—money launderers exploit cash-based businesses and other legal vehicles to disguise the source of their illicit gains, bribe-givers and recipients conduct their illicit transactions through bank accounts opened under the names of corporations and foundations, and individuals hide or shield their wealth from tax authorities and other creditors through trusts and partnerships, to name but a few examples.[1]

While in Chapter 7 we discuss the concept of Business as a vehicle for financial crimes, here we consider the comments of the OECD that corporate vehicles are essential for a market economy and the global economic system and the fact that they recognize there is misuse of such vehicles for money laundering, corruption, diversion of assets, and other types of illegal behavior.

In this chapter, we discuss the specifics of the various types of business entities.

PROPRIETORSHIPS

Of the three main entities, the sole proprietorship is perhaps the most easily started and administered. While the startup costs are minimal, there are drawbacks to this form of business organization—foremost among them is the lack of owner protection.

Unlike the partnership and the corporation, which we will discuss momentarily, the sole proprietorship is not a separate entity. This means quite simply that the owner of the business is in fact the business. As a result, all liability incurred by the business is actually incurred by the owner. As you will see momentarily, this is a concept quite different from that encountered in both the partnership and corporate structures.

In reality, while most easy to begin and operate, the sole proprietorship is probably not the most favorable form of business—because of the unlimited liability problem. As a result, most businesses the investigator will encounter take either the partnership or corporate business structure as their organizational method.

PARTNERSHIPS

In terms of complexity and ease of administration, the partnership can be one step up from the sole proprietorship. Although at its heart the partnership is nothing more than an agreement between two or more persons to enter into a profit-motivated venture, the reality of today's business environment means the investigator may encounter a number of variations on this simple theme.

To begin a partnership, in theory, nothing more need be done than enter an agreement. In reality, most states, following the Revised Uniform Partnership Act (RUPA), require that this partnership be reduced to writing and registered with the state.

Although partnership structure can rival that of even the most multinational corporations, you are likely to encounter only two categories of partnerships—the general partnership and the limited liability partnership.

The general partnership is a partnership in which all partners have unlimited liability for the debts and contracts of the partnership. Conversely, the limited liability partnership limits the liability of those partners holding limited status.

As with all areas of the law, the rules governing partnership liability are very complicated and several paragraphs in an introductory text such as this could not bring out all its niceties; however, there are some basic rules that are fairly uniform.

First, most states require that at least one of the partners in a limited partnership hold general liability. Second, limited partners must refrain from daily operation or management of the firm. If they act as a manager they risk the loss of their limited status.

Assuming the limited partner meets the statutory requirements, what is the benefit of limited status? Probably the most notable is the limit of liability.

As noted in the section on sole proprietorships, and reiterated in the section on general partners, those people have unlimited liability for the debts and misdeeds (civil) of the firm. For example, if XYZ Ltd. enters into a $1 million contract to provide widgets to ABC Corporation and then fails to provide the widgets, they are probably in breach of contract and can be held civilly liable for damages. In a proprietorship and general partnership, under most circumstances the owners' personal assets (car, stocks, bonds, but most likely not their primary residence) will be reachable to satisfy a judgment. Conversely, a limited partner's liability is limited by his investment in the firm. In this case, if partner Jones in XYZ Ltd. invested $150,000 in the firm, he can lose only his investment, and his personal assets are not reachable to satisfy a judgment. As you can see, this limit can provide a very attractive enticement for partnership investors.

As we stated earlier, the complexity of partnerships has grown tremendously since they were first recognized, and the likelihood that you will encounter such a simply structured partnership in the real world is slim. In fact, with the recognition of the Limited Liability Limited Partnership, the Limited Liability Company (which is a hybrid between partnership and corporate structure and we will discuss momentarily), the Professional Association (usually seen with lawyers, accountants, and other professionals), secret partnerships, and silent partnerships, the variety of partnerships one might encounter seems to increase annually. In reality, however, the basic foundations that we have discussed still apply.

As stated earlier, while this form of business association is still very popular, you run a much greater likelihood of encountering our final form—the corporation.

CORPORATIONS

Of all the enterprises we have discussed, the corporation is probably the most prevalent. While the rules regulating corporate governance are complicated and extensive, they provide owners with a very important benefit—protection from liability.

As illustrated in the proprietorship and partnership, ownership can be a dangerous proposition financially. Not so in the corporation, thanks to the legal fiction known as the entity concept.

The entity concept is a legal doctrine that gives corporations personality. By personality, we are referring to the fact that corporations are looked at legally as persons capable of doing everything "real" people can do.

For example, corporations can own property, buy and sell real estate, enter into contracts, get married, get divorced, and even die. In fact, there are very few legal obligations into which a lawfully recognized corporation cannot enter. Understanding of the entity principle is crucial for everything else we know about corporations.

The reason this is such a key, is because recognizing a corporation as its own person means that the owners are insulated from legal actions. In other words, the corporation gets sued, and the owners are unreachable in the eyes of the law.

Let's revisit our XYZ Ltd. example. If, instead of a limited partnership, XYZ were a corporation, then its breach of contract would result in a lawsuit against XYZ Corp. The owners would be untouchable—even if the assets of XYZ Corp. were insufficient to satisfy the judgment against them. In that case, XYZ's ownership would simply walk away having lost only their investment in XYZ stock and nothing more. In certain circumstances, the law allows creditors or claimants to "pierce the corporate veil" and hold the shareholders personally liable. The theory behind this legal concept is that shareholders who muddy the distinction between the corporation and themselves should not be allowed to hide behind the corporate veil.

As expected, while this example is quite oversimplified, it illustrates fairly well the value that corporate structure has. By providing this layer of liability protection the corporate form of ownership is very attractive to legitimate business. Unfortunately, it is also attractive to criminal enterprises. So, once again we revisit the OECD's paper, "Behind the Corporate Veil." Specifically, the OECD noted that "to prevent and combat the misuse of corporate vehicles for illicit purposes, it is essential that the authorities in all jurisdictions have the means to obtain and share, on a timely basis, information on the beneficial ownership and control of corporate vehicles established in their jurisdictions."[2]

Because there is this layer of opacity between the enterprise and the owners, determining who is actually doing what is sometimes very difficult. In the United States, this is not usually that difficult. Most states have state laws proscribing the form and procedures that must be followed in order for a company to avail itself of the corporate protection. Along with these laws they also have databases that list all the legally recognized corporations. Some states, such as Florida, have also expanded this online database to include limited partnerships and limited liability companies.

The beauty of this close regulation is that consumers and investigators are rarely more than a phone call away from knowing exactly who the officers of each corporation are. This can be very valuable in linking people with corporate actions. However, some states have made identifying corporate ownership slightly more complicated.

For example, Delaware has been historically notorious for the favorable treatment that it offers corporations in terms of information disclosure. Nevada is also favorable to securing corporate information. While law enforcement investigations rarely encounter difficulty in determining true ownership of an enterprise in the United States, that is not the case in foreign jurisdictions. As a result, the attractiveness of foreign registration of corporations is becoming more and more common.

In the next section we will build on our knowledge of the entity concept and couple that with certain unique characteristics of international law to show why many modern criminals have gone global.

BUSINESS ENTERPRISES IN THE GLOBAL ENVIRONMENT

Business structure in the international arena has some significant differences from that in the United States. Some of those differences stem from the general nature of international law. Others stem from differences in the legal systems and the way countries view the relationship between businesses and the law. Still more differences exist in the way in which varying accounting standards affect the methods used to report financial stability.

Regardless of the source, they are differences that financial crime investigators are bound to run into during their careers.

The Entities

As in the United States, individual liability for both criminal and civil wrong-doing in the business context will be influenced by the structure of the business. While sole proprietorships continue to exist in the global business world, you are much more likely to encounter the partnership and the corporation.

In countries following the common law system, most partnerships and corporations will be treated much as they are in the United States. In countries following the Romano-Germanic Civil law system you will find a much wider variation among countries. Those countries adhering to Islamic law under the Shari'a may offer a blended approach to matters involving business associations. The most important thing to understand is whether the country in which the business association that you are investigating is located recognizes the entity principle for that particular business structure.

The key to understanding the role that international businesses play in financial crime is remembering the entity principle. It is this entity principle that gives the international business its strong allure. And none have the allure as strongly as the International Business Corporation (IBC). However, before you can understand the IBC, it is important to first understand the offshore haven.

The corporate structure, particularly the existence of the corporation as a legal entity, lends itself well to the task of structuring financial transactions to increase anonymity. Nowhere is this more evident than through the use of offshore entities known as International Business Corporations (IBCs), or entities whose ownership is held through bearer securities.

The International Business Corporation takes the entity principle a step further. It may have nominee directors. Ownership may be held through bearer shares, or ownership may be held through registered owners who are known only to the IBC. By layering several IBCs an individual can render true ownership absolutely opaque.

Further, an air of legitimacy can be constructed in these IBCs by using entities known as "shelf-corporations." These ready-made corporations are corporations that had been created many years earlier and placed on the shelf—hence the descriptive term. In other words, they are not actually assigned ownership, but instead simply exist on paper only. When someone needs a shell corporation to help obscure true ownership, he simply purchases the shelf corporation and assumes ownership. Because the corporation's existence significantly predates the ownership's purchase, an air of legitimacy is conferred through what appears to be a lengthy corporate life.

A trust is similar to a corporation in that it is separate from its beneficiary/ owner. Using this legal fiction, financial criminals can separate legal ownership from beneficial ownership. Although trusts are entirely legal and very powerful estate planning tools, when combined with the IBCs in offshore financial centers they can make determining ownership of business assets and money impossible. By transferring all the assets of a firm into a trust the individual can create the appearance that he or she is no longer in control of them.

Ownership can be further layered by transferring either the corpus (body) of the trust or the profits to an offshore trust. Proceeds from the trust can then be repatriated to the true "owner" using international banks and correspondent relationships.

In conjunction with IBCs and offshore trusts, criminals can use bearer securities to conceal true ownership. Bearer securities consist of bearer bonds and bearer stock certificates. Although the use of bearer bonds to launder money has not been officially documented, the use of bearer stock certificates in legitimate business is commonplace.

In a conventionally created corporation, ownership of the entity is signified by the issuance of registered shares. Registered shares are exactly that: shares whose ownership is registered on the books of the entity. Determination of actual ownership and control of the entity at any given point in time is a simple matter of referring to the books.

Bearer shares, in contrast, are unregistered. They are owned solely based on possession or physical control of the actual share certificate. There is no registered owner, and determination of actual ownership and control of the corporate entity is difficult where possible at all. Although some countries now prohibit the issuance of bearer shares, in a number of countries such forms of corporate ownership are still commonplace.[3] An investigator will often encounter such a structure in less developed countries (LDCs) and *offshore financial centers*. By creating a legally viable entity with bearer shares, a criminal enterprise can almost completely defeat attempts to learn the true identity of the shareholders of the corporation.[4]

Offshore Finance   The term *offshore* simply refers to entities whose legal authority allows them to exist in a host country, but generally, only transact business with non–host country individuals. Offshore is often used to refer to banks, business associations, and trusts.

Because they are generally prohibited from engaging in business in the host country, the host country does not regulate them or oversee their operations.

This fact, combined with favorable, and often very strong corporate and banking secrecy laws in the host nation, makes these entities very popular among people seeking to hide money or conceal ownership.

Given the obvious potential for abuse, why then do host nations continue to allow these entities to operate? One reason is economics. Another reason is complacency. However, whatever the reason, since the events of 9/11 and the "new war on terror," many haven nations have moved toward more transparency. Still, there are some nations that continue to offer shelter to financial criminals looking for protection.

Offshore banking provides the key to the entire financial crime scheme. Simply put, offshore finance is the provision of financial services to nonresidents. Like IBCs, this nonresident restriction on business allows offshore banks to operate largely unregulated by the host country. While many major nations, including the United States, have an offshore banking population, only those with the bulk of their financial sector activity offshore would be called offshore financial centers.

Haven nations pose a challenge for financial crime investigators because bank secrecy laws make access to ownership information, as well as account holder data, impossible to obtain. To add a layer of complexity, it is possible to use shell banks, which are nothing more than mere shells through which money can pass opaquely.

Much like shell companies, shell banks are institutions with no physical presence in the jurisdiction in which they are incorporated. Instead, they are often called brass-plate institutions because they have no affiliation with a regulated financial group, and are frequently nothing more than a brass nameplate on the door.[5]

The use of shell banks places both ownership information and accountholder data out of reach for most investigators. The combination of corporate secrecy, bank secrecy, and lack of regulation by host nations makes offshore financing a very attractive vehicle for financial criminals to execute their schemes.

For obvious reasons, these institutions, while performing marginally legitimate functions, are tailor-made for employment in layering transactions. By using a shell bank, which is often owned and operated in an offshore financial center itself, a correspondent relationship may be established between the shell bank and a registered financial group within the offshore financial center. Once the correspondent relationship is established, the shell bank, acting as a respondent, can essentially transfer limitless amounts of money between banking institutions. This unlimited access to untraceable wire transfers eliminates any audit trail that may have existed.[6]

In other words, correspondent banking is the tie that binds. While offshore finance and nominee ownership allows financial criminals to evade detection and apprehension, it does nothing to ease the need for access to their money. Correspondent banks fill the gap between the offshore bank and the domestic financial criminal.

Correspondent bank accounts are accounts that banks maintain with each other in their own name. In the course of international banking, correspondent banking has a significant legitimate purpose. For example, by establishing multiple correspondent relationships globally, one bank can undertake various financial transactions internationally without the need for a physical presence in a host country. These services include such legitimate transactions as international wire transfers, check-clearing services, and foreign exchange services.[7] However, such relationships are well suited for misappropriation by criminal enterprises.

The indirect nature of the correspondent relationship means that the correspondent bank (the international bank supplying the transfer services to the criminal enterprises' bank) is essentially supplying services for individuals or entities for which it has no verifiable information. In correspondent banking, the correspondent bank must rely on the respondent bank (the bank in which the account holder has funds on deposit) to verify the nature of the transactions and perform the necessary due diligence and monitoring of the customer's account. In some cases, the respondent bank may be providing correspondent services to another institution.

As you can imagine, because a correspondent relationship is a banking arrangement between two banks, criminals can use these arrangements to settle accounts, transfer money, and clear financial instruments. By establishing a correspondent banking relationship between an offshore bank and a domestic bank, the financial criminal can repatriate his cash through a number of schemes.

By capitalizing on time-honored foundations of international law coupled with advances in technology, financial criminals can now move billions of dollars annually at the click of a button.

We discussed earlier in this chapter the OECD's comments as to combating and preventing the misuse of corporate vehicles. To fulfill these objectives, the OECD noted the need for adherence to three fundamental objectives: (1) beneficial ownership and control information to be maintained or be obtainable by the authorities; (2) proper oversight and high integrity of any system for maintaining or obtaining beneficial ownership and control information; and (3) nonpublic information on beneficial ownership and control must be able to be shared with other regulators/supervisors and law enforcement authorities, both domestically and internationally.[8]

SUGGESTED READINGS

Abadinsky, H., ed. *Organized Crime*, 3rd edition. Chicago, IL: Nelson Hall, 1990.

Bauer, P., and R. Ullmann. "Understanding the Wash Cycle." *Economic Perspectives*, 6. Retrieved March 10, 2006, from http://usinfo.state.gov/journals/ites/0501/ijee/clevelandfed.htm.

Cassard, M. "The Role of Offshore Centers in International Financial Intermediation." IMF Working Paper 94/10. Washington, DC: International Monetary Fund, 1994.

Financial Action Task Force—OECD. "Policy Brief: Money Laundering." *OECD Observer*. Paris, France: FATF Secretariat, OECD, 1999.

Financial Action Task Force on Money Laundering. *1998–1999 Report on Money Laundering Typologies*. Paris, France: FATF Secretariat, OECD, February 1999.

Financial Action Task Force on Money Laundering. *1999–2000 Report on Money Laundering Typologies*. Paris, France: FATF Secretariat, OECD, February 2000.

Financial Action Task Force on Money Laundering. *2000–2001 Report on Money Laundering Typologies*. Paris, France: FATF Secretariat, OECD, February 2001.

Gustitus, L.E. Bean, and R. Roach. "Correspondent Banking: A Gateway for Money Laundering." *Economic Perspectives*, 6. Retrieved March 13, 2006, from http://usinfo.state.gov/journals/ites/0501/ijee/levin.htm.

Harvey, J. "Money Laundering and the LDC Offshore Finance Centres: Are They the Weak Links?" Paper presented at the *Development of Economics Study Group Annual Conference 2002*, Nottingham, UK, University of Nottingham, April 18–20, 2002.

International Federation of Accountants. "IFAC Discussion Paper on Anti-Money Laundering." New York: International Federation of Accountants, 2002.

Joseph, L.M. "Money Laundering Enforcement: Following the Money." *Economic Perspectives*, 6. Retrieved May 5, 2002, from http://usinfo.state.gov/journals/ites/0501/ijee/justice.htm.

Lorenzetti, J. "The Offshore Trust: A Contemporary Asset Protection Scheme." *Journal of Commercial Law Review*, 102, no. 2 (1997).

Mahan, S., and K. O'Neal. *Beyond the Mafia: Organized Crime in the Americas.* Thousand Oaks, CA: Sage Publishing, 1998.

Monkkonen, E.H., ed. *Crime and Justice in American History: Historical Articles on the Origins and Evolution of American Criminal Justice. Vol. 8: Prostitution,*

Drugs, Gambling and Organized Crime, Part 1. Munich, Germany: K.G. Saur, 1994.

Pace, D.F., and J.C. Styles. *Organized Crime: Concepts and Control*. Englewood Cliffs, NJ: Prentice Hall, 1975.

"The Ten Fundamental Laws of Money Laundering." Retrieved April 8, 2002 from www.unodc.org/money_laundering_10_laws.html.

United Nations Office of Drug Control and Crime Prevention. *Attacking the Profits of Crime: Drugs, Money and Laundering*. Vienna, Austria: UNODC, 1998.

United States Department of the Treasury. *A Survey of Electronic Cash, Electronic Banking and Internet Gaming*. Washington, DC: U.S. Government Printing Office, 2000.

United States Department of the Treasury, Financial Crimes Enforcement Network. [Electronic version,] *FinCEN Advisory: Transactions Involving Israel*. Issue 17. Washington, DC: U.S. Government Printing Office, July 2000.

Woodiwis, M. *Crime Crusades and Corruption: Prohibitions in the United States 1900–1987*. Totowa, NJ: Barnes & Noble Books, 1988.

NOTES

1. OECD, "Behind the Corporate Veil: Using Corporate Entities for Illicit Purposes," 2001.
2. Ibid.
3. J. Madinger, and S.A. Zalopany, *Money Laundering: A Guide for Criminal Investigators* (Boca Raton, FL: CRC Press, 1999), p. 409. See also FATF, *2001–2002 Report on Money Laundering Typologies*, p. 4.
4. Ibid.
5. J.A. Blum, M. Levi, R.T. Naylor, and P. Williams, eds., "Financial Havens, Banking Secrecy and Money Laundering," in *Crime Prevention and Criminal Justice Newsletter*, vol. 8 (New York: United Nations Publications Board, 1998), p. 65.
6. Ibid.
7. N. Wilkins, *The Correspondent Banking Handbook* (London: Euro money Books, 1993), pp. 11–17.
8. Ibid.

4

FUNDAMENTAL PRINCIPLES
OF ANALYSIS

GOOD ANALYSIS = DUE DILIGENCE?

Pshaw, my dear fellow, what do the public, the great
unobservant public, who could hardly tell a weaver by his
tooth or a compositor by his left thumb, care about the finer
shades of analysis and deduction! [1]

As often as Sherlock Holmes is quoted, so much of his fictional speech rings true in what has taken place in business. Up until the news headlines surrounding Enron, WorldCom, and others, what did the public know about analysis of financial information? Specifically, what did the "non-expert" know about analysis and deduction when it came to financial results and how to interpret them?

Now that we have a basic understanding of financial fraud, how it occurs, who commits it, and some of the underlying principles of accounting and entities involved, we need to consider how a non-expert can undertake financial analysis and explain what it all means.

Analysis can be conducted for two reasons: as part of due diligence before a transaction and as part of an investigation after a fraud has occurred or is believed to have occurred. Typically, the number of specific transactions in a business will prohibit the ability to examine every piece of paper and every underlying action. Analysis may therefore be needed to focus on the problem areas, again, for due diligence before a deal to determine whether certain facets of a business just do meet the "gut feel" test, or to determine where to look further in a fraud situation. It is the latter that is the focus of this book and therefore the focus of this chapter.

If a party suffers a loss, due to the lack of financial due diligence or at least some level of financial analysis, the pain of a bad bargain will live on long after the excitement of the particular transaction has faded to a mere memory. Even supposedly well-trained and experienced businesspeople still enter into transactions not only not knowing much about the parties, but also not understanding the metrics of the underlying data.

In the face of the often mentioned recent multibillion-dollar financial statement frauds, it is clear there still are so few people who truly understand what it all means and understand even the most basic of analyses. The concept of financial analysis, due diligence, call it what you like, is an understanding before a commitment. That commitment could be lending a sole proprietor money to take her business to the next level, it could be buying into a partnership, or it could be investing in a major corporation. It could be joining business with a sole proprietor to create a partnership, or it could be a bank entering into an agreement to provide financing for a new facility. It could even be an investigative journalist trying to get a better understanding of a company's results for a particular story.

The size of business and type of entity may dictate exactly which procedures are followed; however, you must understand the underlying business before you can determine which path to follow.

Any type of financial analysis will obviously involve numbers. However, depending on the needs of the analyst, it may involve more than just looking at the numbers. It may require a deeper investigation that, among other things, looks at the company in its markets, calculates asset values, discovers hidden liabilities, and examines long-term strategy. Sadly, experience shows that even the most rudimentary analysis is conducted after the fact—the famous historic perspective that financial statements offer us. Anyone who has experience as the victim of fraud or investigating fraud will tell you that there are always red flags that are obvious to the trained eye right from the beginning.

WHY DO IT?

Business has changed since the days of Luca Pacioli. It has changed since the advent of computers. And it has certainly changed since the corporate shenanigans of the past few years. But has business really changed? Or has only the underlying way in which results are captured changed? At the root of it all is one thing—money—specifically, the need to make it, keep it, and grow it, and all driven by the human element. Perhaps the ethos is no different today than it was 500 years ago; perhaps just the pressures have changed.

Although the recent scandals have mostly surrounded publicly traded companies, with the perception that they can inflict the greatest hurt on outsiders, let us not forget the private companies, the partnerships, and indeed the sole proprietorships, in whom someone on the outside may soon be having an inside interest. The breakdown of confidence in financial statements and their underlying data should apply across the board, not just to public companies.

What and Whom Can You Trust?

Historically, analysts believed that audited financial statements contained all the information needed for their analysis. This misconception was not only common to companies looking at acquisition targets but was also to be found at banks, bonding companies, vendors' customers, and any other type of business wishing to have some type of fiduciary relationship with another company. The exposed misrepresentations on the financial statements of Enron, World-Com, and others should sufficiently demonstrate that making an investment decision based solely on financial statement analysis can be dangerous.

Financial statement fraud has always been with us, but the recent scandals show that not even the most important companies in the economy can remain untainted. In 1998, then–SEC chairman Arthur Levitt warned in a speech called "The 'Numbers Game'" that aggressive accountants were exploiting the flexibility of generally accepted accounting principles (GAAP) to create misleading earnings reports: "As a result, I fear that we are witnessing an erosion in the quality of earnings, and therefore, the quality of financial reporting. Managing may be giving way to manipulation; integrity may be losing out to illusion."[2]

OTHER FACTORS TO CONSIDER

In the post-Enron era, mere analysis of audited financial statements may not be enough, and other key performance indicators may have to be considered. Margin and other ratio analyses will, of course, always be important, but a thorough examination may have to extend to customers, underlying costs, product lines, and market shares, among many other factors. Additional time should be spent talking to vendors and customers to more fully analyze the industry in which the company operates.

When assessing competitor and market risk, prospective acquirers frequently access and rely on information obtained from analysts and self-proclaimed industry "experts." Recent revelations have shown the significant risk of bias in these sources. In addition, in the eagerness to complete a transaction, human nature inadvertently causes greater weight to be placed on positive information and less on negative. Early warnings of potential problems are frequently ignored.

The analytical process should "drill down" to find out who authorizes individual transactions and to ask why. Skepticism should guide the examination of all questionable transactions. In the case of a prospective acquisition, more emphasis should be placed on analyzing whether there is a real need to acquire the target and what its long-term impact on the existing strategy could be. Many badly advised boards of directors have authorized the acquisition of companies in businesses unfamiliar to their own management but argued to be capable of providing what used to be called "synergies." The results have almost always been disastrous.

Lenders, suitors, or any other agent surveying a company need to be alert to factors they may not have considered previously. The old emphasis on net income should now shift to cash flow. It does not matter how a company records transactions once the money is spent; it is the cash flow that should be more closely investigated.

One area that should receive increased attention is the company's governance practices. A board dominated by a multi-titled, charismatic, and/or domineering chairman, president, or CEO should raise a red flag. How many independent directors are there? Are they truly independent? Are they financially literate? Do they have experience in the company's business sector? How much time and energy are all directors devoting to fulfilling their duties? How effective is the audit committee? Is senior management's compensation excessive? Finding these answers can be a challenge because they are not often transparent. If effective corporate governance is not in place—and there is no control or oversight of senior management—then "buyer beware."

ANALYSIS FOR THE NON-EXPERT

As the chart in Exhibit 4.1 shows, in gauging performance certain ratios can be applied to an entity's financial statements. In this section, we discuss some of the more "popular" or well-known ratios.

EXHIBIT 4.1   Popular Ratios

Liquidity Analysis Ratios

Current Ratio

$$\text{Current Ratio} = \frac{\text{Current Assets}}{\text{Current Liabilities}}$$

Quick Ratio

$$\text{Quick Ratio} = \frac{\text{Quick Assets}}{\text{Current Liabilities}}$$

Quick Assets = Current Assets − Inventories

Net Working Capital Ratio

$$\text{Net Working Capital Ratio} = \frac{\text{Net Working Capital}}{\text{Total Assets}}$$

Net Working Capital = Current Assets − Current Liabilities

Profitability Analysis Ratios

Return on Assets (ROA)

$$\text{Return on Assets (ROA)} = \frac{\text{Net Income}}{\text{Average Total Assets}}$$

Average Total Assets = (Beginning Total Assets + Ending Total Assets) / 2

Return on Equity (ROE)

$$\text{Return on Equity (ROE)} = \frac{\text{Net Income}}{\text{Average Stockholders' Equity}}$$

Average Stockholders' Equity = (Beginning Stockholders' Equity + Ending Stockholders' Equity) / 2

Net Profit Margin

$$\text{Net Profit Margin} = \frac{\text{Net Income}}{\text{Sales}}$$

Earnings Per Share (EPS)

$$\text{Earnings Per Share (EPS)} = \frac{\text{Net Income}}{\text{Weighted Average Number of Common Shares Outstanding}}$$

Business Analysis Ratios

Accounts Receivable Turnover Ratio

$$\text{Accounts Receivable Turnover Ratio} = \frac{\text{Sales}}{\text{Average Accounts Receivable}}$$

(*continues*)

EXHIBIT 4.1   Continued

Average Accounts Receivable = (Beginning Accounts Receivable + Ending Accounts Receivable) / 2

Inventory Turnover Ratio

$$\text{Inventory Turnover Ratio} = \frac{\text{Cost of Goods Sold}}{\text{Average Inventories}}$$

Capital Ratios

Debt-to-Equity Ratio

$$\text{Debt-to-Equity Ratio} = \frac{\text{Total Liabilities}}{\text{Total Stockholders' Equity}}$$

Interest Coverage Ratio

$$\text{Interest Coverage Ratio} = \frac{\text{Income Before Interest and Income Tax Expenses}}{\text{Interest Expense}}$$

Income Before Interest and Income Tax Expenses = Income Before Interest Income Taxes + Interest Expense

Capital Analysis Ratios

Price/Earnings (PE) Ratio

$$\text{Price/Earnings (PE) Ratio} = \frac{\text{Market Price of Common Stock Per Share}}{\text{Earnings Per Share}}$$

Market to Book Ratio

$$\text{Market to Book Ratio} = \frac{\text{Market Price of Common Stock Per Share}}{\text{Book Value of Equity Per Common Share}}$$

Book Value of Equity Per Common Share = Book Value of Equity for Common Stock / Number of Common Shares

Dividend Yield

$$\text{Dividend Yield} = \frac{\text{Annual Dividends Per Common Share}}{\text{Market Price of Common Stock Per Share}}$$

Book Value of Equity Per Common Share = Book Value of Equity for Common Stock / Number of Common Shares

The Ratios

Current Ratio The current ratio is the standard measure of an entity's financial health, regardless of size and type. The analyst will know whether a business can meet its current obligations by determining if it has sufficient assets to cover its liabilities. The "standard" current ratio for a healthy business is recognized as around 2, meaning it has twice as many assets as liabilities.

The formula is expressed as: *current assets divided by current liabilities.*

Quick Ratio Similar to the current ratio, the quick ratio (also known as the "acid test") measures a business's liquidity. However, many analysts prefer it to the current ratio because it excludes inventories when counting assets and therefore applies an entity's "liquid" assets in relation to its liabilities. The higher the ratio, the higher the level of liquidity, and hence it is a better indicator of an entity's financial health. The accepted optimal quick ratio is 1 or higher.

The formula is expressed as: *current assets less inventory divided by current liabilities.*

Inventory Turnover Ratio This ratio measures how often inventory turns over during the course of the year (or depending on the formula, another time period). In financial analysis, inventory is deemed to be the least liquid form of asset. Typically, a high turnover ratio is positive; however, an unusually high ratio compared to the market for that product could mean loss of sales, with an inability to meet demand.

The formula is expressed as: *cost of goods sold divided by average value of inventory.*

Accounts Receivable Turnover Ratio This ratio provides an indicator as to how quickly (or otherwise) an entity's customers/clients are paying their bills. The greater the number of times receivables turn over during the year, the less the time between sales and cash collection and hence, ceteris paribus, better cash flow.

The formula is expressed as: *net sales divided by accounts receivable.*

Accounts Payable Turnover Ratio Converse to the accounts receivable turnover ratio, the accounts payable turnover ratio provides an indicator of how quickly an entity pays its trade debts. The ratio shows how often accounts payable turn over during the year. A high ratio means a relatively short time between purchases and payment, which may not always be the best for a company (the entity would want to make sure it is taking advantage of all discounts, while not at the same time paying for goods before their time). Conversely, a low ratio may be a sign that the company has cash flow problems. However, this ratio, like all others, should be considered in conjunction with the other ratios.

The formula is expressed as: *cost of sales divided by trade accounts payable.*

Debt-to-Equity Ratio This ratio provides an indicator as to how much the company is in debt (also known as "leveraged") by comparing debt to assets. A high debt-to-equity ratio could indicate that the company may be overleveraged and may be seeking ways to reduce debt.

Aside from the other ratios we have noted, the amount of assets/equity and debt are two of the more significant items in financial statements; they are key evaluators of risk.

The formula is expressed as: *total liabilities divided by total assets.*

Gross Margin Ratio The gross margin (or gross profit) ratio indicates how well or efficiently a proprietor, group of partners, or managers of a company have run that business. Have the managers bought and sold in the most efficient manner? Have they taken advantage of the market? A high gross margin indicates a profit on sales, together with cost containment in making those sales. However, a high margin, but with falling sales, could be indicative of overpricing or a shrinking market.

The formula is expressed as: *gross profit (sales minus cost of sales) divided by total sales.*

Return on Sales Ratio This ratio considers after-tax profit as a percentage of sales. It is used as a measure to determine if an entity is getting a sufficient return on its revenues or sales.

Although an entity may make what looks to be a satisfactory gross profit, it still may not be enough to cover overhead expenses. This ratio can provide an indicator of this fact and help determine how an entity can adjust prices to make a gross profit sufficient to cover expenses and earn an adequate net profit.

The formula is expressed as: *net profit divided by sales.*

Concluding Comments on Ratio Analysis Many other ratios are used in the course of financial analysis, but these are deemed to be some of the most commonly used and understood. It must be remembered that ratios need to be considered in their entirety; unlike in the past, even ratio analysis alone is not to be considered the most useful information. So what if a company made a 25 percent gross profit? So what if its current ratio is 2:1? Given the right circumstances and together with other due diligence, an analyst can obtain a good picture of an entity's performance and situation.

The ratio analysis cannot be considered in a vacuum; rather, it is important to consider the entity, the type of entity, the industry, the market, the competition, the management, and then consider the calculated ratios.

Data Mining as an Analysis Tool

While not the focus of this book for the "non-expert," data mining has become an increasingly important tool in the investigator's tool-box. Data mining is defined in a number of ways:

- "The process of analyzing data to identify patterns or relationships"[3]
- "The analysis of data for relationships that have not previously been discovered"[4]
- "Analyzing data to discover patterns and relationships that are important to decision making"[5]

What is most interesting about the above-noted definitions is the progression in their pattern—from identifying patterns or relationships, progressing to identifying those that have not previously been discovered, to those that are important for decision-making. Those mindsets are important when analyzing data from a fraud investigation perspective.

Being able to manipulate electronic data is an essential ingredient of an effective fraud investigation. The ability to analyze statements and produce the ratios we discussed earlier is one thing; the ability to dig down into the underlying data and look at the various relationships is another.

Later on in this book, we discuss the various techniques for interviewing witnesses and maintaining documents. These skills are essential to an effective investigation; so too are the skills needed for effective data mining. It is like any other tool-kit—we can have the most expensive screwdriver and drill bits, but if we do not possess the skills to locate wall studs or the ability to measure effectively, the end result will not justify the state-of-the-art tools.

Just as an investigation consists of the various puzzle pieces put together to form the whole picture, so does the usefulness of data mining fit with the rest of the investigation. These techniques do not negate the need for using one's experience in the area of investigation and analysis; neither do they allow an "armchair only" approach to an investigation.

In *A Guide to Forensic Accounting Investigation*, it is noted that consideration of data mining should be made at the outset of an investigation, specifically to determine:

- What relevant data might be available?
- What skills are available within the team?
- How will the data analysis fit in with the wider investigation?[6]

TO THE FUTURE

Until recent years, there was an accepted profile of companies susceptible to financial statement fraud. The typical fraud company had revenues of less than $50 million, was a technology, healthcare, or financial services company suffering losses or reaching only breakeven profitability, had an overbearing CEO or CFO, a complacent board of directors, and a poorly qualified audit committee meeting as infrequently as only once a year. The discovery of accounting improprieties at a number of large companies shows that even Fortune 500 companies are not immune to poor governance.

The fear that we are moving into an age of untrustworthy and arrogant management bent on looting their companies is probably exaggerated. The aftermath of the great stock market excesses of the 1920s, the "Go-Go" market of the 1960s, and the collapse of 1987 also brought overvaluations and insider trading scandals to light that were shocking in their size and audacity, but none of them proved to be harbingers of greater corruption to follow. The companies most in need of a due diligence investigation will continue to be those with revenues of less than $50 million. However, all companies must be scrutinized with a healthy professional skepticism at all times.

Two recent cases emphasize the point of diligence and the use of data mining. The first involved a former senior government official and a lawyer, sent to prison for their part in an $18.1 million contract procurement fraud at a Navy base in Pennsylvania. As noted in the newspaper story, Department of Defense auditors unraveled the scheme when they used data mining software and found $11 million of payments using government credit cards.[7]

In another case, reported by Reuters, investigators used data mining programs in the fight against insurance fraud; specifically they used "linkage" software to find a common thread between multiple, seemingly unrelated claims.[8] For example, this technique helped solve the case of a woman who claimed she found a finger in her chili at a Wendy's restaurant. The investigators found a woman with a history of filing similar claims for foreign objects in her food.

As we noted in one of our definitions of data mining, it is about the analysis of data for relationships that have not previously been discovered. As the recent news stories show, these techniques are also being used for proactive fraud detection, as well as after-the-fact investigation.

The lessons to be learned from recent corporate fraud are that companies have to be more proactive and cannot assume that the analysis used in the past will suffice in the future. While the acquisition of personnel and the tools necessary will involve the types of proactive expenditures many businesses previously shied away from, the lessons learned in recent years, and many discussed in this book, should drive home the point of the age-old idiom "penny-wise, pound-foolish."[9]

SUGGESTED READINGS

Golden, Thomas W., Steven L. Skalak, and Mona M. Clayton. *A Guide to Forensic Accounting Investigation.* Hoboken, NJ: Wiley, 2006.

Levitt, Arthur. "The 'Numbers Game.' " Speech presented to the New York University Center of Law and Business, September 28, 1998.

Silverstone, Howard. "International Business: What You Don't Know Can Hurt You." *GPCC News, the Newsletter of the Greater Philadelphia Chamber of Commerce,* October 2002.

Silverstone, Howard, and Peter McFarlane. "Quantitative Due Diligence: The Check Before the Check." *The M&A Lawyer,* 6, no. 6 (November–December 2002). Used with permission of Glasser Legal Works, 150 Clove Road, Little Falls, NJ 07424, (800) 308-1700, www.glasserlegalworks.com.

NOTES

1. Sir Arthur Conan Doyle, "The Adventure of the Copper Beeches"; www.lit quotes.com/quote_title_resp.php?TName=The%20Adventure%20of%20the% 20Copper%20Beeches.
2. Arthur Levitt, "The 'Numbers Game,'" a speech presented to the New York University Center for Law and Business, September 28, 1998; www.sec.gov/news/ speech/speecharchive/1998/spch220.txt.
3. https://iomega-eu-en.custhelp.com/cgi-bin/iomega_eu_en.cfg/php/enduser/std_ adp.php?p_faqid=1725.
4. www.creotec.com/index.php?page=e-business_terms.
5. www.jqjacobs.net/edu/cis105/concepts/CIS105_concepts_13.html.
6. Thomas W. Golden, Steven L. Skalak, and Mona M. Clayton, *A Guide to Forensic Accounting Investigation* (Hoboken, NJ: Wiley, 2006), Chapter 20.
7. www.cumberlink.com/articles/2006/03/28/news/news16.txt.
8. http://today.reuters.com/business/newsArticle.aspx?type=ousiv&storyID=2006-03-31T194159Z_01_N31262096_RTRIDST_0_BUSINESSPRO-FINANCIAL-INSURANCEFRAUD-DC.XML.
9. www.goenglish.com/PennyWisePoundFoolish.asp.

5

THE ROLE OF THE
ACCOUNTING PROFESSIONAL

THE IMPORTANCE OF ACCOUNTING PROFESSIONALS
IN THE INVESTIGATION

People always ask me, "Were you funny as a child?"
Well, no, I was an accountant.[1]

There is no doubt the high-profile cases of WorldCom, Enron, and others brought an increased public scrutiny of accountants. The demise of the Arthur Andersen firm was directly related to Enron and probably brought the accounting profession to the fore more than any other single incident.

Much has been written about the state of the accounting profession in recent times, including WebCPA, an online resource for accountants.[2] Comments received by WebCPA from industry leaders provide an interesting insight into the state of the accounting industry. According to Carol Markman, President of the National Conference of CPA Practitioners, "CPAs are also more aware of their own responsibility to maintain an honest and independent perspective when engaged in the audit function." Added Gary John Previts, Professor and Associate Dean, Weatherhead School of Management, Case Western Reserve University, "We have made progress, but we have not yet achieved the level of regard of which we are capable." Jack Ciesielski, publisher of *The Analyst's Accounting Observer*, added "When the profession does things right, it's not noticeable. When things go awry, that's news."

Statement on Auditing Standards (SAS) No. 99, issued by the AICPA in 2002, significantly expanded the information-gathering phase beyond the traditional audit. The standard requires the auditor to assess the entity's programs and controls that address identified fraud risks. Significantly, the standard requires a brainstorming session among the audit team to discuss the potential for material misstatement of the financial statements due to fraud, a greater emphasis on inquiry as an audit procedure to increase the likelihood of fraud detection, expanding analytical procedures, and considering other information, such as client acceptance procedures, during the information gathering stage.

We should keep in mind the ACFE's *2004 Report to the Nation on Occupational Fraud and Abuse*, where only 10.9 percent of frauds were initially detected by external audit. However, almost 24 percent were detected by internal audit, which should tell us that utilizing similar skill-sets and a skeptical mindset should assist in overall detection. The most important qualities the accounting professional can bring to any fraud investigation are an investigative mindset and skepticism. In the past, external accountants have been criticized for a lack of skepticism for fear of upsetting a client and possibly losing them. One would hope that in the wake of recent accounting scandals, accountants are beyond that fear, especially in light of SAS 99.

Toby Bishop, immediate past President and CEO of the ACFE, and Joseph Wells, founder and Chairman of the ACFE, believe that "one of the most difficult issues facing the auditing profession is that there are no auditing procedures that can provide absolute assurance in detecting all fraudulent financial reporting." Bishop and Wells believe that "the public and the auditing profession could be better served by adopting a more holistic approach to the deterrence of fraud." Their concept, the "Model Organizational Fraud Deterrence Program," employs a best practices approach to fraud prevention.[3]

Bishop and Wells emphasized several areas of concentration, including anti-fraud education and research, anti-fraud specialists on public company audits, and financial transparency for boards, insiders, and executives.

The skeptical mindset is something that has long been inherent in forensic accountants and other internal investigators when looking for evidence of fraud. The investigator historically has asked a set of questions different from those of the conventional auditor, who is monitoring the financial statements to see whether they are in compliance with GAAP and thereby fairly represent the financial condition of the company.

With the emergence of SAS 99 and under increasing scrutiny, the external auditor is now being pushed to think like the forensic accountant—to think like both a thief and a detective and be constantly looking for the weak links in the accounting system and among the people who staff it. In the course of the investigation, the forensic accountant must be prepared to reach far beyond the company's books to industry and government information, proprietary databases, court records, and to any source that might throw light on the case.

The investigative accountant should bring independence and objectivity, as should the auditor. Since fraud is a breach of standards of honesty, the investigator must be of irreproachable personal integrity and without allegiance to anyone or anything but the truth. Everyone encountered in the course of the investigation must be dealt with impartially and evenhandedly.

Any fraud investigation is part art and part science. The science element comes, of course, from academic training in accounting theory, especially the audit side, and from knowledge of business practices and legal processes acquired through experience. This serves as the foundation for the investigator's task. As for the art element, many may argue that accounting is an art, not a science, but that is not a discussion for this book!

What turns a well-trained and experienced accounting professional into a good financial investigator, however, is the knowledge of human behavior and a sixth sense for red flags and a good intuitive feel for the significance of evidence. The skeptical mindset should raise questions about the reasonableness of all transactions and the evidence that underlies them. Since the magnitude of amounts taken in a long-term fraud, for example, is often invisible except for a small irregularity in the accounts, the financial investigator must be curious and tenacious enough to follow up even the most initially unpromising clues. The judgments made through this skepticism will open up new hypotheses or close down old ones by testing them against the accumulating evidence until only one explanation is left. "When you have eliminated the impossible, whatever remains, however improbable, must be the truth."[4]

To highlight part of the convergence of the forensic accountant's and auditor's mindset, the AICPA recently published an excerpt from "Auditing for Internal Fraud" by Michael Connelley, CFE and CPA. The article highlighted common fraud types and their red flags (i.e., warning signs of fraud). Among the exhibits to the article were identification of fraud schemes, their symptoms, and detection methods. As an example, for the fraud scheme of skimming, symptoms included cash sales or receipts differing from normal or expected patterns, and unusual patterns of cash shortages. The detection methods included spotters and surveillance, gross profit analysis, and inventory comparisons. Interestingly, surveillance was used as a detection method, something once used only by investigators, but now recommended for auditors!

Accounting professionals play two important roles in any forensic investigation: as lead financial investigators and, potentially, as expert witnesses in any subsequent civil or criminal trials. In the first instance, they are the *key* people in any fraud investigation because they understand accounting systems and internal controls and know how to trace the flow of funds into, through, and out of the company. They are also in a position to provide an independent, objective critique of the corporate organization. This critique should not only cover the problems in the accounting system that permitted the fraud to occur in the first place but also address the integrity of the people at the heart of the process. As experts assisting in case strategy and testimony, accounting professionals know the rules of evidence, what documents to request, whom they should interview, and, in civil cases, how to do any associated damage quantification arising out of a particular situation.

The good financial investigator must be knowledgeable about fraudulent practices both in general and for a specific industry. A wide experience of how frauds are committed enables the investigator to act quickly in deciding which classes of documents will be most useful and who needs to be interviewed. Because some industries such as insurance, construction, and banking are especially prone to fraud, some investigators may specialize in those fields.

Since so much information is now created and stored electronically, a good knowledge of computers and information technology is an essential part of the investigator's tool-kit. Computer forensics techniques are now also commonplace as part of financial investigations. These techniques can assist in recovering "deleted" information such as e-mails and proprietary information transferred to unauthorized computers. Then, when the evidence has been gathered and the suspects have been identified, good communication skills are needed to write a report that ties the whole story together and makes a well-supported argument in clear language. The ability to translate complex accounting issues into language the layperson understands is especially important when giving expert testimony. A judge or jury not familiar with accounting concepts and terminology must receive the information in clear, understandable form.

When fraud is suspected, the first job of the investigative accountant is to discover and review the evidence to prove or disprove the allegations. Since the reputations of the suspected principals are at stake, the evidence-gathering process must be extremely discrete. Evidence must also be gathered and preserved in such a way that it can meet the standards-of-proof tests of any court; this is the forensic standard to which investigative accounting is held. In criminal cases, the evidence must establish guilt beyond a reasonable doubt; in civil cases, liability is established by the less rigorous standard of the balance of probabilities. Nonjudicial regulatory authorities, boards, and tribunals have yet other standards with which the investigator should be familiar.

Evidence will typically come from two primary sources. The first is the accounting records and any underlying documentation that may exist. In many cases, evidence found in these records might suggest additional research in external databases such as public records and court documents, as mentioned above. The investigator's experience should indicate what issues are well supported, which ones need additional evidence, and which are merely circumstantial.

The second source of evidence is gained through the interview process. Interviews may be conducted with key internal personnel, outside sources, and, ultimately, the suspects and any outside parties such as vendors or contractors who have done business with the individuals in question. The nature and timing of the interviews will be driven by the conduct of the case. (Interviews are discussed at greater length later on in this book.)

The financial investigator must also be a good psychologist and be able to assess the greater or lesser likelihood that any given suspect is a fraudster. The paper and electronic evidence may show that accounting irregularities exist, but unless the evidence is connected to individuals, no fraud can be established. The investigator must be able to pick up on the motivational and behavioral clues that define a suspect. A winter tan, a better car, an affair, domestic financial worries, and a thousand other clues can all raise suspicions that might develop into a picture of criminal activity. Again, this process is discussed later in this book.

> He preferred the precision of a balanced ledger, its promise of fiscal transparency, its devotion to a world defined by generally accepted accounting principles, to the wild, terminal justice of a hollow-tipped bullet.[5]

THE AUDIT PROCESS

Every fraud has an institutional context. Fraud is less likely to occur in an ethical corporate culture created by a principled management that respects the law and its employees, pays them adequately, and deals fairly with its customers and suppliers. A permissive corporate culture driven by greedy and even charismatic management that turns a blind eye to cutting corners, overlooks infractions of regulations, and has an inadequate accounting system gives unscrupulous employees the green light to commit fraud.

Some frauds show amazing ingenuity, but most are quite straightforward if the investigator knows where to look. Many very clever people have committed fraud but have been caught because every fraudster leaves a trail and makes mistakes. Since only a small proportion of fraud is actually discovered by investigation, most of the investigator's initial work involves checking out preliminary information.[6] This is especially true of so-called off-book frauds (i.e., bribery and kickbacks), which do not leave an audit trail and are often discovered by tip-offs.

The fraud itself may be entirely internal, directed against outsiders, or directed by outsiders against the company. Internal frauds are usually abuses of the accounting system to steal cash. Frauds directed against outsiders frequently take the form of misrepresentations of financial information to creditors, shareholders, or insurance carriers. Outsiders defrauding the company are most often vendors, contractors, and consultants who supply shoddy goods, overbill, or seek advantages through bribing employees.

Given the statistics and the fact that approximately 11 percent of initial fraud detection is through external audit (and approximately 24% is from internal audit), together with over 18 percent from internal controls, one would hope that we have all learned from the lessons of the past and have become smarter and better equipped to detect fraud. Certainly, the American Institute of Certified Public Accountants and the accounting bodies have gone a long way to instill the fraud mindset in external auditors. Through Statements on Auditing Standards (SAS) 53, 82, and, most recently, 99 (Consideration of Fraud in a Financial Statement Audit), auditors have been given expanded guidance for detecting material fraud.[7]

As stated by the AICPA, "The standard reminds auditors that they must approach every audit with professional skepticism and not assume management is honest. It puts fraud at the forefront of the auditor's mind."[8]

SAS 99 provides primarily for an increased professional skepticism; the auditor must plan for brainstorming how fraud can occur and put aside prior mindset as to management's honesty and integrity. At the planning stage, the auditor is required to identify the risks inherent in the client organization and to keep in mind the essentials of fraud factors, such as incentive, opportunity, and rationalization. In addition, there must be discussions with management, and inquiry must be made as to the risk of fraud and as to whether management is aware of any fraud. Auditors must also talk to employees and outside management, and give people a chance to bring to light problems that may exist (the concept of whistleblowing). This particular factor emphasizes the psychological deterrent to potential perpetrators of knowing there is a better chance they will be turned in if people who are aware of the problem have a chance to provide information in a controlled, somewhat anonymous forum.

SAS 99 also places emphasis on surprise testing of locations and accounts that might otherwise not be tested, and that would therefore come as a surprise to management and employees alike. The standard also includes procedures for auditors to test management's potential override of controls.

From a historical perspective, the debate on the auditor's role as "watchdog" versus "bloodhound" and the auditor's responsibilities is nothing new. Two AICPA committees, the Cohen Commission of 1978 and the Public Oversight Board of 1978, were established to look at the public perception of the auditor and his perceived role versus his actual role. In addition, the AICPA held a conference in 1992 called the Expectation Gap, which identified fraud as a problem in the industry. It was found that the public truly believed that the independent auditor would detect material misstatements owing to fraud.

The Cohen Commission also noted that users of financial statements were confused as to the respective responsibilities of auditors versus those of management. The most troubling aspect of the Cohen Commission's findings was the confusion that appeared to be prevalent among what could be considered educated users such as bankers, analysts, and shareholders.

It was hoped that the Auditing Standard Board's Statement of Auditing Standards No. 58, Reports on Audited Financial Statements, would clarify the understanding of management and auditor responsibilities. However, as business transactions became more complicated and entities more complex, it became clear that the nature of business left prior perceptions behind. Perhaps because of this business complexity, the standards began to address the role of the auditor, specifically in detecting fraud, and emphasized that the concept of the professional skeptic had to be spelled out not only for the auditor to understand, but for the users of financial statements, who needed to comprehend the auditor role and its separate existence from management.

Sadly, the accounting shenanigans discussed in earlier chapters once again brought into question the auditor's role and the perceived value of an audit. It is the users and the regulators who want the auditor to probe deeper, and it is out of this need and expectation that SAS 99 was born. Auditors must use analytical techniques during the planning of their audit. These results can now be used in conjunction with other evidence gathered for purposes of identifying material misstatements.

So what does all this mean in the context of understanding basic accounting concepts, the concept of fraud, and the use of analytics in conjunction with all other knowledge? What it means is that today's auditors must think like their investigative accounting counterparts. They have to think like a potential fraudster. They have to be experienced in understanding the concept of fraud and must continually be the skeptic. Although this will put pressure on other aspects of the audit—such as staffing and budgeting (a subject near and dear to most clients' hearts!)—it will hopefully narrow the expectation gap that has existed for so long.

INTERNAL CONTROLS

Internal controls are part of the protective system against fraud. They are designed to prevent irregularities and ensure early detection. Indeed, the Association of Certified Fraud Examiners' *2002 Report to the Nation on Occupational Fraud and Abuse* noted that "a strong system of internal controls was viewed as the most effective anti-fraud measure by a wide margin."[9] In its 2004 survey, the ACFE noted "strong internal controls can have a significant impact on fraud and a well-designed control structure should be a priority in any comprehensive anti-fraud program."

Internal controls become a concern to both the auditor and financial investigator when these controls are either absent or vulnerable to manipulation by fraudsters. Controls ensure that transactions are carried out only with appropriate authorization and are recorded correctly according to transaction type, amount, and time of execution. With good internal controls, restricting access and segregating responsibilities should safeguard assets. Access to data processing centers and to the computers themselves should be strictly controlled. Assets are further controlled through comparing physical inventory counts with the financial records.

So what do we make of cases like Computer Associates, where executives admitted they fraudulently recorded hundreds of millions of dollars' worth of contracts to inflate earnings? How about Krispy Kreme or Parmalat or many other companies, who in recent times have been accused of accounting irregularities?

In light of these recent events in the business and accounting world, one of the more important controls over the accounting system has to be the ethical conduct of management. It cannot be stressed enough that the ethical tone of the company is established at the top and works its way down. Good management should ensure that employees are properly trained, that they read and abide by a written code of conduct, and that they know that a policy of integrity will be enforced. The owners must also ensure that the board of directors is composed of financially experienced and honest people. It is especially important that the audit committee include financially educated and sophisticated members who meet regularly and carry out their responsibilities conscientiously.

Hiring at all levels should be done carefully through screening processes in which HR people or background-check specialists actually make the phone calls to verify education and experience claimed on the application form. All employees must take their vacations. This is one of the most basic tenets of business, but also one that is not readily enforced and has been shown to be the roadmap to fraud on so many occasions.

Although the costs of good controls can be significant, they should not be more than their anticipated benefit. Smaller companies are sometimes forced to combine duties that would be separated in larger firms. The audit committee as well as the internal and external auditors should be aware of this fact. People with multiple responsibilities must be supervised closely. Many companies have introduced the concept of self-audit, whereby different groups or locations within a company audit each other on a monthly basis, checking certain aspects of each other's business. This process demonstrates not only that controls are actually in place, but also that any fraud likely to be perpetrated would then have to comprise more people in its collusive manner, hence increasing the difficulty of its execution.

Another simple concept, but one that is easily missed, is that of preparing an organizational chart that defines responsibilities. This eliminates "I didn't know that was my job" from the excuse and/or rationalization stage. In addition, forms used within the company should be designed for accurate recording of data. The data as recorded should be complete enough to be accepted as evidence in court. Accounting personnel should be rotated to different duties on a regular basis. Recordkeeping should not be handled by operating personnel, and there should be a clear records management policy with a schedule for retention, archiving, and destruction that meets statutory, legal, and regulatory requirements.

Special attention should be paid to the control of cash and inventory, two of the most common targets of fraud. Only a reasonable amount of cash should be kept on hand at any time, and the custodian should have no access to the accounting records. Cash receipts should be deposited by way of a lock box arrangement with a bank. Where a lock box is not practical due to company size or nature of business, cash should be deposited daily by bonded custodians and bank accounts should be properly authorized. The cashier should have no accounting duties. Cash disbursements should be made only through computer-generated checks, and all signing authorities should be limited. Inventory counts should be made by employees other than those responsible for managing the stockroom or warehouse. Insurance coverage should reflect the real value of the current inventory at all times. Periodic counts should be compared to the perpetual record.

So many times we hear about the red flags of fraud, the quotes of management playing Monday-morning quarterback, the specialized sense of hindsight of the "should have known" variety. Through qualified professionals, a healthy serving of professional skepticism, suitable guidance from the accounting profession, and adequate assistance from business itself, business can minimize the chance of fraud occurring. However, as we have seen and will continue to see throughout this book, none of these factors is mutually exclusive, and none of the players are mutually exclusive.

Clearly, the accounting professional plays a key role in all aspects of a company's business; and while the same accountant or accounting firm under Sarbanes-Oxley can no longer fulfill all the roles for one client, the profession itself has a significant role to play in all aspects of protecting companies' financial well-being.

I have no use for bodyguards, but I have very specific use for two highly trained certified public accountants.[10]

NOTES

1. Ellen DeGeneres, comedian, b.1958; www.thinkexist.com.
2. www.webcpa.com/.
3. Toby J.F. Bishop, CFE, CPA, FCA, and Joseph T. Wells, CFE, CPA, "Breaking Tradition in the Auditing Profession" (September/October 2003), ACFE.
4. Sherlock Holmes in Sir Arthur Conan Doyle's *The Sign of Four.*
5. Christopher Reich, *The Devil's Banker* (New York: Bantam Dell, 2003), lead character Adam Chapel's reaction when discussing guns.
6. Bologna and Lindquist state that 90 percent of fraud is discovered by accident. See G. Jack Bologna and Robert J. Lindquist, *Fraud Auditing and Forensic Accounting: New Tools and Techniques* (New York: John Wiley & Sons, 1995), p. 32. This estimate has changed in recent years as reported by the Association of Certified Fraud Examiners. Of the 532 cases whose discovery was studied for the *2002 Report to the Nation: Occupational Fraud and Abuse*, only 18.8 percent were found by accident. This figure is especially startling because it is higher than those discovered by internal audit (18.6%), internal controls (15.4%), or external audit (11.5%). Tips from employees were the single largest source of information that fraud was suspected (26.3%); www.cfenet.com/media/2002RttN/.
7. As defined in Statement of Financial Accounting Concepts No. 2 (FASB, May 1980), materiality is "the magnitude of an omission or misstatement of accounting information that, in the light of surrounding circumstances, makes it possible that the judgment of a reasonable person relying on the information would have been changed or influenced by the omission or misstatement."
8. Barry Melancon, AICPA president and CEO.
9. www.cfenet.com/media/.
10. Elvis Presley, American singer and actor, 1935–1977; www.thinkexist.com.

PART II
FINANCIAL CRIME INVESTIGATION

6

BUSINESS AS A VICTIM

INTRODUCTION

Business can be a victim of both internal and external fraud. Internal fraud is perpetrated by employees at any level from bookkeepers writing checks to themselves to the complex collusion to steal inventory by manipulating computer data and shipping the stolen goods to offsite locations. External fraud is deception committed by an outsider against the company. Insurance companies are common victims of this type of fraud through false applications and false claims. Banks are also frequently victimized, as are government agencies.

The key factor is to recognize the warning sign of fraud; to understand how fraud is committed is to understand how to minimize its possibility. Unfortunately, the statistics still show that many businesses do not understand the red flags of fraud.

> You only pay a nuclear physicist two million dollars for one thing these days and it wasn't to build a better mousetrap.[1]

As indicated in the 2004 report of the Association of Certified Fraud Examiners mentioned in Chapter 1, asset misappropriation accounts for an overwhelming 92.7 percent of all occupational fraud. Corruption schemes are a distant second at 30.1 percent, and fraudulent statements represent 7.9 percent.[2]

EMPLOYEE THEFTS

Cash

Cash is the favorite target of fraudsters and accounts for 93 percent of all asset misappropriations according to the 2004 ACFE study. Much is taken by outright cash larceny and skimming, but the majority is stolen through more elaborate disbursement schemes, including some manipulation of the billing and payroll systems or falsification of expense reimbursements and check tampering.

All accounting cycles pass through the cash account at some time. The cash produced in these processes becomes either petty cash or demand deposits, such as checking accounts, interest-bearing accounts, certificates of deposit, or other liquid investments. The mechanism of these thefts is usually quite simple. Petty cash is stolen by forging authorizing signatures or creating false vouchers for reimbursement.

Dishonest employees often manipulate receipts being prepared for deposit. This is common in small companies where the same person is responsible for booking the cash receipts and writing the checks for deposit. It is not uncommon for the long-term "trusted employee" to become an "opportunity taker" type of fraudster in the face of this temptation. Because the money is so available and no one appears to be watching, the fraudster frequently rationalizes the theft as "borrowing" with the intent to return the cash later. Of course, since the money is easier to take than to return, the accrued amount stolen soon becomes too great to replace and the fraudster becomes locked into an endless round of theft and cover-up. Perhaps the ultimate conclusion is that the fraudster never intended to return the money and this is indeed a weak response when they are ultimately questioned about their activities.

Case Study: Like Pulling Teeth

A receptionist/bookkeeper at a small dental practice was the only person who understood the proprietary software used to track patient data, as well as being the one who prepared deposits of receipts for the bank. The bookkeeper noticed that she could input data (checks, insurance receipts, credit card receipts) and prepare a deposit slip for the owner to take to the bank, before inputting cash into the system. The deposit slip given to the owner of the practice did not show certain cash receipts, and hence he had no idea the bookkeeper had in fact pocketed the money. She entered the cash into the system after printing the deposit slip, just in case a patient should ever be questioned about his or her account.

The bookkeeper left the practice after six weeks for a better-paying job. However, she did not factor into her scheme a patient who returned to the dental office asking for a receipt for the cash she had paid two weeks before. The new receptionist/bookkeeper, not yet being familiar with the computer system, obtained the deposit slip used by her boss to make the deposit on that particular day and, of course, the cash was nowhere to be found. They then went into the computer file and realized what had happened. A call to the police ensued!

Case Study: How the Worm Got into the Apple

A husband and wife started a small printing business, having been in the printing world for quite some time and with an excellent relationship with their bank. They owned their own house, had a large loan to start the business, and had various lines of credit. At that stage of the business, the wife kept the books. As the company grew and prospered, they decided to hire a bookkeeper so the wife could spend more time marketing the business. The bookkeeper was a gem—the books were always in good order and she was easy to work with. Her responsibilities were gradually increased and she became controller with a suitable salary and bonuses.

The owners had also adjusted their accounting system to permit her to write checks, which would be signed by the husband or wife. Unfortunately, their trust and friendship with the bookkeeper blinded them and made them careless. They did not review the monthly bank statements. They left the collection, banking, and check-writing in the hands of the same person. However, this was not a classic fraudster; this was a 44-year-old divorced woman waiting for the good life to come her way. She started to forge the owner's signature on checks and hid them from the owners. She paid her own credit card bills along with legitimate business payables. This fraud continued for four years and almost $500,000—money that was not available for reinvestment, for maintaining loan covenants and paying off debt, or for salary increases or bonuses.

Ultimately, the bookkeeper was taking more money than the company had coming in, generating overdrafts and NSF fees. When she realized she could not repair the damage, she disappeared. On the day she left, the bank's relationship officer called the owners to discuss the overdrafts and huge NSF fees, $1,600 in the last month alone. Upon further investigation, the owners wanted to know why the bank had honored checks with such obviously forged signatures. A lawsuit ensued, demanding reimbursement of the NSF fees and the $500,000 withdrawn by the bookkeeper. The bank asserted it was up to all customers to be aware of the usual disclaimers and that the Uniform Commercial Code protected banks from the negligence of their customers by limiting liability for forged checks to one year and even then only if the customer identified the checks and signed a forged check affidavit. The case was settled after the bank offered some small restitution to the owners.

The lessons to be learned from this case study are that the owners should have been more responsible for their financial affairs and should have checked the monthly bank statements. As the ACFE points out in its 2004 survey, 93 percent of asset misappropriation cases involved cash. Also, a fidelity bond policy (employee dishonesty) would have helped minimize the financial impact of the loss. Closer monitoring by the relationship manager at the bank, and asking questions as the company grew, could have also helped the owners through their growing pains.[3]

Case Study: All in the Family

Mary was married to Ron. Over the years, as Mary's father, Ben, continued to age, Mary would assist her father with the paying of his bills, the writing of checks, and similar tasks. During this same timeframe, Mary and Ron were getting themselves deeper and deeper into credit card debt, not unlike many young couples these days.

Mary and Ron both worked at good jobs, earning good incomes, but were living beyond their means. As Mary's father became more and more dependent on Mary's help, Mary and Ron fell deeper and deeper into debt. And instead of working on their spending problem, they sought out an easy and quick fix.

One day, when Mary was in the process of paying her dad's bills and balancing his checkbook, she took the opportunity to jot down some pertinent information, namely the account number and bank routing number as well as the next available check number from her father's checking account. Of course she was also privy to the available balance in the account.

Her next act was to call her credit card company and offer them a payment by phone, a method of bill paying that has become widely practiced these days by busy (too busy to write a check a week or so before it's due and drop it in the mail) people. Mary used the information gained from her father's checkbook to issue an electronic check for payment against her credit card account. Her father had no knowledge of what Mary was doing—stealing her father's money!

To add even more fuel to this crime, Mary authorized a payment of $29,000 from her father's account, roughly $20,000 more than she and Ron owed on that credit card. As is the practice by most credit card companies, they refunded the excess payment amount to Mary and Ron about two months later. Mary and Ron's credit card bill was paid in full, and they had $20,000 more to spend. Ben, on the other hand, had been robbed, but was unaware of the theft, as Mary, his trusted, loving daughter, was balancing his checkbook.

Ben's lifestyle was simple, and his financial needs were easily covered by his Social Security checks that were directly deposited into his checking account each month. Mary continued to pay her father's bills each month as she had been doing for years.

Ben, although growing old, was not feeble, and one day decided to look over his checking account statement to see how much he had sitting in the bank that had been accumulating from his excess Social Security deposits. That's when he saw the theft of his $29,000. He called his daughter, and he called his bank.

An investigation ensued, and the bank told Ben that the draft from his account was paid to a credit card company, and that the draft was complete and proper: It contained the correct account name, the correct account number, the correct routing number, and was made out for an amount that was within the current balance at the time, and therefore, it was honored by the bank.

Based on the information contained in the telephone payment draft, which the bank disclosed to Ben, as it was Ben's account the money came from, Ben then confronted the credit card company with his demand for reimbursement. After all, Ben didn't owe any money to the credit card company. And based on the account number that was credited with the funds, Ben found out that the money was used by his daughter, Mary.

Now, Ben had a dilemma. He was out $29,000, no small sum for a retired man. The credit card company accepted his money, but without his permission, and applied it to his daughter's, (and son-in-law's) balance owing. His bank allowed the money to be withdrawn from his account, again without his permission. But Ben also realized that it was his daughter who stole the money from him. What's a father to do?

Ben sued the bank and the credit card company. He wanted his money returned, but he didn't want to see his daughter go to jail, and knew she no longer had the money with which to reimburse him.

The bank was able to legally transfer liability to the credit card company and was deemed not liable for any wrongdoing. The credit card company defended itself, and hired a banking expert to assist in its defense. The credit card company was, in fact, not liable for anything, and acted within allowable and legal banking standards. The case was settled before trial when the credit card company agreed to make a small cash settlement with Ben.

Case Study: The Bank Teller

The huge amounts of cash passing across the counter every day at any bank branch frequently provide all the temptation a teller may need to become dishonest. A client complained she could not account for the withdrawal of several thousand dollars recently deposited following the sale of her car. She remembered the name on the tag of the teller who had processed the deposit. The employee was interviewed and confessed she had obtained the client's identifiers (her mother's maiden name and birth date) and created a duplicate bankbook.

This was a particularly sad case because the teller was just in her early twenties. The motive for her theft was her large credit card debt, which left her without enough money to pay her rent. She was dismissed from the bank but was not prosecuted.

PAYROLL FRAUD

Fraud through the payroll department is commonly committed by using ghost employees, inflating hours of work and overtime, as well as overstating expense accounts or medical claims.

Case Study: Simple Payroll Fraud

The bookkeeper of a construction company knew there were hundreds of transient workers on the payroll at any given time. She also knew that at any point in time, many workers dropped off the payroll and many more joined. She also knew that no one was checking her work. She handled the payroll, used the owner's facsimile signature stamp on checks, and hand-delivered the checks to the various jobsites!

The bookkeeper kept a handful of former employees on the payroll, both male and female. She even paid their union dues and payroll taxes! However, instead of delivering these checks to the jobsite, where of course the employees no longer worked, she endorsed the back of the checks and deposited them into her bank account. She was friendly with one particular teller at the bank branch and used this teller exclusively to deposit the checks. Several people at her employer were curious as to her new executive automobile, new home, and rumored house at the beach, which she passed off as the result of her husband's large win at the casino.

However, it took an enforced prolonged illness and absence from the office for a temporary bookkeeper to question why non-employees were still on the payroll. Ultimately, the company recovered just about all of its lost funds, including refunds from the union and the IRS together with recoveries from the bank and the fraudulent bookkeeper.

Case Study: Expense Report Fraud

For some reason, expense accounts have been the most overlooked and least controlled area of many companies. Some supervisors give these reports a cursory review and if they pass the "smell test," they are authorized.

Imagine the horror of a company that discovered that a particular employee's "authorized" expense reports had not in fact been authorized. She had forged the signatures of her supervisors and hand-delivered her expense reports to the accounting department, each time concocting an excuse why they did not come through the customary route of other employees' expense reports.

The embezzler was later described as a "smooth talker" who distracted others with her line of conversation. Over the course of four years, she submitted expense reports with several hundred thousand dollars of falsified expenses. She even went as far as creating false invoices submitted with her expense reports as support for her expenses. She included vouchers for business publication subscriptions, where she would show her credit card as having been used to incur the original expense, when in fact she hadn't even submitted the application for the subscription.

As is typical in many of these situations, her scheme was never found out while she was in the company's employment. She actually was dismissed for a totally unrelated insubordination issue. In the interim, she had become bold and mailed an invoice to the company from a fictitious vendor using a post office box, which did not reach the bookkeeping department until after she had been dismissed. A keen and skeptical clerk ran some Internet searches and internal reports and discovered the post office box had actually been used by the now former employee. After further investigation, her entire scheme was discovered. The company recovered much of its loss from its insurance carrier and the perpetrator was sentenced to time in prison.

FRAUDULENT BILLING SCHEMES

These frauds are usually committed by outsiders such as vendors, suppliers, and contractors of various kinds. They are perpetrated through submission of false invoices for goods or services not supplied or inflated invoices for goods or services of inferior quality. These frauds often involve collusion between outsiders and internal employees and can become quite complex. Collusion allows controls to be circumvented.

Case Study: Construction Fraud

Because the competitive bidding process for construction contracts often makes profit margins razor thin, contractors may be tempted to increase their profits through fraud. A developer negotiated a $550 million guaranteed maximum-price contract with a prime contractor and subcontractors to erect a 40-story building. To the developer's surprise, the allowances and contingency holds for unexpected costs and emergencies were exhausted before even the core and shell had been completed. This left the interior work unfunded. Puzzled and suspicious, the developer hired private investigators who discovered the prime contractor had bribed the architect and they were now colluding to defraud the developer. The contractor was purchasing goods and services beyond those required for the developer's building, diverting the excess to other jobs on which he and the architect were working and submitting the invoices to the developer. The excess expenses were approved and explained away by the architect. The contractor and the architect had convinced themselves that the developer's cost controls were shortsighted and would make the job unprofitable for them. When the architect and contractor were confronted with the evidence of the private investigation, they agreed to pay for the remaining construction from their own funds rather than be prosecuted.

The developer did not press charges against either the architect or the contractor, but he did report the architect to the licensing board. At the hearing, the investigators produced the evidence they had discovered for the developer and the architect received a written reprimand. This effectively put the architect on an industry blacklist, which made it difficult for him to find well-paying jobs. As with other fraudsters, the consequences of the dishonest architect's fraud affected his family. He was no longer able to keep his children in private school, and he had to drop a club membership he had enjoyed with his wife. Life went on, but not at the carefree level the family had enjoyed before.

FRAUD COMMITTED BY OUTSIDERS

Credit card and insurance fraud are perpetrated against companies by outsiders. Credit card fraud is estimated to have caused $650 million in losses to American business in 2001.[4] The impact of this type of fraud can be especially devastating to small retailers. According to the Coalition Against Insurance Fraud, fraudulent claims now cost the U.S. insurance industry an estimated $80 billion annually.[5] Bogus property and casualty claims alone account for $24 billion, or 10 percent of all property and casualty claims paid.[6] The insurance industry is at risk not just from paying on fraudulent claims but also from providing coverage where the real risk of loss is actually greater than can be actuarially determined on the basis of the false data in the original application.

Case Study: Insurance Fraud

A medium-sized clothing manufacturer had a warehouse fire in which it lost its summer inventory and financial records. The insurer became suspicious and started an investigation when a multimillion-dollar claim was filed less than two weeks after the fire. The investigators found the inventory was three times as large as that of the previous year, despite the fact that the industry was suffering a downturn and everybody was cutting back. The only records lost in the fire were those related to the inventory; everything else had been moved to another building a few weeks earlier. On the last renewal date before the fire, the insured had tripled the coverage. The documents submitted in support of the inventory valuation proved to have been created by the owner's brother allegedly for the owner's wife in an angry divorce action. The owner had, in fact, paid his brother $100,000 for the valuation. When the fire marshall's investigation proved arson, the insurer refused to pay the claim. The owner was convicted of arson and sentenced to prison.

With the building destroyed and the insurer refusing to pay the claim, the clothing manufacturing business was worthless. The only value lay in the land on which it had stood. The fraudsters had taken a huge risk and lost everything. They now had to lay off warehouse staff and bookkeepers as well as cutters and other skilled employees. Suppliers lost a customer and were forced to lay off part of their workforce.

MANAGEMENT THEFTS

Fraud by management can be extremely serious since senior personnel can override the controls that have been put in place to prevent the very fraud they are committing. The effects of management misconduct can also have severe consequences for the company's overall morale and set a negative model for employees farther down the company ladder.

Case Study: A Misused Credit Card

A disgruntled employee in the accounting department informed the new president of the publishing company that the secretary-treasurer was defrauding the company through misuse of her credit card. The secretary-treasurer was then covering her tracks by manipulating the accounting records. The new president realized immediately this was a political hot potato that could not be left uninvestigated but could also destroy his effectiveness if it proved to be untrue. He was unknown, and the secretary-treasurer had been with the company for seven years. Forensic accountants were brought in to examine her accounts. They discovered that she had charged personal items to a general corporate expense account and to the advance accounts of several employees. (The company permitted employees to charge personal expenses to their advance accounts from which they would be deducted later.) The false journal entries were in the secretary-treasurer's own handwriting. On the basis of the investigators' evidence, the president was successful in persuading the board of directors to dismiss her.

The departure of the secretary-treasurer created problems for everyone. When confronted by the board, she admitted taking the money and signed a promissory note for the full amount. She threatened a suit for wrongful dismissal but dropped it when confronted with the evidence uncovered by the forensic investigators. She now faced disgrace and loss of employment and was forced to live on her savings for 18 months before she found another job in an inferior position at a lower salary with a less prestigious company.

Those at the publishing house lost a friend and colleague. The company was now faced with the expense of an executive search and the prospect of hiring an unknown for a sensitive position. Everyone was shocked that such a trusted person should have committed fraud. The company incurred the additional expense of developing an educational program for employees in fraud prevention and detection and reviewing its accounting controls.

Case Study: Meaty Matters

A medium-sized meatpacking company in a small Texas town began to experience financial difficulties following a fire that did extensive damage to the plant. The insurance company promptly settled the property damage claim but a lengthy delay in coming to an agreement on a $1 million business interruption claim caused significant hardship as customers were forced to look elsewhere for their meat. The owners were concerned that a decline from their $40 million in annual sales and its effect on accounts receivable would jeopardize their line of credit with the banks. To keep their working capital ratio healthy, they began pre-billing and inflating inventory records.

When the company was eventually forced into bankruptcy, the receiver discovered only $2 million in inventory instead of the stated $10 million and $6 million in accounts receivable from clients who denied owing anything. No money, however, had been diverted to the personal use of the owners; they had acted solely to save the business.

The two owners pleaded guilty to fraud and received prison terms. The lives of two otherwise productive citizens had received blows from which no one ever really recovers. Their families were not only deprived of the presence of two husbands and fathers, but the lives of their wives and children were completely changed. The fraudsters' families were ostracized as they suffered the reflected disgrace of the two men. The wives who had not worked in 20 years now had to find jobs to support their families. The children became the target of other children's taunts. In the end, the situation became unendurable, and both families moved away to start new lives elsewhere. When the men came out of prison they had no money and were forced to begin again at a much lower standard of living. One of the couples divorced.

The effect of closing the meatpacking plant reached far beyond the immediate families of the convicted fraudsters. The company had been a major employer and had a significant impact on the local economy through its own spending and that of its employees. Of the 50 or so employees at the plant, only about 10 were able to get jobs in the town. Others found it difficult keeping up their mortgage payments and were forced to take odd jobs or look for employment in the next major center, which was about an hour's drive away. The local retailers suffered a noteworthy loss of business.

Case Study: The Whole Shebang

A manufacturing company was headquartered on the East Coast of the United States but had its main facility in the Midwest. Consequently, there was little day-to-day communication between the board of directors and senior management with management of the main operation in the Midwest. The chief financial officer, based in the Midwest, had been with the company for many years and had worked his way up from bookkeeper to assistant controller to controller and ultimately to CFO.

What was most interesting about the CFO's role is that with all the promotions leading finally to CFO, he retained custody over the bank reconciliations. For all the best practices discussed in Chapter 2 of this book, the company, perhaps unwittingly, allowed its CFO to authorize contracts with vendors, approve payments, actually print and sign checks, receive bank statements, and perform the bank reconciliation.

It was no surprise, then, that over seven years the CFO was able to embezzle over $600,000 through almost a dozen different schemes. The schemes ranged from a falsified employee workers' compensation claim (under which the CFO paid for his children's braces) to an expense account fraud whereby the company paid the CFO's credit card bill through a corporate check, while at the same time he submitted the charges on his expense account and was therefore reimbursed twice. He also paid for lavish family travel and entertaining on the company's expense and was part of a scheme with vendors whereby he received kickbacks in return for giving them various contracts.

When questioned how these schemes could go unnoticed for so long, it became apparent from his former staff that he had created a barrier between himself and anyone who worked for him. In addition, his physical size and manner reportedly intimidated anyone who wished to confront him. The schemes were ultimately discovered when a disgruntled secretary approached Human Resources and informed them that she thought something was peculiar about the handling of the CFO's expenses. She also questioned why he was still handling the bank reconciliation. An internal investigation ensued, and the schemes were discovered.

The company ultimately recovered $500,000 of its losses under a fidelity bond; an agreement was made between the company, the bonding company, and the U.S. attorney to keep the principal out of jail and working at another company in a nonfiduciary position, where he was able to start making restitution.

CORPORATE THEFTS

Corporate fraud is committed by senior management to benefit the corporation as a whole. This type of fraud includes financial statement fraud, antitrust violations, securities fraud, tax evasion, false advertising, environmental crimes, and the production of unsafe products.

Financial statement fraud is usually committed in order to improve the earnings and hence the stock price of publicly traded companies or the ratios supporting loan covenants at private companies. Generally accepted accounting principles (GAAP) provide accountants with a certain amount of interpretive leeway in creating their accounts. What can be justified as a liberal but understandable interpretation of GAAP can easily become a policy of deliberate earnings management and ultimately slip across the line into fraudulent manipulation. Managements of publicly traded companies are often under pressure from Wall Street analysts to meet earnings expectations by showing steady growth despite any downturns in the economy. The Equity Funding and Enron cases discussed earlier in this book are examples of what can happen when real life cannot perform up to expectations.

Antitrust laws, starting with the Sherman Antitrust Act of 1890, are designed to encourage competition by preventing monopolies or conspiracies to monopolize. The willingness to enforce these laws has varied from administration to administration. The principal instrument of monopoly power is price fixing.

Case Study: Price Fixing

Although price fixing has been discovered in many industries, one of the most outstanding recent cases was that of Archer Daniels Midland. The company paid a $100 million fine after pleading guilty to felony charges alleging a conspiracy with other producers of citric acid, lysine, and other commodities. It was estimated that makers of soft drinks, processed foods, detergents, and other products paid $400 million extra to buy citric acid from ADM and its co-conspirators between 1992 and 1995. Poultry, swine, and other livestock producers paid an extra $100 million in the same period for lysine, a growth additive used in feed.[7]

During the late 1940s through the 1950s, electric equipment manufacturers, including General Electric, Westinghouse, Allis-Chalmers, and Federal Pacific, conspired to fix prices in a market worth $1.75 billion annually.[8] Utilities, all levels of government, the military, and industry were victimized by prices that rose by double and sometimes even triple digits, despite slow growth in the wholesale price index. Four grand juries handed down 20 indictments against 45 individuals and 29 companies. The power of rationalization and "neutralization" referred to in Chapter 1 is well exemplified in the remarks of some of the industry executives. One company president defended his actions this way: "It is the only way a business can be run. It is free enterprise." Another, in a statement worthy of Yogi Berra, said: "Sure, collusion was illegal, but it wasn't unethical."[9]

IDENTITY THEFT

Identity theft is one of the fastest growing crimes. As much as the Internet has made access to our personal information a lot quicker, from almost anywhere in the world, so has it made such information accessible to the criminal element. Between January and December 2005, Consumer Sentinel, the complaint database developed and maintained by the FTC, received over 685,000 consumer fraud and identity theft complaints. Consumers reported losses from fraud of more than $680 million.[10] Of these, 63 percent were fraud-related and 37 percent identity theft.

Identity theft is defined as "the deliberate assumption of another person's identity, usually to gain access to their finances or frame them for a crime."[11] It has also been defined as "someone else using your personal information to create fraudulent accounts, to charge items to another person's existing accounts, or even to get a job."[12]

In his testimony before the U.S. House Government Reform Committee's Subcommittee on Technology, Information Policy, Intergovernmental Relations and the Census (September 22, 2004), Steven Martinez, Deputy Assistant Director of the FBI, noted the many ways in which identity theft has manifested itself. These included large-scale intrusions into third-party credit card processors, theft of printed checks from the mail, theft of preapproved credit cards from the mail, credit card skimming, and other crimes.

What is key about these schemes is that they can be inflicted on individuals and corporations. Whereas many of the fraud schemes discussed in this book relate primarily to business, identity theft is an intrusion on the corporation and therefore may take longer to be discovered than when against an individual. According to Toby Bishop and John Warren, "theft of personal information can be committed by hackers and other criminals outside your organization, or by employees, contractors and others working inside the company."[13]

One of the more prevalent schemes is to create a false website; indeed, outside vendors now offer services that include monitoring corporate websites to prevent the corruption of legitimate sites. In a scam in the United Kingdom, Internet banking customers of several major banks received e-mails that appeared to come from their bank. The e-mails contained a link that took the user to a replica of the legitimate site and extracted the customers' user names and passwords! Unfortunately, many individuals are still not sophisticated enough in Web technology to differentiate between a bogus e-mail and website and the real thing.

One solution that has been offered to the bogus e-mail/website scam is for companies to ensure they own various permutations of their name online, as well as educating individuals as to what a legitimate e-mail looks like, versus a bogus e-mail. Additionally, companies, especially banks and credit card companies, are reminding their customers about submitting personal data online and warning them of suspected scams.

Frank Abagnale, whose "paperhanging" or check fraud schemes were brought to the big screen in *Catch Me If You Can*, provides insight on how to reduce the risk of identity theft. As you look over this list, remember that they can apply equally to individuals and corporations. The onus on corporations is to ensure someone within the company is watching this information and taking the same steps as an individual should. Specifically, Mr. Abagnale suggests:

- Guard your Social Security number. Author's note: This also applies to a company's EIN (employer identification number).
- Monitor your credit report.
- Shred old bank statements and credit card statements.
- Take bill payments and checks to the post office to mail to avoid having these items stolen from a mailbox outside your home or office.
- Examine credit card charges before paying the bill.
- Never give credit card numbers or personal information over the phone unless you have initiated the call and trust that business.[14]

Toby Bishop and John Warren remind us that background checks are essential when hiring anyone who is going to be in a position to have access to personal information. While many white-collar criminals are first-time offenders, it still adds a layer of protection, especially by identifying someone with a major credit problem or a personal bankruptcy, for example. Companies should also have written policies on aspects such as data security, as well as training programs on security and sensitivity. Companies should also have a policy on the ramifications of a breach of such policy.

Identity theft has crossed the threshold from being just a consumer problem to a real problem for businesses. This is yet another aspect of fraud that companies need to plan for; as with all frauds, it means putting the right controls in place, recognizing the red flags when the controls fail, and being able to respond quickly.

Perhaps Charles Caleb Colton summed it up best some 200 hundred years ago, when he said, "There are some frauds so well conducted that it would be stupidity not to be deceived by them."[15]

SUGGESTED READINGS

http://insurancefraud.org/site_index_set.html; www.insurancefraud.org/news/study021303_set.html.

"The Growing Toll of Identity Theft." *Credit Card Management*, 15, no. 6 (September 2002): 13; www.aba.com/industry+issues/ealertii20.htm.

Simon, David R. *Elite Deviance*, 6th edition. Boston: Allyn & Bacon, 1999.

NOTES

1. Christopher Reich, *The Devil's Banker* (New York: Bantam Dell, 2003).
2. The sum of percentages exceeds 100% due to cases involving multiple schemes falling into more than category.
3. This case example originally appeared in "Fraud at a Customer's Business Could Mean Litigation for the Bank," an article in the February 2003 issue of *RMA Journal*, by Steven Butler, CFE.
4. "The Growing Toll of Identity Theft," *Credit Card Management*, 1, no. 6 (September 2002), p. 13; www.aba.com/industry+issues/ealertii20.htm.
5. http://insurancefraud.org/site_index_set.html.
6. www.insurancefraud.org/news/study021303_set.html.
7. David R. Simon, *Elite Deviance*, 6th ed. (Boston: Allyn & Bacon, 1999), p. 107.

8. Ibid., p. 108.

9. Quoted in ibid., p. 110.

10. www.consumer.gov/sentinel/pubs/Top10Fraud2005.pdf.

11. http://en.wikipedia.org/wiki/Identity_theft.

12. www.investordictionary.com/definition/identity+theft.aspx.

13. Toby Bishop and John Warren, "Identity Theft: The Next Corporate Liability Wave?" (February 2005), Association of Certified Fraud Examiners.

14. www.bankrate.com/brm/news/advice/20030124b.asp.

15. Charles Caleb Colton, 1780–1832, British clergyman, sportsman, and author of the *Lacon (Many Things in a Few Words)*; http://en.proverbia.net/citastema.asp?tematica=489.

7

BUSINESS VILLAINS

INTRODUCTION

The knee-jerk reaction upon first hearing the phrase "financial crime" is to think of a business enterprise as the victim. While that is true in many cases, it overlooks a fundamental tenet of financial crime investigation: Businesses are frequently the vehicles through which criminals operate. Throughout this chapter we will try and help you overcome any stereotype you may harbor about the difference between organized crime and big business by highlighting where crime has been, and where it is, and by predicting where it may be headed. Through it all you will notice one underlying theme: Crime is all about money. What this chapter is also about, but in a much less noticeable way, is the fact that money is often all about crime, as well.

ORGANIZED CRIME AND BUSINESS

When people hear the phrase *organized crime*, the words conjure up images of ruthless ethnic criminals with names like "Sammy the Bull," "Fat Tony," and "Jimmy the Weasel." While it may be true that "The Sicilian Mafia, or La Cosa Nostra, is the most famous organized-crime group in the world,"[1] its nearly 5,000 known members who are divided into roughly 180 families are neither the first, nor currently the most significant, organized criminal enterprises in the world.[2]

It is unclear why the collective consciousness of American minds has this distorted view of organized crime. Perhaps it stems from the impact of modern cinema. Films such as Martin Scorsese's *Goodfellas* and Mario Puzo's *Godfather* trilogy have immersed us in the seedy and often glamorous world of the Italian Mafia. Or, perhaps it is because the Italian Mafia is the most well-established and geographically diverse group of organized criminals.[3] Whatever the reason, the mistaken belief that most people retain is that the Mafia is today's typical organized criminal enterprise.

The truth of the matter is that the Italian Mafia plays a much less significant role in the larger picture of modern organized crime. Today, financial crime investigators are likely to find much greater diversity among organized criminal enterprises. For example, groups from a variety of ethnicities such as Hispanic, Chinese, Japanese, Mexican, and most recently, Eastern European now account for a significant majority of crime attributable to organized groups.

Today, the world lacks borders. True, sovereign nations still maintain control over their own territories, but the globalization of the marketplace, combined with technological advancement, has made those technical distinctions much more illusory. As a result, the ethnic categories, modes of operation, and areas of specialty are different from those traditionally associated with individual groups of organized criminals.

The organized criminal enterprise of today is much different from the enterprise of yesterday. Likewise, the enterprise of tomorrow will likely be much different from that of today. In fact, some of the very definitions we use to understand organized crime have changed and will continue to change. To help understand the changes we expect to occur in the future, we should first look at the past.

The Life Cycle of Organized Crime

Although a narrow definition of organized crime would probably exclude the members of the social group known as the Tammany Society of New York City, their involvement in criminal activity and reliance upon domination through violence necessitates some discussion.

Originating as a patriotic and fraternal club in the early 1780s, the Tammany Society took its name from the legendary Delaware Indian Chief Tammany, and eventually grew to become a powerful influence in nineteenth-century politics.[4] Their membership, in keeping with the cycle of immigration from Europe near the turn of the nineteenth century, was composed overwhelmingly of Irish immigrants. In fact, the Tammany Society is largely credited with the rise of the Irish in early American politics.[5] As new immigrants began to arrive, Tammany Hall would offer protection from persecution by earlier immigrants in return for loyalty. These favors led to jobs, licenses, and political perks as well. It was through a cycle of violence and a ready supply of fresh immigrants that Tammany maintained a stranglehold on politics in New York City throughout the mid-nineteenth century.[6] And, as commonly occurs, unbridled power coupled with greed leads to crime, corruption, and abuse.

Instrumental in the elections of a number of local, state, and national leaders—Aaron Burr, John Adams, and Andrew Jackson to name but a few—their political power and influence was based largely on violence and intimidation.[7] Utilizing street-gangs like The Short-Tail Gang, the Dead Rabbits, the Plug Uglies, and the Five-Points, Tammany dominated the city and influenced the outcome of countless local elections and more than a few state contests.[8]

Slowly, ethnic succession weakened Tammany's grasp on the political machine. Social scientists have developed the term *ethnic succession* to describe the mobility struggle and the ensuing transition of power from one organized criminal group to another.[9] As waves of new non-Irish immigrants reached America's shores, the struggle for power began, and the luck of the Irish began to run out. The new players in the game—the Jewish immigrants from Eastern Europe—began to take hold of the reins of power.

Like most social processes, the transition of power from one ethnic group to the next was neither neat nor quick. In fact it was not even orderly. During this time, Jewish immigrant Arnold Rothstein became close friends with Monk Eastman, namesake of the Eastman Gang.[10] Rothstein quickly discovered his latent talents for both lending money and gambling. A consummate pool shark and craps shooter, Rothstein enlisted the tougher Eastman to help him collect delinquent loans. Rothstein recognized the need for sponsorship early on, and began to develop a close association with a powerful Tammany insider named "Big Tim" Sullivan.[11]

Over the years, Sullivan was good to Rothstein and provided protection for his growing gambling and loan-sharking rackets. However, through a series of political maneuvers culminating in murder, Sullivan wound up dead.[12] This unfortunate turn of events also sent Captain Charles Becker, one of Sullivan's right-hand men and a notoriously corrupt police officer, to prison for an unrelated murder.[13] A power vacuum existed. Quickly, Arnold Rothstein was tapped to fill Becker's former position and became the new middleman between Tammany Hall and the criminal underworld. As a result, Rothstein's syndicate of gambling houses and loan-sharking operations continued to grow.

Meanwhile, the turn of the twentieth century also brought prosperity to Italian immigrants, including Alphonse "Al" Capone, Johnny Torrio, Frankie Yale, and Charles "Lucky" Luciano. This group of Italian street hoods was running a small section of Manhattan as members of Paul Kelly's (Paolo Antonio Vacarelli) Five-Points Gang.[14] This street gang changed the way gangs in America operated, and is credited with originating the modern-day Mafia.[15]

Eventually, Johnny Torrio would leave the gang and head for Chicago. Capone and Luciano remained under the continuing influence of Frankie Yale. Yale took Capone and Luciano under his wing and both men proved to be quick studies. Eventually, Capone followed Torrio out west, but Luciano remained in New York with Kelly and Yale. Albert C. Marinelli, another of Tammany Hall's powerful elite, recognized the power that the members of the Five-Points Gang wielded among the Italian immigrants and enlisted their help in all sorts of errands ranging from leg breaking to money deliveries to intimidation.[16] During the early years of the twentieth century, Lucky Luciano's power and prestige among his fellow gangsters continued to grow.

After Congress passed the Volstead Act in 1919, Luciano's power among the world of gangsters and thieves solidified, and his reputation as a consummate gangster was forever forged. Luciano's reputation and skill at bootlegging and narcotics smuggling gave him an introduction to other powerful underworld figures such as Benjamin "Bugsy" Siegel, Frank Costello, and ultimately, Joe "the Boss" Masseria—the boss of bosses.[17] It was Luciano's association, and subsequent disagreement, with Masseria that would eventually lead to his affiliation with Arnold Rothstein.

One of the principal differences of opinion that Luciano had with Masseria, who represented the old-school Mafiosi known as "Moustache Petes," stemmed from Masseria's refusal to deal with non-Italians.[18] This, in Luciano's mind, limited the organization's opportunities for growth. Masseria stood in the way of Luciano's vision of a unified national network of crime. It was this disagreement that led to the Castellammarese War, in which the two bosses in New York, Masseria and Joseph Maranzano, battled over which direction the Mafia would take.[19] At the end of the Castellammarese War, Lucky Luciano and his close associate Frank Costello sat at the top of the Mafia food chain. Sitting with them was Luciano's childhood friend, Meyer Lansky.[20]

Meyer Lansky, sometimes called the mastermind of the mob, had been friends with Luciano since their early days on the streets. As a Russian Jew, Lansky, who immigrated to America with his family in 1911, could remain above the fray between the Italians before the days of the Castellammarese War.[21] After the war, his friendship with Luciano and service as his advisor served to bring together two of the most powerful men in organized crime— Charles Luciano and Arnold Rothstein.

In 1933, the Volstead Act was repealed. Many would have predicted this to have been the death knell for organized gangsters, who made a fortune from bootlegging, but it served instead to rocket them to greater heights of power. A resulting union between the Italians and Jews arose that would change the face of organized crime in America forever. Once liquor became legal, Luciano and his crew needed to find an alternative business through which to generate the tremendous profits that they had realized during the prohibition days. Arnold Rothstein had the answer—gambling.[22]

With the teaching of Rothstein, the managerial know-how of Lansky, and the muscle of Luciano, this Italian-Jewish syndicate would take over both the illegal and legal gambling rackets in the United States, and later Cuba. Starting with illegal gambling in Saratoga, New York, they later expanded into the realm of legal gambling in those jurisdictions that had seen fit to legalize it.[23] Lansky, with the help of his friend and associate, Benjamin "Bugsy" Siegel, colonized the city of Las Vegas in the name of the Luciano organization. In addition, the shrewd negotiating skill and business acumen that Lansky possessed allowed him to establish a Mafia beachhead in Havana under the approving eye of dictator Fulgencio Batista.[24] Then, in 1928, Arnold Rothstein was murdered. With his death, Lansky, Meyer, and Luciano took over his syndicate and concentrated power in one of the most powerful Mafia families in the history of the underworld.

By the mid-1950s, ethnic succession was complete. Power had transferred from Tammany to an Italian-Jewish–dominated business-like organized criminal enterprise. As America entered the sexual revolution and the Age of Aquarius, a new criminal threat was emerging. Throughout the 1960s and 1970s, Latin-American, African-American, and Asian gangs began to emerge on the organized crime scene.

Organizations such as the Cali and Medellin cartels changed the face of how Americans perceived organized crime. Violence became the calling card of the organized criminal.

Ruling their territory through unprecedented violence, the Colombian Cocaine cartels turned the streets of Miami, New York, and Los Angeles into a
new "wild west."[25] Bringing with them horrific phrases such as the "Colombian Necktie,"[26] the *narcotraficantes* of the late 1970s and 1980s revolutionized the way in which desertion and infidelity to the organization were
punished.

Unlike the Mafia before them, the Colombians visited violence not just
upon the transgressor, but on his whole family. Mark Bowden notes that "in
Colombia it wasn't enough to hurt or even kill your enemy; there was a rit-
ual observed. . . . Before you killed a man you first made him beg, scream,
gag . . . you killed those he most loved before his eyes. To amplify fear, victims were horribly mutilated and left on display."[27] It was this departure
from the norm and their extraordinary indifference toward death that distinguished them from their earlier organized crime ancestors.

On the heels of the rise of the Latin crime organizations followed the Ja-
maican Posses.[28] Credited with a greater propensity for violence than even the
Colombians, the Posses capitalized on the crack cocaine epidemic to earn
themselves a place among the most feared and violent organized criminals in
history.[29] While no true ethnic succession had taken place, the influence of
these new ethnic groups had imprinted the personality of organized crime in
America. As the end of the twentieth century approached, an even more dras-
tic evolution was about to occur.

The Changing Face of Organized Crime

As the new millennium approached, law enforcement officials began to see the
emergence of a new type of organized criminal. Although these new groups
were still highly ethnocentric organizations, they had begun to change. While
the rapid dissolution of international borders had paved the way for quick expansion of territory, there still remained, for the time being at least, a strong
ethnicity in the emerging organizations.

Among these ethnic criminals were Asian criminal enterprises. These
groups included traditional Tongs, Triads, and the Yakuza, as well as nontraditional hybrid affiliations between ethnic groups.[30] The Yakuza, for example, are the Japanese answer to the American Mafia. Based upon the
eccentric bands of roving Samuari known as "Boryokudon," these organized
criminals can be traced back into the 1600s.[31] However, it was not until the

mid-1960s that the power of the Yakuza as an organized criminal element began to grow.

Today, this organization with a family-based structure similar to the American Mafia is estimated to be responsible for nearly $500 million per year in crime.[32] The Yakuza enmesh themselves in both legitimate and illegitimate businesses from which they can control their illegal enterprises, which often consist of gambling, prostitution, extortion, and narcotics.[33] More recently, the FBI has indicated that these Asian criminal enterprises are engaged in crimes such as fraud, money laundering, and trafficking in humans.[34] Asian criminal enterprises were not the only emerging players in the international arena—there were also the Eastern European criminal enterprises.

With the fall of communism in Eastern Europe came a tremendous vacuum of power, goods, and social structure. A number of highly placed government officials, who were likely already criminals and kleptocrats in the first place, stepped in to fill the void and answer the new-found demands of the market economy. Capitalizing on their knowledge of the black market infrastructure and the Shadow Market that had emerged during the lean years of Stalinist Russia, these former KBG officers and "apparatchiks" formed associations with the *Vory y Zakone*, Russian for "thieves in law," who had existed in Russia for hundreds of years.[35] While some journalists have reported that the Russian Mafia is a recent phenomenon, the reality is that existence of a world of thieves dates to Czarist Russia. The fall of communism in the last decade of the twentieth century merely fueled its meteoric rise.[36] Since that time, the Russian Mafia has been able to penetrate legitimate business and government in Russia at a historically unprecedented rate.

Experts have noted that Russian criminal enterprises are very good at financial crimes, money laundering, and trafficking in humans. Corruption and violence are also defining characteristics of their organization, and their influence over businesses in Russia, both public and private, is overwhelming the economy.[37] In the early 1990s, official FBI estimates placed Mafia-controlled ownership of private business at 40 percent and state-owned business at 60 percent.[38] More recently, the figures have risen to estimates as high as 85 percent voting control of all corporations in Russia. More startling is the estimate that Russian organized crime controls over 400 of Russia's banks, allowing them to launder over $250 million a year.[39]

The emergence of these new multinational criminal enterprises requires us to change the way we think about organized crime. Whether the change was precipitated by the erosion of the political order in Eastern Europe, the unification of Europe, or as some have speculated, by the rapid advance of technology, the end result is the same. Organizations that were once ethnocentric and national have become multicultural and international. This same phenomenon has been observed in the business world.

The Business of Organized Crime

As both the traditional organized crime families and the new world order have shown us, crime is all about business. The involvement of Italian organized crime in legitimate business through gambling in Las Vegas provided the perfect opportunity to exploit their knowledge of gambling, coupled with the business acumen developed during prohibition, to churn out previously unheard-of sums of money. In fact, history is filled with examples of organized crime figures involving themselves in legitimate business. Al Capone used a single used-furniture business to conceal his illegal activity and Joe Profaci, long-time head of the Profaci crime family, maintained America's largest olive oil importation business.[40] These are just two of many examples that have occurred throughout history. And, as in any business, the better organized you are, the more successful you become. In the late twentieth century, organized crime became much better organized. In the late twentieth century, organized crime became a business enterprise.[41]

Enterprises like the Mafia, Rothstein's Syndicate, and many of the crime families that have followed in their footsteps do not give us much trouble in terms of defining organized crime. The arrival of more loosely aligned organizations such as some of the hybrid Asian enterprises and the Eastern European groups that associate on an ad-hoc basis, however, sometimes proves problematic. Not to mention the fact that the traditional definition of organized crime completely ignores businesses and corporations such as Enron, BCCI, and WorldCom.

Leading scholar and organized crime expert Howard Abadinsky identified a number of common attributes that exist in all law enforcement definitions of an organized criminal enterprise. First, the organization must be nonideological, meaning they exist for the purpose of aggregating money and power, not for some other more ideological or political reason. Second, the enterprise must be hierarchical: The organization must have a somewhat vertical power structure based on permanent ranks established independent of the person holding the rank. Third, membership in the enterprise is granted on a limited or exclusive basis. Fourth, the organization must be self-perpetuating. There is permanence to the group that exists beyond the current membership. Fifth, the group shows a willingness to use illegal means such as bribery and violence to accomplish its mission. Sixth, the organization uses specialization and division of labor. And, finally, the enterprise must endeavor to monopolize the area of specialty.[42]

As you can see, the traditional definitional elements identified by Abadinsky, while fitting our corporate criminal enterprise fairly well, fall short in several areas when tested against the emerging criminal enterprises of Eastern Europe. Therefore, it will be beneficial to our continued discussion of financial crimes to redefine who we include in our definition of organized criminal enterprise. For that we turn to Interpol.

Interpol defines an organized criminal enterprise as "any enterprise or group of persons engaged in a continuing illegal activity which has as its primary purpose the generation of profits and continuance of the enterprise regardless of national boundaries."[43] This definition provides a much more liberal framework, and encompasses both our corporate criminal enterprise and our Eastern European criminal enterprise quite well. Now, using this definition, our discussions of organized crime can begin to focus on the underlying assumption made about criminal enterprises and corporations. Interpol's definition makes this underlying assumption clear by defining an organized criminal enterprise as one whose "primary purpose [is] the generation of profits."[44] It is this profit motive that the traditional organized criminal enterprise shares with the corporation that explains their historical intermingling. Now having laid this assumption bare, we are prepared to discuss how both corporate criminal enterprises and traditional organized crime address this problem of profits.

MONEY LAUNDERING

Because money laundering by its nature is a crime of concealment, the scope of money-laundering activity is not precisely known. It is safe, however, to assume that huge sums of illegal funds course through the international economy on a daily basis. The International Monetary Fund (IMF) has estimated that, annually, laundered funds are equivalent to roughly 3 to 5 percent of the entire world monetary output. Given a worldwide economic output of nearly $43.8 trillion for 2005, criminals laundered between $800 billion and $2.2 trillion during the same period. In the United States alone, it has been estimated that more than $2 million in laundered funds flow through the U.S. economy daily.[45] These figures, though imprecise, are a sobering illustration of the degree to which law enforcement in this area is seemingly a needle-in-a-haystack effort.

Money laundering, though a distinct crime in its own right, is also a collateral crime associated with many forms of organized crime. As we discussed earlier, the large sums of cash that criminal activity tends to generate pose logistical problems for criminal enterprises. In order to ensure the continued existence of the enterprise, its managers must quickly and surreptitiously convert this mountain of dirty money into legitimate-appearing income. Money laundering is the process by which criminal enterprises accomplish this task—more or less successfully depending on the efficacy of the laundering scheme employed. Generally speaking, the more successful a money-laundering operation is at imitating the patterns and behaviors of legitimate transactions, the less likely the operation will be exposed. For an investigator, this rule-of-thumb is the key to success.

No matter how hard the criminal enterprise tries to emulate the patterns of legitimate business activity, however, appearances will eventually break down. Many times, the cracks in the armor will be imperceptible unless you as the investigator are knowledgeable about the legitimate patterns of activity and behaviors of an actual going concern. Armed with this knowledge, you are poised to spot the impostors through financial analysis paired with conventional investigative techniques.

It is widely accepted, and rightly so, that the investigation of money-laundering activity is an effective means to dismantle any criminal enterprise. It wasn't until "Deep Throat," the key informant in the Watergate scandal, urged Bob Woodward of the *Washington Post* to "follow the money" that the phrase "money laundering" even appeared in print.[46] However, this approach to investigating had been employed successfully in all types of criminal enterprises ranging from traditional organized crime networks to modern terrorist cells. As early as 1932, law enforcement had applied this collateral attack technique to solve the predecessor crimes. For example, Bruno Richard Hauptmann was eventually arrested for the Lindbergh kidnapping because his efforts to launder the ransom money were unsuccessful.[47]

This collateral attack is in essence a "reverse engineering" method that is predicated on the idea that once the origin of laundered funds is uncovered, both the source of the money and the persons responsible for generating the illegal income will be revealed. Much like the laundering process itself, the success of the investigative process depends largely on the efficacy of the scheme employed and on the skill of the financial bloodhound tracking the source of funds.

From the perspective of a financial investigator, money laundering may be broken down into a series of three stages—placement, layering, and integration.[48] Within these three stages, which may overlap, various methods and techniques are employed to accomplish the individual goal of that stage. These methods vary widely in complexity and detail, but when combined, they can produce a total break in the link between illegal activity and assets.

Step One: Placement

Placement is the introduction of the dirty money into the global financial system. It is the starting point of all money-laundering activities, and because of the volume of funds involved, it is often the most difficult stage. It is at this stage that the form of the funds must be converted to hide their illegal origin. Since most illegal activities generate large sums of cash in small denominations, criminal enterprises must break these large amounts of dirty money into smaller, less conspicuous sums. This is accomplished in a variety of ways.[49]

In theory, the criminal enterprise's creativity is the only limit to the ways in which placement can be accomplished. In practice, launderers try to make their choices reflect, as closely as possible, the profile of legitimate businesses in the areas in which they operate. In addition, the criminal enterprise's choices as to placement methods will often depend on the magnitude of the criminal activity. The methods of placement used to integrate small sums periodically will vary greatly from the methods used to place large sums regularly.

If the sums are small, or the nature of the revenues is generally infrequent, there are a number of techniques that efficiently combine all three stages into the placement stage. For example, small sums can be placed, layered, and integrated using the racetrack method.

In this scheme, the criminal enterprise purchases winning betting slips from patrons at local racetracks for a percentage over the actual payout: The criminal enterprise in turn redeems the slips for face value, instantly legitimizing the funds as gambling earnings. For obvious reasons this method is limited in the amount of cash that can be legitimized efficiently.

In the past, one of the most common methods of placement for larger, more regularly occurring cash flows was a technique known as smurfing. Smurfing is accomplished by dividing large sums of cash into smaller amounts—less than the currency transaction reporting (CTR) requirement.[50] These bundles are distributed to a large network of "mules," who take the allotted cash and deposit it into special accounts set up for that purpose. By keeping the deposits below the CTR threshold (currently $10,000 in a single transaction or multiple structured transactions to that limit), and distributing the sums across a wide geographic area, the criminal enterprise can fly under the radar of most watchdog agencies. Once the cash is successfully placed into the financial system, the first link between illegality and the money is broken.[51]

Criminal can avoid some of the red flags associated with large-value cash deposits by associating it with legitimate sources of income such as cash businesses or charities, thus concealing the illegal nature of the money. Therefore, the links tying the money to its source—illegal activity—are no longer visible.

Popularized by the drug cartels of the 1980s, smurfing has its limitations. As the operation grows, more mules are required, and the probability of detection increases—both through betrayal and by suspicious bank personnel. Smurfing has become much less popular. Instead, financial investigators, fraud auditors, and criminal investigators are more likely to encounter the next technique—placement through legitimate businesses.[52]

This technique employs cash-intensive legitimate businesses as fronts for the placement operation. The complexity of this operation may run from the occasional mingling of dirty cash with legitimate receipts to complete support of the business with illegal proceeds. In keeping with the criminal enterprise's desire to mirror the profile of legitimate businesses, bars, restaurants, casinos, and other cash-only businesses are prime targets for laundering activity. Large cash deposits of small-denomination bills are expected by the local bank, and, absent inside information, local officials rarely notice anything out of the ordinary.

Although not exhaustive, the following methods are commonly employed, either individually or in tandem, to accomplish the successful placement of dirty money:

- Exchange of cash for money orders and other negotiable instruments
- Smuggling hordes of currency across the border to a haven nation for deposit
- Conversion of cash into high-value/low-bulk items such as diamonds and precious gems

- Collusion with banking officials to avoid reporting of large-value deposits
- Use of parallel banking systems
- Conversion of cash into insurance products and long-term capitalization bonds
- Concealment of cash in trading losses of derivatives and securities brokers

Regardless of the method employed, the goal remains the same: Insert large amounts of cash into the global financial system. By keeping this goal in mind, the financial investigator is much more likely to recognize the potential for money-laundering activity at this stage.[53]

Step Two: Layering

Once the funds are introduced into the system, the criminal enterprise must further conceal their origin and ownership in an attempt to destroy the audit trail. This is accomplished through layering. Layering consists of moving the funds through a series of transactions within the financial system—often more than a dozen.[54] At first glance, these transactions appear to be normal business transactions and routinely pass unnoticed by even the most watchful eye.

Similar to the placement stage, the criminal enterprise's options are often limited only by the creativity and imagination of the money movers. Recently, with the advent of smart cards and e-cash, a whole new area of financial transaction has become ripe for exploitation by sophisticated criminals.

In the conventional scenario, a criminal enterprise will shift funds between various banks using electronic funds transfers (EFTs). Electronic funds transfers are instantaneous and, given the sheer volume of daily EFT activity, practically invisible. According to the Federal Reserve Board of Governors Annual Report for 2004, there were more than 125 million domestic wire transfers initiated in 2004. These transfers moved nearly $470 trillion at an average of $1.8 trillion per day.[55] With that volume of activity, it is no wonder criminal enterprises feel secure in their anonymity.[56]

It is at this stage that shell corporations, offshore financial centers (OFCs), and Non-Cooperative Countries and Territories (NCCTs) play a significant role. In addition, the advent of online banking services, electronic cash payment systems, and smart cards has combined to greatly complicate the financial investigator's job.

Step Three: Integration

After completion of the first two phases, all connection with illegal activity is broken. The criminal enterprise must now reintroduce the money into the economy. After all, the end motive for the criminal enterprise is profit. Without access to the money, the existence of the criminal enterprise would be pointless.

The techniques for integration, like the first two stages, can range in complexity from simple repatriation schemes to a series of complex financial transactions. The methods used vary, but the goal is the same. The laundered money must be reunited with the members of the criminal enterprise in a manner that emulates legitimate business activity.[57]

To this end, criminal enterprises often establish additional shell corporations. It is at this point that the members of the criminal enterprise wish to establish a legitimate connection between the clean funds and themselves. They must convince the authorities that they have a legitimate source of revenue to justify their lifestyle. Establishing a cash-intensive business is a start toward accomplishing this objective.[58]

Using cash-heavy businesses, such as bars, nightclubs, vending machine businesses, and casinos, the criminal enterprise mixes the laundered funds with legitimate income and reports the entire amount as legitimate earnings. In addition to the use of front businesses, other popular techniques include loan-back schemes, import/export operations, and real estate or luxury item transactions.

In the loan-back scenario, the criminal enterprise arranges for the shell bank to extend a business "loan" to the domestic business controlled by the criminal enterprise. The loan proceeds, which are in reality the laundered cash, are transferred to the criminal enterprise's business as a business loan. Once the loan is executed, the criminal enterprise begins repayment with funds consisting of dirty money (often commingled with legitimate business receipts). In effect, the criminal enterprise is repaying the loan, including the tax-deductible interest, to itself. In this way, the loan-back scheme may also become a component of the placement process.[59]

In the import/export scenario, the criminal enterprise establishes a domestic corporation engaged in the business of exporting. The domestic exporter in turn engages an offshore importer (occasionally also owned by the criminal enterprise) and exports goods at overvalued prices. Occasionally, no goods will be exchanged; however, it is much safer if the goods actually exist but are highly overvalued. A slight variation of this scheme involves the financial takeover of a legitimate, reputable foreign importer. This method allows the criminal enterprise to assume the sound business reputation of the going concern, gaining immediate business legitimacy as well as a viable source of legitimate income with which to commingle dirty money for placement.[60]

Once all three stages have been completed, what began as traceable—and forfeitable—fruits of a criminal activity have evolved into untraceable, legitimate-appearing income—the holy grail of all organized criminal activity.

The concept of money laundering has changed under the influence of the Internet and the globalization that has accompanied it. Although the basic framework, the motivations, and the end goal have not changed, the methods used have been heavily influenced by the advent of electronic commerce and Internet banking.

Emerging Trends in Money Laundering

As the face of financial crime in America changes, so does the nature of money laundering and we must constantly adapt our way of thinking about money laundering.

In the 1950s, Lucky Luciano and Meyer Lansky were washing money through the Las Vegas casinos. In the 1970s and 1980s, the Colombians carried cash across our borders by the box load. At each stage of that evolution, financial crime investigators identified chokepoints and studied methodologies in order to capitalize on vulnerabilities in the launderer's operations.

September 11, 2001, marked another turning point in the evolution of money laundering. The nineteen terrorists who stole four commercial airlines and blew up the World Trade Center and the Pentagon did so with a mere $500,000. That includes such activities as flight school, travel, rental cars, food and lodging, and all living expenses for several months before the attacks.[61] While $500,000 sounds like a sizable sum of money, in the money laundering picture, it is hardly a blip on the radar. The adage, "follow the money," no longer means what it used to. Terrorist financing differs from traditional money laundering in some significant ways. First, the volume of money involved is much lower for terror financing. For example, in a recent DEA investigation a Colombian drug cartel was laundering roughly $10 million dollars in drug money through south Florida businesses and banks.[62] These proceeds, fairly common among illegal drug smugglers, are uncommon in the terrorist financing operation. Terrorist groups usually operate with a much smaller amount of money. As mentioned previously, the entire budget for the 9/11 operation was just over $500,000—roughly 5 percent of the Colombian operation. Lower budgets translate into fewer red flags. As discussed in the section on money laundering in general, one of the chokepoints for illegal money is in the placement stage. Given the large sums of money that criminals normally need to wash, the $10,000 CTR threshold was traditionally viewed as being adequate. However, the comparatively smaller sums of money generally involved in the terror financing operations routinely fall well below the threshold level and, as a result, fail to send out warning signs to authorities. A second difference between terrorist financiers and traditional money launderers is the direction of the pipeline. In a traditional criminal enterprise, the flow of money is always away from the criminal activity. For example, the Colombian drug lord is trying to make the money he receives from selling heroin move as far away from the source of contamination as possible. Conversely, terrorist financiers are moving the money in the direction of the illegal activity. Law enforcement has not been trained to look for money flowing in that direction, and as a result, many of what investigators would later identify as defining characteristics of the operation fall through the intelligence cracks. A third difference is the source of the funds. In traditional money laundering schemes the money involved in an operation is derived from illegal activity. Drug dealing, gambling, prostitution, or any number of illegal endeavors produce money. Many times, law enforcement officials may encounter the money laundering operation as a collateral matter when pursuing the other, more easily noticed crimes. In the area of terror financing, many times there are not illegal activities generating the money.[63] Since the needs of terror financing are different from those of the traditional money launderers, their methodologies differ as well. As these methods change, investigators must become more aware of the pressing need to follow the trail of the money. Since these methodologies often mirror conventional business practice, which from a financial crime investigator's vantage point can make identification very difficult, you must maintain your awareness. It is a key step toward identification.

CONCLUSION

The face of criminal activity has changed forever. What began as low-tech familially structured organizations based strongly on ethnicity has evolved into highly globalized, multiethnic conglomerations more resembling multinational corporations than the humble patriarchal groups from which they came. Whether the transitions were precipitated by the erosion of once-solid political ideology, or the rapid advance of technology, is immaterial. What matters is that criminal enterprises have changed.

Criminal enterprises are more like corporations. With this change has come the need to reassess how we view organized criminals and their behavior. The once-distinct line between criminal enterprise and big business has disappeared. Scandals like Enron have illustrated well the fact that organizations, no different from people, can engage in criminal activity the end goal of which is profit accumulation. The shrinking of this distinction has ushered in a new way to view the relationship between the criminal and the corporation— and consequently how we as investigators view financial crimes.

Terror added to the change. September 11, 2001, for all that it did to America's collective psyche, also helped shift the way in which we view the role of money in relation to criminal activity. Before the terrorists, "follow the money" stood as a mantra representing the adage that you could find the criminal, after the fact, by following the trail of money leading away from the crime. Since Osama Bin Laden and those like him have become household names, the money trail now leads in a different direction: It now points proactively toward criminal activity.

Change will continue. As rapidly as financial criminals have changed, those charged with investigating their conduct have adapted. While not always happening quickly, progress has occurred and officials have rededicated themselves to their efforts. However, as history reminds us, life is fluid and the changes we have witnessed in the past century will not be the last. Many changes are yet to come.

However, even accounting for all the changes, one thing remains the same—money. As investigators it is imperative that we continue to heed the advice given to Bob Woodward so long ago—"follow the money." If we do, we will surely have an advantage over those who have gone before us. As you continue with this book keep that thought as a reminder of why this topic is of such great importance.

SUGGESTED READINGS

Bauer, P., and R. Ullmann. "Understanding the Wash Cycle." *Economic Perspectives*, 6. Retrieved May 5, 2002, from http://usinfo.state.ov/journalsl/journala.htm.

Cassard, M. "The Role of Offshore Centers in International Financial Intermediation." IMF Working Paper 94/10. Washington, DC: International Monetary Fund, 1994.

Financial Action Task Force—OECD. "Policy Brief: Money Laundering." *OECD Observer*. Paris, France: FATF Secretariat, OECD, 1999.

Financial Action Task Force on Money Laundering. *1998–1999 Report on Money Laundering Typologies*. Paris, France: FATF Secretariat, OECD, February 1999.

Financial Action Task Force on Money Laundering. *1999–2000 Report on Money Laundering Typologies*. Paris, France: FATF Secretariat, OECD, February 2000.

Financial Action Task Force on Money Laundering. *2000–2001 Report on Money Laundering Typologies*. Paris, France: FATF Secretariat, OECD, February 2001.

Gustitus, L.E. Bean, and R. Roach. "Correspondent Banking: A Gateway for Money Laundering." *Economic Perspectives*, 6. Retrieved May 5, 2002, from http://us-info.state.gov/journals/jounala.htm.

Harvey, J. "Money Laundering and the LDC Offshore Finance Centres: Are They the Weak Links?" Paper presented at the *Development of Economics Study Group Annual Conference 2002*, Nottingham, UK, University of Nottingham, April 18–20, 2002.

International Federation of Accountants. IFAC Discussion Paper on Anti–Money Laundering. New York: International Federation of Accountants, 2002.

Joseph, L.M. "Money Laundering Enforcement: Following the Money." *Economic Perspectives*, 6. Retrieved May 5, 2002, from http://usinfo.state.gov/journals/journala.htm.

Lorenzetti, J. "The Offshore Trust: A Contemporary Asset Protection Scheme." *Journal of Commercial Law Review*, 102, no. 2 (1997).

Mahan, S., and K. O'Neal. *Beyond the Mafia: Organized Crime in the Americas*. Thousand Oaks, CA: Sage Publishing, 1998.

Monkkonen, E.H., ed. *Crime and Justice in American History: Historical Articles on the Origins and Evolution of American Criminal Justice. Vol. 8: Prostitution, Drugs, Gambling and Organized Crime, Part 1*. Munich, Germany: K.G. Saur, 1994.

Pace, D.F., and J.C. Styles. *Organized Crime: Concepts and Control*. Englewood Cliffs, NJ: Prentice Hall, 1975.

"The Ten Fundamental Laws of Money Laundering." Retrieved April 8, 2002, from www.unodc.org/money_laundering_10_laws.html.

United Nations Office of Drug Control and Crime Prevention. *Attacking the Profits of Crime: Drugs, Money and Laundering*. Vienna, Austria: UNODC, 1998.

United States Department of the Treasury. *A Survey of Electronic Cash, Electronic Banking and Internet Gaming*. Washington, DC: U.S. Government Printing Office, 2000.

United States Department of the Treasury, Financial Crimes Enforcement Network. [Electronic version,] *FinCEN Advisory: Transactions Involving Israel*. Issue 17. Washington, DC: U.S. Government Printing Office, July 2000.

Woodiwis, M. *Crime Crusades and Corruption: Prohibitions in the United States 1900–1987.* Totowa, NJ: Barnes & Noble Books, 1988.

NOTES

1. J.R. Richards, *Transnational Criminal Organizations, Cybercrime, and Money Laundering* (Boca Raton, FL: CRC Press, 1998).
2. Ibid.
3. Ibid.
4. H. Abadinsky, *Organized Crime*, 3rd ed. (Chicago: Nelson-Hall Publishers, 1990).
5. Ibid.
6. Ibid.
7. Ibid.
8. Ibid.
9. Ibid.
10. Alan May, "Arnold Rothstein," Court TV Crime Library: *Gangsters and Outlaws: Mob Bosses*, http://www.crimelibrary.com/gangsters_outlaws/mob_bosses/rothstein/index_1.html.
11. Ibid.
12. Ibid.
13. Ibid.
14. Bardsley, "Al Capone: Made in America," Court TV Crime Library: *Gangsters and Outlaws: Mob Bosses*, http://www.crimelibrary.com/gangsters_outlaws/mob_bosses/capone/index_1.html.
15. Ibid.
16. Abadinsky, *Organized Crime*, 3rd ed.
17. R. Nichols, "Cosa Nostra," Court TV Crime Library: *Gangsters and Outlaws: Mob Bosses*, http://www.crimelibrary.com/gangsters_outlaws/mob_bosses/luciano/index_1.html.
18. Ibid.
19. Ibid.
20. Ibid.
21. M. Gribben, "Meyer Lanksy: The Mastermind of the Mob," Court TV Crime Library: *Gangsters and Outlaws: Mob Bosses*, http://www.crimelibrary.com/gangsters_outlaws/mob_bosses/lansky/index_1.html.
22. Ibid.
23. Ibid. See also Abadinsky, *Organized Crime*, 3rd ed.
24. Gribben, "Meyer Lansky"; see also Abadinsky, *Organized Crime*, 3rd ed.
25. Howard Abadinsky, *Organized Crime*, 7th ed. (Chicago: Nelson-Hall Publishers, 2004), p. 167.

26. Ibid.
27. M. Bowden, *Killing Pablo: The Hunt for the World's Greatest Outlaw* (New York: Atlantic Press, 2001), p. 14.
28. M.D. Lyman, and G.W. Potter, *Organized Crime*, 2nd ed. (Upper Saddle River, NJ: Prentice Hall, 1999), p. 328.
29. Ibid., pp. 328–329.
30. See generally, Abadinsky, *Organized Crime*, 7th ed., pp. 206–213.
31. See generally, Richards, *Transnational Criminal Organizations*, pp. 11–13.
32. Ibid., 12.
33. Abadinksy, *Organized Crime*, 7th ed., p. 206.
34. Federal Bureau of Investigation, Asian Criminal Enterprise Working Groups and Initiatives, http://www.fbi.gov/hq/cid/orgcrime/aace/aceworkgrp.html.
35. See generally, Abadinsky, *Organized Crime*, 7th ed., pp. 191–193.
36. Ibid.
37. Ibid., p. 204.
38. BBC News, "The Rise and Rise of the Russian Mafia," BBC Online Network, November 21, 1998; http://news.bbc.co.uk/1/hi/specialreport/1998/03/98/russianmafia/70095.stm.
39. See generally, Richards, *Transnational Criminal Organizations*, pp. 11–13.
40. See generally, Abadinsky, *Organized Crime*, 7th ed.
41. Ibid. Abadinksy, *Organized Crime*, 3rd ed.; See also Abadinksy, *Organized Crime*, 7th ed., p. 267.
42. See Abadinsky, *Organized Crime*, 7th ed., pp. 2–3.
43. P.J. Ryan, *Understanding Organized Crime in a Global Perspective: A Reader*, George E. Rush, ed. (Thousand Oaks, CA: Thousand Oaks Publications, 1997), p. 137.
44. Ibid.
45. Financial Action Task Force on Money Laundering (FATF), *2001–2002 Report on Money Laundering Typologies* (Paris, France: AFT Secretariat, OECD, February 2002).
46. Richards, *Transnational Criminal Organizations*, pp. 28–40.
47. Ibid. pp. 152–157.
48. Ibid. pp. 46–47.
49. Ibid. pp. 47–48.
50. Ibid. pp. 122–123.
51. Ibid. See also R.E. Grosse, *Drugs and Money: Laundering Latin America's Cocaine Dollars* (Westport, CT: Praeger Publishers, 2001), p. 4.
52. Grosse, *Drugs and Money*, pp. 4–7.
53. Ibid.
54. Richards, *Transnational Criminal Organizations*, p. 49.
55. Federal Reserve Board, *Annual Report*, Federal Reserve Board of Governors, 2004, http://www.federalreserve.gov/PaymentSystems/FedWire/fedwirefunds trfann.html; see also Federal Reserve Board, *Quarterly Statistics*, Federal Reserve

Board of Governors, 2005, http://www.federalreserve.gov/PaymentSystems/
FedWire/fedwirefundstrfqtr.html.

56. Richards, *Transnational Criminal Organizations, Cybercrime and Money Laundering*, (1998), pp. 48–50.
57. Ibid.
58. Ibid.
59. Ibid. p. 57.
60. Ibid. p. 55.
61. Jonathan M. Winer, "Globalization, Terrorist Finance, and Global Conflict: Time for a White List?" in *Financing Terrorism*, Mark Pieth, ed. (AA Dordrecht, The Netherlands: Kluwer Academic Press, 2002), p. 5.
62. J. Lebovich, "Operation Cali Exchange Busts Drug Ring, Leads to Arrests in South Florida, Officials Say," *Miami Herald*, December 8, 2005.
63. See generally, T. M. Hinney, "The Cyber-Front on the War on Terrorism: Curbing Terrorist Use of the Internet," *Colum. Sci. & Tech. L. Rev.* 5, no. 3 (2003–04).

8

THE INVESTIGATIVE PROCESS

INTRODUCTION

All investigations share similarities. Whether the investigation centers around financial crimes, burglary, or even murder, each must pass through the same general stages. All cases go from initiation, to planning, to execution, to prosecution, and finally to reflection. In some cases the stages overlap. In others they are abbreviated. However, in every case each stage plays a key role in how well, or poorly, the outcome matches the expectations.

Understanding these similarities and the roles each play in the overall investigation is crucial to success. In every investigation, there will be mistakes. Whether they are mistakes in planning, mistakes in execution, or simply errors in judgment, they will occur, and they will influence the outcome of the case. Failures in the planning stage can result in cost overruns, and mistakes in the execution stage can result in a nolle proscqui, or worse, an acquittal. By understanding what must occur during each stage of a case you can reduce the number of errors and minimize their impact.

Understanding these stages is more important in financial crime investigations than any other. In most nonfinancial crime investigations like burglary, robbery, and even murder, there are challenges. Each is unique in its own right, and all require tremendous skill and experience. Financial crime investigations, however, generally result in higher volumes of evidence and more complicated theories than their nonfinancial cousins. This unique set of challenges will tax the organizational and investigative skills of even the most experienced investigator.

By the end of this chapter you will have a better understanding of the stages through which each case will progress. Beginning with initiation we will examine how cases catch your attention. From there, we will discuss the important role that planning plays in the overall process, followed by a look at the investigative plan. Additionally, we will explain how reflection can pay dividends in future investigations.

CASE INITIATION

Investigations of financial crimes may be divided into two general categories: reactive and proactive. Traditionally, reactive investigations occur as the result of victim/citizen-initiated actions. They are investigations that result from external notification that a crime has occurred. Whether initiated by disgruntled employees, lovers or former spouses, or, as occasionally happens, by auditors, stockholders, or corporate management, the investigator reacts only after the crime has been committed.

The suspect may or may not still work for the firm. In some cases, the victim will notify you only after the suspect has been terminated. In others, the suspect may still work for the firm, and be relatively unaware of his employer's suspicions. Both situations offer their own unique problems. Both will involve different concerns and logistical approaches.

Conversely, proactive investigations occur as the result of investigator-initiated action. In a proactive posture, the investigator discovers the financial crime in progress independent of a victim report. Sometimes, as in the case of many money laundering cases, the investigator may be following leads on another case and discover the financial crime accidentally. At other times there may be generalized suspicion that something is afoot, leading to a deeper probe and the discovery of illegal financial activity.

Sometimes the manner of discovery will dictate the method of investigation. For example, an auditor from XYZ Company may report that he has discovered a possible discrepancy in the company's accounts receivable. He suspects that an employee has been engaging in theft from clients' accounts. Although this case may be approached from a strictly reactive posture by collecting invoices and stitching together a paper trail of documents, a proactive approach might work equally well.

Investigative techniques such as surveillance and undercover operations are not usually thought of as the bread-and-butter of financial-crime investigators. Sometimes, however, they may yield invaluable evidence that can prove to be the smoking gun in an embezzlement that would otherwise be difficult to prove. Techniques such as covert surveillance of suspect employees and keystroke logging might prove valuable in narrowing suspicion or identifying members of a conspiracy. In fact, surveillance may be the essential element necessary to tie a specific employee to specific acts.

In today's business world where computers often control the entire revenue generation cycle, identifying individual perpetrators is tough. As more and more transactions are documented digitally, assigning responsibility, and in the case of investigations, culpability, for a specific transaction may be difficult through traditional methods. Long gone are the days when forensic document examiners were the most essential components of financial crime investigations.

In today's digital environment, linking an employee to a transaction is often done with no more than a secret code or password. In the day-to-day business world, the audit trail left by most software and computer systems is more than adequate for productivity and "business" purposes. However, from the viewpoint of an investigator, poor information technology security, or ITSEC, can make proof of culpability impossible as a practical matter.

Poor network security can hinder attempts to link individuals to transactions. Although it may be desirable for productivity purposes to allow clerks to log in under other employees' ID numbers, it destroys all hopes of conventionally following the forensic audit trail and indisputably assigning a specific transaction to a specific employee. Sometimes this happens with tacit approval. At other times, it may be done clandestinely by informal employee agreements. In either case, when an investigator is faced with such a situation, a combination of reactive and proactive techniques might help bridge the gap.

Actual surveillance of the employee, combined with the documentary evidence produced by the computer audit log, can reliably link a suspect employee to each and every suspect transaction. Therefore, as crucial as reactive techniques are to a fraud investigator, it is essential to remember the value that proactive techniques can add to many cases.

Once the case has come to your attention, you must evaluate its merits. The old adage, "where there's smoke there's fire," while often true, is not sufficient grounds for initiating a full-blown investigation. Sometimes, the motives of the complainant are suspect. Other times, your personal observations can be misleading. Either way, the original tip must serve only as a starting place. From there it is very important to evaluate the viability of the case.

CASE EVALUATION

In financial crime cases, reactive investigations often result from reports by investors, insiders, or auditors who have discovered an imbalance in the accounts. Often, these reports are sketchy at best and contain a mixture of fact, speculation, and hyperbole. Therefore, this stage requires that the fraud investigator sort through the superfluous information and extract the essential elements of the allegation. The resulting information must then be applied to the law. Just because a complaining witness feels aggrieved does not necessarily mean the suspect's conduct is legally cognizable.

Without a legally cognizable claim, the investigator's efforts are essentially wasted. In addition, civil liability may stem from an unwarranted investigation resulting in defamation of the suspect's character. In either case, although the complainants may feel good to have proven that the suspect in fact committed the alleged act, peace of mind will be of little solace when they realize that no legal action may be taken. Therefore, as the first step in any investigation you must determine the cause of action.

The basis for most investigations will be the commission of a crime. In today's society crimes are defined under statutory law. Whether federal or state, these statutes define precisely what conduct is prohibited as well as what penalty will be imposed for their commission. They are passed by legislative bodies and apply to all areas of our daily lives. For example, most states have statutory laws that prohibit theft. There are a number of subcategories of this general category, and most people are aware of their existence.

When a crime has been alleged, some prosecutorial authority will become involved. Whether you are an investigator hired privately by a client or a criminal investigator for a law enforcement authority, the goal of any criminal investigation is the prosecution of the offender. Prosecution is ultimately handled by state and federal prosecutors.

Sometimes there will be no criminal statute implicated. Occasionally, the allegations confronting the investigator will not rise to the level of a crime. That does not necessarily mean that further investigation is unwarranted. In some cases, civil torts might in fact be the basis for an investigation.

Torts are civil wrongs. While the line between the civil and criminal systems can become blurred because there are often areas of overlap, the end goal is often the most clearly discernable difference. In the criminal venue, the end goal of the prosecution is imprisonment of the offender, a serious fine, or both.

In the civil system the goal is repair of damage to the victim. Money damages are a common result of a successful civil prosecution.

In the civil system, there is no representative of society. Unlike the criminal prosecutor who is the attorney for society, the civil attorney represents an individual. In the case of financial cases, that individual is most often the business victim. While many of the allegations may sound substantially similar to those advanced by a state or federal prosecutor, the end result is different.

Regardless of whether the allegations of wrong are civil or criminal, the law defines the offense. Each offense consists of individual elements that must be proven in order to secure a successful prosecution. In the criminal venue, those elements are explicitly defined through the statutory laws mentioned previously. In the civil venue, the elements of the offenses are largely defined through common law and case decisions. While statutory law is often easier to pinpoint due to codification, neither is more or less important than the other.

It is imperative that you know the elements of the offense; otherwise, a successful prosecution is unlikely. Sometimes knowing the precise elements of the offense will be difficult—especially when you are investigating an area of crime unfamiliar to you. Other times, the elements of the offense will be quite familiar. In those cases where the elements of the offense are unclear it is imperative to consult with the attorney who will be prosecuting the case.

After you have nailed down the elements, you must examine the likelihood of a successful outcome to the case.

Solvability Factors

Solvability factors are those characteristics of an incident that help to predict how successful an investigation will be. Unfortunately, not all cases are solvable. Whether in the private or public sector it is necessary to help identify those unsolvable cases as soon as possible. After the unsolvable cases have been identified they can be discarded, allowing more time for investigating cases with a higher probability of solution. Generally, there are two types of solvability factors, weighted and unweighted.[1]

1. *Weighted solvability factors.* Weighted systems recognize that not all factors are as important in determining solvability. For example, the existence of a fingerprint at the scene might be more important in

determining outcome than the availability of a witness. As a result, the fingerprint factor is weighted more heavily.[2] The weights are determined in advance based on both statistical research and anecdotal experience. Stanford Research International's (SRI) Felony Investigation Decision Model for Burglary and Robbery is an example of a system using weighted factors.[3]

2. *Unweighted solvability factors.* Conversely, systems relying on unweighted factors do not assign any particular importance to individual factors. In other words, each factor is as relatively important as the next. The existence of one or more factors determines whether the case receives further attention. Most unweighted solvability schemes are particular to each agency and are based on anecdotal data.[4]

Regardless of whether you use a formal system of evaluation involving weighted factors, or an informal system, you must evaluate each case.

GOAL SETTING AND PLANNING

Once the need for investigation becomes apparent, its flow must proceed as logically and efficiently as possible. Although every investigation is unique, with its own intricacies and obstacles, success depends entirely on a combination of the skill and knowledge of the investigator with the soundness of the investigative process. A skillful and knowledgeable investigator who proceeds in a haphazard manner with slipshod techniques is no more likely to succeed than one who is inexperienced and ignorant and yet proceeds with a carefully designed investigative plan. Armed with an understanding of the unique nature of financial crimes, and an awareness of the logical flow of a successful investigation, it is possible to produce reliable and consistent cases.

The beginning of every investigation, regardless of whether it is generated proactively or reactively, results from a complaint. In the proactive posture, the investigator generates the complaint; in the reactive posture, a reporting party generates the complaint.

Since the investigator's task is entirely results oriented, it is imperative to define the goal of the investigation in terms of legally cognizable actions.

Setting the Expectations and Goals

Goal setting includes identification of the complainant's goals. For the fraud investigator in the criminal arena, this goal is often clearly defined. In most cases, the complaining party is seeking a combination of reimbursement and the proverbial pound of flesh—incarceration. Although from a goal-setting perspective this makes the investigator's job easier, in the client expectation area it adds another dimension of complexity. For the civil fraud investigator, the goals may not be so clearly defined.

Complainants are customers. Although few investigators readily admit it, crime victims are customers—they are involuntary customers but customers nonetheless. As customers, crime victims seek out the services of fraud investigators with certain preconceived notions about both obtainable results and acceptable outcomes. Whether their expectations are reasonable or unreasonable will determine whether you have a satisfied customer.

Where these expectations are reasonable and rational, the outcome is often satisfactory. However, when the customer arrives with unreasonable expectations, in terms of either obtainable results or acceptable outcomes, the conclusion of the investigation will result in a customer who is unsatisfied. Therefore, customer expectations make goal setting a bit trickier. In this context, we will briefly define what we mean by obtainable results and acceptable outcomes.

- *Obtainable results.* An obtainable result is one that can be reasonably expected to be achieved in any given investigation, given the circumstances surrounding the allegation coupled with the current state of technology. In the context of financial investigations, it is necessary to redefine the term *current*. Here, current means not merely what is in cognizable existence now, but also what is foreseeable within the life cycle of the investigation in question. Currency must be defined in that way simply because financial crime investigations can, and frequently do, span periods of time in which technological discovery surpasses preconceived expectations. When that occurs, obtainable results shift.

- *Acceptable outcomes.* An acceptable outcome in the arena of the criminal allegation is that final end product of the investigation that is reasonably expected given the current state of the law. In this context, the term *current* is in fact that period of time delimited by the actual criminal acts under scrutiny. This definition of currency is necessarily limited by constitutional constraints based on the prohibition against ex post facto laws. If we expanded our definition of currency to include the life span of the investigation, an acceptable outcome might well include a punishment that was not in existence at the time the crime was committed. Not considering for the moment the notion of a course of ongoing criminal conduct, the customer might harbor an unreasonable expectation of a more severe punishment than allowed under the law.

Now that we have defined our terms, let us explain how they factor into the investigative goal setting.

The effectiveness of every fraud investigator, in pursuing either criminal or civil fraud investigations, is ultimately judged by how closely—and consistently—she reaches or exceeds her investigative goals. In the criminal milieu, this effectiveness is often measured by the clearance or arrest rate—how often the bad guy is identified to a legal certainty. In the civil sector, effectiveness is much less easily determined. One measure of success is the depth and monetary value of the investigator's client list—investigators who consistently reach or exceed the customer's expectations generate greater volumes of business.

If goal setting occurred in a vacuum, there would be little, if any, need for further discussion. For example, if the investigator alone were responsible for setting the goals of the investigation, there would be very little chance that the goals would be poorly defined. This is because the trained investigator usually has an innate feel for both obtainable results and acceptable outcomes. But life abhors a vacuum, and customers' preconceived expectations complicate what would otherwise be a straightforward process.

Although less like investigative work and more like customer service, the fraud investigator's job includes customer education. Education must include defining both obtainable results and acceptable outcomes. It is only through education that both investigator and client can reach common expectations about the result of the investigation. Once you have established common expectations, you must clearly identify the goals. These goals allow both the customer and the investigator to fairly and objectively assess the progress of the investigation as well as the acceptableness of the case's outcome.

The investigator's job at this stage is that of an educator; it is therefore vital that she possess the highest level of skill in the investigation of financial crimes. These skills must include a strong working knowledge of investigative methods and technology. In addition, she must also have a thorough understanding of not only the rules of evidence, but also the legal burdens of proof necessary to successfully prosecute a case—criminally and civilly.

Armed with these tools, the fraud investigator is well equipped to clarify the customer's expectations. By defining or redefining the obtainable results and acceptable outcomes and clarifying areas of confusion where necessary, the investigator can help guide the customer in determining whether there is adequate justification to proceed further. Many times making things more clear at this stage can result in a much more cooperative client.

In a potential criminal investigation, the end result of this process might be a determination that the conduct alleged by the victim is not in fact criminal. Not all clients understand or recognize the fact that while objectionable, not all activity is illegal. If you don't make this determination now—and clearly convey it to the victim—the victim will internalize unreasonable expectations about the acceptable outcome. This will become a source of dissatisfaction at future stages of the investigation. Conversely, if the fraud investigator clearly identifies the legal components of the allegation as falling below the threshold for criminal prosecution, the victim, though probably disenchanted with the announcement that the conduct is not criminally prosecutable, can explore other investigative options such as suing in civil court.

Aside from establishing reasonable customer expectations, goal setting provides a solid basis for the fraud investigator to build an investigative plan. These goals are the foundation of the investigation. If the investigative goals of the case are poorly designed or unsound, then the entire investigation suffers from a poor foundation.

Why Plan?

Once you have clearly established your goals, it is essential that you develop an investigative plan. In trying to stress the need for investigative planning, we are forced to borrow from the old adage, "no one plans to fail; they simply fail to plan." This is especially true in the area of financial investigations.

By their very nature, financial crimes often involve large volumes of information. This information quickly becomes unwieldy without a well-thought-out plan. When it does become unmanageable, it will bury you under a mountain of financial documents. By preparing a strong yet flexible investigative plan, it is possible to control the flow of the investigation, adapt the investigation to the inevitable changes that occur during its life cycle, and manage the massive sea of evidence on which all unsuccessful financial investigations founder. A good investigative plan has three major goals: to maintain focus, control growth, and promote adaptability.

1. *Focus.* A strong investigative plan should focus your efforts in line with the goals of the investigation. A strong focus ensures that neither duplication of investigative efforts nor oversight of leads hamper the progress of the case.

2. *Control.* Financial crime investigations are living, breathing entities. Once they are brought to life, they take on a character of their own. If you let them, they will grow tendrils that crawl into every crevice of your office and attach themselves to every case file in your filing cabinet. They will give birth to other cases or marry themselves to operations throughout your office until they have taken over every inch of your life if you let them. A strong investigative plan recognizes this characteristic of fraud investigations and helps you manage it. It is not always preventable; however, careful management through planning can make its inevitable arrival less catastrophic to the underlying investigation.

3. *Adaptability.* In keeping with their living nature, financial crime investigations evolve. They may grow (always) or they may shrink (rarely); however, they will change. For that reason, all good investigative plans must have some built-in adaptability. Without adaptability, slight changes in the circumstances surrounding the investigation will render the plan useless. Once this happens, the alternatives are to either operate ad hoc or take the time to reevaluate and replan. Either alternative is unfavorable. By ensuring that the investigative plan has built-in adaptability, changes in the course of the investigation do not necessarily require wholesale changes in the investigative plan.

Planning the Case

Develop an Investigative Plan Preplanning cannot ensure against compromise; however, it can relocate the task of assessing operational compromise to a time when study and deliberation may be made, avoiding the need for reactionary decision making. When you determine ahead of time what potential outside support you require, you reduce ad-hoc decisions and overall integrity is increased. Decisions made under the pressure of time often lack the depth of vision that leisurely study affords. Therefore, to the extent that such decisions can be made in the comfort of the planning office, the investigation can proceed with fewer bumps in the road.

FINANCIAL PLANNING Investigative planning can help save money. Preplanning for investigative resources is fiscally responsible. Regardless of the context of the investigation, whether undertaken at the behest of a private client or under the auspices of the local district attorney, money is always an issue. Regardless of the size of the investigation, there is rarely enough money to do the job in the way you would like.

Therefore, like almost everything in an investigation, cost is a matter of compromise. Identification of potentially expensive issues early in the investigation allows you to make key fiscal decisions at a time when alternative approaches can be easily considered. For example, although a phone tap might be the perfect investigative tool to achieve your overall investigative goal, failure to examine the net cost of that approach could be costly—both in terms of financial resources and in terms of wasted investigative man-hours.

If you undertake financial analysis during the planning phase, alternative techniques can be considered. Too many times perfectly viable investigations begin in the hope that money will eventually come through. When it does not, the investigation bogs down with no hope of achieving the initial objective. When you fail to identify alternatives to costly investigative procedures, the results are usually compromised outcomes—either failure to achieve the stated objective or expenditure of more funds than reasonable. Either outcome produces dissatisfaction and failure to achieve customer expectations.

PERSONNEL PLANNING Early identification of personnel issues help to ensure an efficient investigation. Once you have mapped out the overall scope and direction of the investigation, it is much easier to predict the staffing needs and to assemble an investigative team designed to efficiently proceed with the investigation. Whether you anticipate that the investigation will be protracted or short, it is essential to identify key personnel requirements early. For long-term, complex cases this is imperative.

At this stage, it is important to consider the use of outside experts. Although you will be well prepared to handle almost any financial crime after reading this book, situations may arise in which financial transactions are beyond your investigative ability. In those situations, you need to enlist the help of financial professionals as either consultants or expert witnesses. In addition to accountants, the investigator should consider the use of experts in the area of stocks and securities transactions, corporate governance and structure, and international financial transactions.

Technology experts can also prove invaluable. In today's high-tech world, the odds of encountering computer-based information are very high. It is unreasonable to expect that even the most well-trained investigator will be capable of handling every possible scenario. For that reason, it may be necessary to arrange for outside personnel to act as an investigative resource. Whether in the area of network topography, computer security, cryptography, or individual proprietary software, the investigator must often tap into the wealth of community resources.

Experts in both these areas, and others, frequently come from outside law enforcement or security agencies. When they do, depending on the sensitivity of the investigation and the nature of the support required, integrity concerns may arise. For example, if you anticipate encountering encrypted data, your case may require outside expertise in that area. This can lead to an operational concern about the integrity of the independent source. Without some assurance about the consultant's integrity, both the evidence and the investigation itself may be compromised beyond repair.

The help of experts can greatly simplify your job. Although none of these topics are beyond the ability of dedicated investigators who have studied the subject, utilizing outside expertise in these very technical areas can save valuable investigative time. In addition, if you contact these outside sources early, they can often provide sharper focus and stronger direction when planning your case.

TECHNOLOGY PLANNING   Although shoe leather is often still the best investment an investigator can make in a case, today's investigations often require more. The image of the gumshoe knocking on doors and following down leads still has its place; however, as technology advances and the world is caught up in the digital revolution, investigators must employ more than muscle power. Many times this requires an investment in technology.

Whether this investment is temporary or permanent you must plan for it. Sometimes, the need for high-tech equipment will be short-term, such as rental of expensive camera equipment to obtain surveillance photos of your target piloting the yacht he purchased with company proceeds. Other times, the investment must be more long-term. An example of such an investment would be computer upgrades. While investments in new technology must always be evaluated based on cost/benefit, and usually occur at predetermined intervals, those temporary investments are not so predictable.

Looking at your next case from a technology perspective can help even out those technology expenditures. When you plan your case, you can identify areas in which you may need to invest money. For example, if the case involves a computer geek with all the newest gadgets, you may need to invest in the technology to properly secure and analyze the digital evidence you are likely to encounter. Likewise, identifying particular technological concerns in advance reduces their logistical impact.

Compatibility issues can ruin an otherwise simple investigation. While hardly insurmountable, differences between computer operating systems, video encoding systems, and electronic communications equipment can seriously hamper the progress of an investigation. If you operate in a PC environment and your client or suspect uses a UNIX system, the investigation may stop dead in its tracks until you migrate one way or the other. Planning will not eliminate the problem but will minimize its impact.

Murphy's Law does exist. Although careful planning is essential to the successful completion of a complex investigation, some investigations defy all attempts to map out their destiny. Murphy's Law is as active in the investigative realm as it is in everyday life and will invariably insinuate itself into your investigation at the most inopportune time. Even the most careful planning overlooks some eventualities. This is not to say that planning is helpless against Murphy's Law; it assuredly is not. By carefully planning the investigation, however, the eventual unforeseen detour will become the exception rather than the rule. You can eliminate the obvious hurdles in advance, and the investigator's best efforts can be directed at dealing with the inevitable unforeseen obstacles. In other words, planning will not prevent investigative obstacles, but it will make those inevitable hurdles much more manageable.

INVESTIGATION

Once you have completed the planning, you may begin the investigation. This is traditionally where you perform the bread-and-butter investigative work. You identify witnesses, collect documents, and analyze and assemble them into exhibits. Eventually, if all goes to plan, you will charge a suspect. This is the traditional venue of perseverance, legwork, and solid nuts-and-bolts police work—often backed by a healthy dose of intuition. Many facets of this stage are substantially similar to the investigative process for other types of crime. There are, however, some fundamental differences in investigative technique that mark financial crimes apart from other, nonfinancial crimes.

Regardless of how well the planning stage is undertaken, your investigation will be in a constant state of flux. Changes in direction happen in large part because of the nature of the investigative process. It is a process founded in evolution. It begins with a preconception of a finite set of facts. As the investigation progresses, your knowledge about what happened evolves to include new facts, theories, and knowledge. And as knowledge grows, you must reevaluate hypotheses and theories of the case. With the learning of new facts, avenues of proof are either reinforced or weakened. Those that are bolstered rise in importance in the hierarchy of proof; those that are lessened get relegated to subtheories, alternative theories, or, if completely refuted, are discarded as disproved hypotheses. Indeed, knowledge is an ever-changing entity.

The investigation and analysis of evidence will be a constant process throughout the investigation. Even after the investigator feels confident that all witnesses who have anything relevant to say have been interviewed, and all documents with relevant data have been collected, he cannot close the door on the case. Transposing analysis of what has been collected against what witnesses will say yields new theories. Even the most meticulous investigator will discover new potential witnesses and sources of documentary evidence as analysis takes place. This process of discovery often results in going back to the planning stage. However, as long as you have undertaken goal setting properly, these inevitable discoveries will require only slight modifications in the investigative plan.

The investigation should flow in an orderly fashion. You will find that the various investigative tasks occur in a particular order. This is no happenstance. Instead, we have listed each in the order we find most likely to result in success. Can you deviate? Yes, of course. There may be circumstances when you need to contact some key witnesses before you have completed the background investigation. Or, perhaps you need to interview the principal suspect while some documents are still outstanding. These are the inevitabilities of criminal investigation and, while not ideal, they will not cause the earth to stop spinning.

Instead, view these as outlines. If you understand the reason behind each step, you can adapt them, or change their order. It is not particularly the order that is important; instead it is the underlying logic that will serve you well.

Background

We cannot stress enough the value of laying the proper groundwork for an investigation. This is true more for financial crime investigations than any other type. Not only are financial crime investigations more evidence heavy, they are frequently very complicated. There are two main reasons for this.

First, myriad permutations of fraudulent schemes exist. As an investigator, you will undoubtedly confront some basic recurring themes in your investigations; however, the number of variations on these themes is limited only by the ingenuity of the suspects. What may initially appear to be a simple Ponzi scheme may mutate into something much more intricate.

Second, the business world can be a very confusing place. Not only are new forms of business associations evolving constantly, so are things such as debt and equity instruments. It has only been recently that forms of association such as the limited liability company have gained universal acceptance. Likewise, the creation and evolution of different types of investment vehicles like real estate investment trusts is a never-ending process.

All this change means you will quickly fall behind the curve. Staying abreast of the rapidly changing world of business and finance requires a substantial amount of time—even for professionals. Accountants, lawyers, and business managers invest hours each week reading journals and studying new business models. Even then, there are advancements that seem to creep onto the business scene. As an investigator, you will likely have your hands full maintaining proficiency in the art of investigation. Staying current in the business world is asking too much.

Instead, learn the basics. Reading texts such as this is a good start. Build your basic vocabulary of business topics and learn them well. There are some fundamental concepts that are perennial and will always form the basis of most of what you will need to know. From there, developing a specialty is probably worthwhile. Then, as you encounter new business concepts, or variations on old ones, you can build on the knowledge you have already developed. Building on that knowledge is where the background stage of the investigation comes in.

Understanding the Case Your goal in the background stage is to develop your knowledge of this particular case. While you may have a strong grasp of the phantom vendor scheme, you are unlikely to encounter the prototype of that operation every time. It is more likely that there will be variations of that scheme tailored to the specific victim. Whether the variation is because the business structure is different, or because the accounting process is slightly different from the typical enterprise, your knowledge of the phantom vendor scheme will be tested.

You must understand the business. What is the business structure? Knowing the underlying structure of the business can tell you a number of basic things about the business. Its structure may tell you about who makes the decisions. It may also tell you where to look for particular documents that will be valuable later on. Additionally, knowing how the business claims to be operating may reveal deviations. For example, knowing that a particular company is organized as a chapter 501(c)(3) nonprofit corporation should automatically send up a red flag when you locate a canceled company check to Senator Jones's reelection campaign since 50 percent charitable organizations are prohibited from political activities.

Next, you must become familiar with the business processes. Not only is the business structure important, so are the processes the business uses. Between these two tasks this is probably the more difficult; however, it can pay tremendous dividends in the long run. When doing your background work pay particular attention to the method of accounting the firm uses. Are they a cash basis or accrual basis firm? Knowing how often they send invoices to clients, what accounting controls are in place, and who processes deposits are all invaluable in understanding how things are supposed to work. And, as we noted earlier, knowing how things are supposed to work makes spotting variances much easier.

Chart your progress. Do not be afraid to use visual aids. As you will learn later on, we are tremendous supporters of visual analytical tools in investigations. Drawing a flow chart or an organizational chart can be very helpful in making abstract concepts concrete. Additionally, when you create a chart you can solicit input from company insiders to help correct or confirm your vision of how the firm is operating.

After developing an understanding of the business structure and processes, turn your attention to the industry. While you can learn volumes by analyzing the company itself, you can take your knowledge to the next level by investigating the industry. Every industry has standards. For example, the accounting industry has FASB, lawyers have the ABA, and doctors have the AMA. These organizations represent the industry itself, and are often responsible for setting standards and procedures for adoption by all members.

There is rarely a better source of information about how something is supposed to be done than an industry's watchdog organization.

Even nonprofessional industry organizations have value to the investigator. While the ABA, AMA, and FASB play a role in regulating their respective professions, there are a number of industry-specific organizations that do not. In fact, most industry-based organizations also have monthly publications that serve as guides for their members. When conducting the background portion of your investigation make it a point to identify any groups that may have relevance to both your victim and suspect. If you cannot readily identify them, ask someone from the firm what organizations are available.

Once you understand the business you can move on to better understanding of the suspect. After you lay the foundation by examining the business structure and business processes in place, and then comparing those to the industry as a whole, you will have a fairly strong foundation from which to build. From here, you can expand your general knowledge to include background information on the suspect—a process we call the intelligence gathering phase.

Intelligence Gathering   The value of strong intelligence cannot be overemphasized. An unfortunate, yet vivid example of the value of intelligence is found in the events of September 11, 2001. The failings of our intelligence process arguably resulted in thousands of deaths. While intelligence gathering in financial crime investigations rarely has such dire consequences, it can be extremely valuable.

Do not look at this process as static. While our earlier admonition remains true, we should note that these intelligence gathering techniques can sometimes prove valuable as a supplement to your case evaluation. Because none of them are overly intrusive, nor do they implicate invasions of an individual's right to privacy, they can in fact be undertaken as an adjunct to help determine whether a full-blown investigation might be warranted. Occasionally, the results of your evaluation will be inconclusive. In that case, a little intelligence gathering might provide the information necessary to make a confident decision.

We have broken the intelligence gathering process into three areas: surveillance, database searches, and trash collection. Please note that they are a starting point, not an exhaustive list, and you should feel free to add more tools as you discover them.

SURVEILLANCE Surveillance can provide a wealth of general information. Consider conducting covert surveillance of the suspect, the victim, or the suspect's associates to learn more about your case. As a result of your surveillance you are likely to uncover such important items as:

- Banking or financial institutions
- Cars, boats, and other valuable assets
- Homes, buildings, and other real estate
- Other associates or acquaintances with whom you may wish to conduct later interviews

All of these things, while readily visible to the naked eye, might be invisible to the paper trail. Uncovering them early can sometimes provide you with some very powerful "hole cards" for future negotiation.

DATABASE SEARCHES Databases are a wealth of information. We are a society that lives and breathes data. We create them, collect them, and collate them. We use data for tracking people, predicting their buying preferences, and changing their behavior. Without data our market economy would become inoperable. Whether using your debit card to purchase your groceries or renewing your driver's license, chances are very strong that some tiny piece of discrete data will be created and stored in a database somewhere. Given that fact, it is natural for investigators to seek to tap into this wealth of personal information to try and piece together a picture of their target. Generally, these databases may be divided into two categories: private and public.

1. *Private databases.* For the purpose of this book we have chosen to define private databases as those databases to which access is restricted. Private databases include both commercial and government sources. For example, access to most states' driver's license information is restricted. Additionally, credit reporting services like Experian qualify as private databases.

    Private databases are very powerful repositories of data. Unlike many public databases, which we will discuss momentarily, private commercial databases usually contain a broad range of information. Their files may contain such diverse information as real property, Uniform Commercial Code liens, and telephone listing information. One example of a commercial private database is the Autotrack service provided by Database Technologies. While access to some areas is restricted to law enforcement personnel for legitimate law enforcement purposes, private individuals can download page after page of information—for a fee.

2. *Public databases.* Balanced against the speed and power of many of the commercial private databases is the low cost of public database access. As society moves forward in the digital age, more and more government entities are making public record information available over the Internet. Property and tax assessment records are routinely available through county clerk's offices. Civil and criminal histories are often available on a county-by-county basis, and in most states, corporate filings are only a mouse-click away. While some agencies charge a nominal copying fee for getting these records, most will allow searches for free, and many provide free downloads.

The trade-off is convenience. Nothing in life is truly free. Such is the case with public databases. As mentioned earlier, private commercial databases usually offer a one-stop-shopping approach to intelligence gathering. Public database searches, however, usually must proceed on an entity-by-entity basis. For example, if I wanted to know if my suspect owned any property in Florida, I would need to conduct a county-by-county search of each property appraiser's office in order to find out. Commercial databases do all the legwork for you—for a fee. Convenience versus cost, the choice is up to you and your client.

No discussion of database searches would be complete without a mention of the greatest public access database in the world—the World Wide Web. Most people don't think of the World Wide Web as a database. The reality is that it is probably the most robust and wide-ranging database available—not to mention the fact that it is expanding by leaps and bounds every day. While you cannot type in a suspect's name and expect a detailed criminal history, or a downloadable copy of her driver's license, you can obtain an unprecedented amount of information at the click of a button.

In today's information-rich world, everyone is on the Net. Perhaps your suspect has her own website. That could be very valuable information to know considering many people place personal information about family trips, vacations, and other intimate happenings on their websites. In addition, the rise of the blog culture has given everyone a forum to express themselves. Perhaps your suspect participates in a particular blog.

Business information is readily available for free. Many companies maintain corporate sites listing employee names and profiles. Sometimes companies are lax about updating them, but this could still be a good source of previous employment information on your subject. Take advantage of the power of search engines like Google and Yahoo! in your intelligence gathering. In fact, put down this book and Google yourself; you might be surprised at what you find.

TRASH COLLECTION The very mention of collecting someone else's trash as a means of intelligence gathering sends most people running for cover. The job is dirty, smelly, and frankly, it can be a bit degrading. However, the value that discarded trash can have as an intelligence gathering tool should not be overlooked. People routinely discard papers, receipts, and other personal items that, while by themselves meaningless, when taken together can offer a detailed picture of the suspect's activities.

While there have been some occasional challenges to trash surveillance, the legal system has come down squarely on the side of the collector. In 1988, Billy Greenwood challenged a warrantless search of his trash by the Laguna Beach police, which resulted in a subsequent search of his home, arrest, and conviction for narcotics charges.[5] After carefully considering a number of arguments by Greenwood, numerous amici, and the state prosecutor, the United States Supreme Court decided that people have no expectation of privacy in items that they have discarded.[6]

Even though the search was conducted by the police, private investigators can take some comfort in the Supreme Court's decision as well. Mr. Greenwood's challenge was based on the U.S. Constitution's Fourth Amendment prohibition against unreasonable searches and seizures.[7] The foundational tenets of Constitutional law require that for any cause of action to exist, there must be state action.[8] In the Greenwood case, state action was clear. In a case involving a private investigator there is no state action, and therefore no Fourth Amendment problem. Even if the private investigator later turned over the information to the police, it is doubtful that the evidence would be suppressed.[9]

In regard to searches of trash by private individuals, the courts are likewise unlikely to hold an investigator liable. The courts generally recognize an individual's right to be free from outside intrusions. These intrusions include things such as overly intrusive meddling and searches of private places by private citizens. However, given the Court's explicit recognition that people have no expectation of privacy in trash that has been abandoned, it is unlikely that a private investigator who takes a suspect's trash will be held liable under most state invasion of privacy laws.[10]

That does not mean that you can proceed with reckless abandon. Even though the Supreme Court has been clear about our expectations of privacy in trash, you must be very careful about how and when you collect the trash. For example, if the trash has been hidden behind a fence, secured in the garage, or even waiting on the driveway to be placed out, there is a reasonable likelihood that the person still has an expectation of privacy.[11] However, courts have routinely found no expectation of privacy once the trash has been placed in the street for collection by the trash collector.[12] With that in mind, investigators who are contemplating a trash search should be very careful about where and how they collect the garbage.

Having that in mind, covert trash collection can be a valuable adjunct to your intelligence gathering process. As noted above, journalists, police, and busybodies have been stealing peoples' trash for many years. People discard everything from documents, to contraband, to evidence. Many of these items can help you fill in the gaps in your intelligence. Sometimes, they may even provide the smoking gun necessary to establish your case.

CONCLUSION

The preliminary investigation phase establishes a strong foundation for the rest of the case. By paying particular detail to the early stages of the investigation, it is possible to make the rest of the investigation flow more smoothly. As we have explained, evaluation and planning are crucial to a successful conclusion to the investigation. Likewise, setting goals for the investigation will ensure that both you and the client stay on track. Finally, early intelligence gathering will pay great dividends as the investigation moves forward. By learning as much as possible about the victim, the business, the suspect, and the alleged crime, you can more accurately plan for the resource and time demands of the investigation.

Therefore, as this chapter has stressed, some of the most important work occurs before any actual interviews have been conducted or documents have been collected. Many investigators stress the importance of the interview and document collection phase of an investigation. While this is extremely important, we hope to make clear the real value in preinvestigation preparations.

This chapter has offered a basic framework for ordering the early stages of the investigation. While it is far from exhaustive, we have sought to provide you with some very useful tips to use as guides and points on which to build. As you develop your experience and encounter new types of cases, you will need to massage these building blocks in order to extract as much mileage as possible. Armed with this framework, you can now move forward into the investigation.

SUGGESTED READINGS

Albrecht, W.S., and C.O. Albrecht. *Fraud Examination*. Mason, OH: Thomson South-Western, 2003.

Albrecht, W.S., K.R., Howe, and M.B. Romney. *Detecting Fraud: The Internal Auditor's Perspective*. Altamonte Springs, FL: Institute of Internal Auditors Research Foundation, 1984.

Albrecht, W.S., G.W. Wernz, and T.L. Williams. *Fraud: Bringing Light to the Dark Side of Business*. Burr Ridge, IL: Irwin Publishing, 1988.

Bintliff, R. *Complete Manual of White Collar Crime Detection and Prevention*. Englewood Cliffs, NJ: Prentice Hall, 1993.

Eck, J.E. "Rethinking Detective Management: Why Investigative Reforms Are Seldom Permanent or Effective." In D.J. Kenney and R. McNamara, eds., *Police and Policing*, 2nd ed. Westport, CT: Praeger, 1999, pp. 171–186.

Hudzik, J.K. *Criminal Justice Manpower Planning: An Overview*. Washington, DC: U.S. Department of Justice, Law Enforcement Assistance Administration, 1981.

Propper, E.M. *Corporate Fraud Investigations and Compliance Programs*. Dobbs Ferry, NY: Oceana Publications, 1999.

NOTES

1. H. J. Miron, R. Wasserman, and T. Rickard, *Managing Criminal Investigations* (U.S. Department of Justice, Law Enforcement Assistance Administration, December 1979), pp. 32–33.
2. Ibid.
3. Ibid.
4. Ibid.
5. *California v. Greenwood*, 485 U.S. 35 (1988): 35–36.
6. Ibid.
7. Ibid.

8. M. Zalman, *Criminal Procedure: Constitution and Society* (Upper Saddle River, NJ: Prentice Hall, 2002), p. 69.

9. See generally, H. Wingo, "Dumpster Diving and the Ethical Blindspot of Trade Secret Law," *Yale Law & Policy Review* 16 (1997): 195.

10. *Greenwood*, 37, n. 4.

11. Ibid.

12. See generally, Zalman, *Criminal Procedure*.

9

INTERVIEWING FINANCIALLY SOPHISTICATED WITNESSES

INTRODUCTION

During the course of practically every case, it will become necessary for the investigator to sit down and interview a living, breathing person. Whether that person is an eyewitness, a records custodian, or, ideally, the suspect himself, you will embark on the task of attempting to elicit information using an interrogatory method of some type. Methods of questioning vary in complexity—depending on the subject and purpose of the interrogation—from simple question and answer to a veritable game of psychological survivor.

In this chapter, we hope to provide a framework that the financial crime investigator can use to successfully build an effective interview process. Like all good models, it must be adapted to differing scenarios. However, it can help the investigator navigate the often choppy waters of interpersonal communication that is unique to this setting. In addition, we will offer some valuable tips for approaching interviews with the financially sophisticated witnesses you are likely to encounter in a financial crime investigation.

This chapter is divided into three sections. The first introduces the fundamentals of the interview process such as whom to interview and why. The second section addresses the dynamics of the interview process, including such problems as witness memory, and maximizing the interview environment, and briefly discusses the theory of cognitive interviewing techniques that are applicable to both suspect and nonsuspect interview modes. Finally, the third section provides the reader with financial crime–specific strategies for conducting successful and productive interviews in white-collar crime cases.

THE INTERVIEW

What Is an Interview?

It has been said that an interview is essentially nothing more than a conversation with a purpose.[1] Though true, this statement overlooks the fact that human dynamics intervene in the interview process to inhibit the parties' attempts to successfully realize their purpose. Regardless of whether the interview is being conducted with a suspect or merely a witness, there are many psychological barriers to the efficient communication necessary to reach the interview's goal.

It is the investigator's job to eliminate these barriers or at least to minimize them, to the greatest extent possible, and to open a clear channel of communication. It is no longer acceptable simply to approach a witness, notepad in hand, and implead in a monotone, "Just the facts, Ma'am," expecting the minutiae of observation to roll off the witness's tongue. Even the most cooperative witness will generally have difficulty remembering details to the degree expected by most police officers.

In innumerable instances, police investigators resort to questioning witnesses by using prehistoric methods that are more reminiscent of Adam 12 than modern police procedure, only to throw up their arms in disgust when the befuddled witness fails to respond with the appropriate reply. Is it any wonder that interviewing officers fail to obtain decent accounts of crimes and accurate descriptions of suspects during a seven-minute-long canvassing interview done with all the finesse of a bull moose?

Human memory is a complex and labyrinthine system. Concrete answers to questions about how we store and access information continue to elude science, despite extensive psychological studies. It is still largely unknown how the human brain matches discrete observed events with instantly recallable memories.[2] This bewilderment as to memory accounts, in large part, for poor witness performance.

Beyond the psychological barriers, an interviewer must overcome social and environmental hurdles that impede the flow of information. Witnesses and victims often fail to provide candid interviews for a number of reasons. Some may not want to be involved in an adversarial process in which they may eventually need to testify against a neighbor, a loved one, or other close acquaintance. Others may be reluctant because they themselves are hiding information to which they would rather the authorities remain oblivious. Yet others may be complicit in the crime—or perhaps they may fear reprisal from the suspect. There are as many reasons for reluctance as there are witnesses. Whatever the reason, however, interviews of both witnesses and suspects can be accurately characterized as a psychological tug-of-war.[3]

This does not mean that you should approach all interviews in a confrontational, accusatory manner under the assumption that the witness is hiding information or is intent on being uncooperative. Instead, you should be cognizant of the dynamics of human behavior and proceed in a nonconfrontational way with the underlying recognition that natural barriers to a totally forthright exchange do exist.

As an investigator, it is ultimately your responsibility to break through these barriers and distill all the superfluous information down into a set of facts that can be used to prove or disprove the case.

Unfortunately, in addition to these natural barriers to a free flow of information, the financial crime investigator must confront another barrier—language. When interviewing a financially savvy witness, the witness is naturally going to speak in terms that are familiar to him. Often these terms define concepts that have both unique and unfamiliar meaning to people who are not proficient in the financial arena. In an ordinary conversation, the listener can merely edit out the data that is uninteresting or not understood, and continue the conversation with a moderate level of comprehension. Investigators, however, do not have that luxury. The data they edit out or misunderstand could be the key element in understanding the entire case. In order to help reduce these barriers and increase the level of communication, it is important to plan the interview in advance.

Planning the Interview

Who? Determining the interviewee—without this stage the interview will not take place. In the context of investigational interviewing, in contrast to scientific or research interviewing, these choices are usually fairly obvious. However, because financial crimes often involve witnesses and evidence that are not routinely encountered in other, nonfinancial crimes, a brief discussion is in order.

In preparing a list of potential interview subjects, the investigator should keep in mind that there are relatively few eyewitnesses in financial crimes. There are two reasons for this. First, the overwhelming number of financial crimes is based on one variety of fraud or another. By definition, fraud is a surreptitious crime involving concealment and stealth. In contrast, nonfinancial crimes often involve an affront to a specific individual. Murder, robbery, assault, and even burglary—when unsuccessful—involve witnesses who theoretically can provide a description of the suspect and a more or less detailed account of what happened. The secrecy with which fraudsters ply their trade is designed to avoid eyewitness accounts.

Second, to the extent that a person may witness a discrete act by the suspect, they will likely regard the person's actions as falling within the bounds of routine business activity. The problem of a witness's inability to identify aberrant behavior stems from the fact that successful embezzlers attempt to mimic as closely as possible the patterns and activities of legitimate business. When they are successful, their activities are often indistinguishable from routine daily operations—even to a well-trained observer. For those reasons, the list of interview candidates should include a much wider range of potential information-holders.

Although a witness who can actually place the CFO's hand in the proverbial cookie jar is ideal, it is much more likely that the investigator will have to reconstruct that visual image using circumstantial documentary evidence. In this case, people with very little or no direct contact with the suspect may provide some of the most powerful and damning evidence—exactly who these people are, and what their role within the investigation is, will vary wildly from investigation to investigation and by type of crime. However, you should never overlook such potential witnesses as external auditors, accountants, banking personnel (including tellers and branch managers), mortgage and loan brokers, and business consultants. In short, any individual or firm that may have information about how the business is running, or should be running, is a potential source of information. This fact holds true regardless of the nearness of the witness to the suspect or his business. It should not be necessary at this point to present a laundry list of potential witnesses; it should be sufficient to remind the reader to use both creativity and logic when selecting candidates to be interviewed.

As you prepare your list of potential interviewees, always include both currents and formers. There are few investigators who would forget to interview current employees, co-workers, and intimates of the suspect. However, it is the true professional who also remembers to include in their list of potential candidates the formers as well. Aside from providing greater depth to the investigation, former bosses, co-workers, and significant others can often provide very detailed information without fear of ruining their relationship with your suspect.

A warning about interviewing formers: As you begin to interview former associates and acquaintances of your suspect, keep in mind that formers often have animosity and may have an axe to grind with your suspect, and as a result might tend to either embellish, or worse, fabricate information that they think you want to hear. While currents can be just as deceptive, often for different reasons, you should naturally seek some corroboration of negative statements about your suspect from formers. Some interviewees to consider:

- Victims
- Co-workers, including bosses and subordinates
- Suppliers and vendors
- Customers
- Spouses (and former spouses)
- Significant others
- Relatives
- Attorneys (depending on attorney–client privilege and work-product)
- Accountants
- Bankers and stock brokers
- Regulators, including SEC, if applicable, and other industry watchdogs
- Competitors
- Industry leaders and group representatives

What?   Once you have determined who you are going to interview, you must think about what he or she is likely to know. Even though figuring out whom to interview and what they are likely to know is a reflexive process, you should give considerable thought to what information the witness is likely to be able to provide you with. Most investigators, especially those who are new to financial crime investigation, think about witnesses' knowledge in terms of actual observation of the act in question. While that would be great, as mentioned earlier, the nature of financial crimes makes that unlikely. Instead, you must condition yourself to think in terms of other areas of your case in which the witness might be able to fill in gaps.

Some witnesses who are far removed from the actual crime might have the best information. While the banker and the stock broker may not have access to the smoking gun you need to prove the CFO tinkered with the accounts receivable, they may have even more valuable information in regard to where the money went. We have mentioned several times the value of following the money. Most financial criminals will put that money somewhere, and who better to know where than the suspect's local banker. Even with the stringent restrictions on financial information disclosure imposed on financial institutions, there are often pieces of information that you can gather that will help you track down sources of funds, expenditures of funds, or even motives for the theft.

Thinking about the *what* in advance helps you organize your interview. When you are dealing with witnesses who have access to collateral financial information, you cannot shoot from the hip unless you want to risk causing yourself more work—and probably requiring re-interviews of the same witnesses. When you understand what potential documents the witness may have access to, and what information they may be able to supply, you can prepare probing follow-up questions and obtain things such as subpoenas or other legal process in advance. If you embark on the interview without thinking about *what*, you may have to terminate the interview, get the subpoena, and then reschedule—in today's busy world few witnesses will appreciate this added inconvenience.

Why? *Why* is also closely integrated with both *who* and *what*. Figuring out why you need to interview this particular witness is closely related to who they are, and what information they are likely to have. In fact, by figuring out what they are likely to offer your case, you can answer the question of why they are important.

Part of *why* must include *why now?* In deciding why the witness must be interviewed, consider the order in which you are moving through the list. Interviews with some witnesses are more valuable for background information, or during your intelligence gathering phase, while others will be important in nailing down the fine points. Accountants, bankers, and stock brokers might give you a big-picture perspective, while the Accounts Payable clerk might be able to actually reveal details of individual transactions. Both vantage points are equally necessary, but not always in the same order.

When? Figuring out when to interview a suspect involves more than just figuring out in what order you will interview them. As we mentioned previously when discussing *why*, *why now?* is a planning concern for all witnesses.

However, in addition, you must consider when you should interview a suspect in relation to things such as time of day.

When is the perfect time to interview? The answer is: never. But, some times are clearly better than others. Consider the CFO who is preparing for a presentation to the board of directors. Clearly, his schedule will be very tight indeed. Likewise, a stock broker or banker can be expected to be relatively flexible during certain times of the day and week. Accountants, however, are all but sequestered between the months of December and May for obvious reasons.

When you recognize and give some thought to what particular times are most hectic, and consequently the worst times to schedule interviews, you can help create a more amicable atmosphere with your witness. Professionals are used to squeezing in a working lunch or taking a last-minute meeting when the bottom line may improve. They will most likely view sitting still to answer a raft of questions about John Doe's financial dalliances a waste of valuable time—theirs and the company's. Their impatience will translate into a poor atmosphere for information gathering. If you do your best to work around your witness's schedule, within reason, you will minimize this effect as much as you can. What is the best time? Simply ask.

Where?   Where you conduct your interview is also important. You have several options when deciding where you want to conduct the interview. You can use your witness's place of business, his office, his home, your office, or some neutral forum. Whichever you decide, each will have pros and cons.

Home-field advantage might be important. Additionally, the role that the witness played in the crime may influence how comfortable you want him to feel. Ancillary witnesses such as non-party bankers, brokers, and professionals will likely be most comfortable in their office or in a neutral forum. Suspects and those who might become suspects will likely be most comfortable on their turf as well. However, strategically, you may not want the suspect/potential suspect to be too comfortable.

The proper setting can help to leverage the psychological pressure. It is common for investigators to manipulate the pressure placed on a suspect in order to reduce his resistance to confession. While some might argue against this practice, it is commonly done, and when not abused, can be quite effective. One very powerful tool to manipulate the pressure is taking the suspect out of his element and putting him into yours. Whether it is your office, a police precinct, or an attorney's office, the pressure placed on the witness is likely to be greater.

How? Finally, you must consider how you are going to conduct the interview. In terms of logistics there are several options at your disposal. You can audiotape it, videotape it, or have it stenographically recorded. All three options are quite acceptable. One option that you do *not* have is not recording. Every interview should be recorded for a number of reasons.

Recording protects the investigator. There is no room for he said/she said when an accurate recording of the interview exists. Accusations that you made threats or offered promises to entice a suspect to confess are much easier to disprove when review of the tape shows otherwise.

Between audio and video recording, video is usually preferable. Even though an audiotape captures the identical audio information that a videotape does, the ability to watch both the investigator's and suspect's/witness's expression and body language can dispel any implication that the interview environment was overly coercive or intimidating. The adage, "it's not what you said, but how you said it," offers testimony to the fact that nonverbal communication is a very powerful tool. Your proximity to the suspect and the physical barriers, or lack of them, between you and the suspect are all points of particular importance to defense attorneys arguing against the voluntariness of a statement. Likewise, a dropped book, palm slammed on the table, and other loud noises, sound oddly like coercive beating when unaccompanied by the video image.

Recording also protects the witness. With an accurate recording there is no question of what was said. This can be important to the witness because it gives him some comfort that you will not twist his words into something they are not. When confronted with a witness who balks at the thought of "going on tape," explaining the value of a tape from his point of view is often enough to overcome his hesitation.

Finally, recordings don't forget. Even though tape recordings can get misplaced, destroyed or, in rare cases, altered, they are generally much more resilient than the average investigator's memory. When cases pile up, and dozens of witnesses' statements run into each other, there is no better memory clarifier than the actual tape of the interview. When the time comes for report-writing and trial preparation, reviewing interview tapes will greatly enhance your recollection of critical details and lower the possibility that you will mistakenly include or exclude some pertinent detail. Another *how* consideration is the tone of the interview. As we suggested earlier, there will be different goals with different interviews. You will most likely conduct suspect interviews and witness interviews differently. Psychological pressure and demeanor are both characteristics that will vary depending on the type of interview you are conducting. Along with the psychological aspect of the interview, you will adopt a different tone. By deciding in advance how you wish to approach the witness, you can have a better understanding of how best to capitalize on the psychological pressure of the situation.

Now that we have offered some tips on planning the interview, it is time to move into the interview proper.

The Interview Process

Traditionally, interviews have been categorized as either suspect or witness.[4] Often these interviews are distinguished from each other by use of the terms *interview* and *interrogation*, with interview signifying nonsuspect, and interrogation signifying suspect. Suspect interviews, usually called interrogations, are exactly as they sound—interviews with a person or persons who are suspected of committing some misdeed. Witness interviews are slightly different. The term witness interview encompasses witnesses, victims, and other people who are not immediately suspected of committing a misdeed. The reader should note the use of the term *immediately* in the preceding sentence. Much as a homicide investigator is trained to approach every death investigation with the assumption that there is foul play, every interview should be conducted with the subliminal notion that every witness may, at some point, mutate into a suspect. We don't mean to instill in the reader an "everyone is guilty" mentality; in fact, studies have shown that such bias leads to false determinations of deception.[5] We simply recommend that the financial crime investigator maintain a healthy level of professional skepticism. This attitude can prove invaluable when the comptroller, once believed to be nothing more than a reporting party, becomes ensnared in a web of his own deceit. If you approach every interview from a position of professional skepticism, it is much more likely you will avoid hasty supposition and incorrect assumptions—the bane of any good investigation.

Interviews are conducted for myriad reasons—scientific, psychological, journalistic, or investigative. But regardless of the purpose, certain dynamics exist between the interviewer and the respondent.

As stated earlier, the interview has been defined as a conversation with a purpose. This purpose, regardless of the reason for the interview, is to elicit information.[6] The process of eliciting this information requires verbal inter-action. This interaction necessarily entails discourse. Discourse in turn is the exchange of a commodity. In the case of the interview, this commodity is language.

People exchange words to communicate. Communication is possible because words have shared meaning. However, words—components of the language—have culturally dependent value. This value, unique within the culture, signifies a specific meaning to members of that culture. The culture in this case is the financially astute community. The CPA, the comptroller, the bookkeeper, or the chief financial officer all speak a very unique dialect within their native language.

The interview may take many different forms, from open-ended to focused and predetermined.[7] The most common form in the investigational setting is the semistructured interview. This format allows the interviewer, guided by a set of basic questions and goals, to explore the issues as they arise within the broader context of the structure of the interview.

Conducting the Interview

For many years, police interviewers were trained, when trained at all, in a classic, question-and-answer style of witness interviewing. This procedure consisted of an interviewer-controlled session of closed-ended questions often requiring yes or no answers. The interviewer, in this case the police officer, asked the witness a series of pointed questions designed to elicit a specific factual response relating directly to a relevant fact in the investigation. "What color was the suspect's hair?" "Did he have a gun?" "What was the license plate number?" These are all questions one would reasonably expect to hear in a classic police interview scenario.[8]

Often these questions resulted in inaccurate answers or an inability for the witness to recall the details of the event. Unfortunately, after such an ex-change, the witness was left feeling unhelpful, and the investigator was left feeling appalled at the witness's poor observational skills. What is more dis-heartening is that the officer was left with little hope of developing further investigative leads based on the witness's observations. Any information the witness was able to give was likely to be only marginally accurate.

Fortunately, advances have been made in the study of cognitive behavior and applied psychology.[9] These advances, relating to the manner in which humans store and retrieve information, have direct correlation to how witnesses store and recall observed events. One of the most promising advances in this area is the development of a memory facilitation technique known as the cognitive interview.[10]

The Cognitive Interview In 1984, Dr. R. Edward Geiselman, a professor of psychology at UCLA, his associate, Dr. Ronald P. Fisher, and several colleagues developed the theory behind cognitive interviewing. This new approach to questioning provided a breakthrough in interview technique and was based in part on a concept known at the time as the structured interview (SI). The cognitive interview expanded the SI paradigm and added a number of strategies designed to enhance the efficiency of witness recall.[11]

The strategies that underpin the cognitive interview have several theoretical bases. First, it is hypothesized that remembered (referred to as encoded) information is stored in "records" or discrete units containing event-relevant data. These records are indexed by headings and may be searched using descriptions until the matching record is found. It is believed that information about context, the environment in which the event was recorded, is part of this description information. The reinstatement of the context, or recreation of the environment, therefore aids the individual in accessing the description information and the record.[12]

Second, it is theorized alternatively that, instead of discrete units, our memories are comprised of a network of associations. As a result, it is possible to access the memories from several different places. For instance, it may be possible to trigger recall of an event by shifting the temporal perspective such as starting in the middle or end of the event and regressing.[13]

The last model incorporated into the cognitive interview process is known as the schema theory. This theory holds that familiar events have a script that guides how they are encoded in our brain. If we observe a familiar event, that event is organized into a hierarchy of slots according to this script. New events are stored in slots based on the familiar slots already scripted by the brain. This allows the brain to encode information based on prior expectations and to fill in slots with default information.[14]

The cognitive interview is essentially a systemized approach to exploiting these models of information encoding and retrieval in order to enhance witness recall of event information. Although it has its detractors, the cognitive interview has met with statistical success and has been shown in several studies to increase correctly recalled details by as much as 45 percent over noncognitive interview formats.[15]

Procedurally, the cognitive interview is a multiphase approach incorporating communication facilitation techniques. Phase one consists of free report; phase two is questioning; and phase three is known as second retrieval. Within this procedural context, the interviewer utilizes memory recall techniques that are consistent with the cognitive approach.[16]

During phase one, it is crucial that the interviewer emotionally transfer control of the interview to the witness. In this reporting phase, the witness is encouraged to do the majority of the talking. This may be accomplished by the use of open-ended questions that allow the witness to dictate the pace of the interview. At this point, it is important that the interviewer avoid interrupting the witness's narrative by timing his comments and any necessary questions carefully.

During phase two, the interviewer can begin basic questioning based on the witness's free-report recollection of the event. This form of questioning differs substantially from the standard police interview in which the interviewer approaches the interview with a specific, script-like list of questions designed to fill-in-the-blanks on the report. Although some structure is desirable and necessary to ensure that the *who*, *what*, *where*, *why*, *when*, and *how* are covered, the bulk of this phase should be determined on the fly as the witness recreates the event in her own narrative.

Finally, in phase three, once the interviewer's basic questions have been covered, the witness is directed to make a second attempt to retrieve the information she could not recall during the initial free report.[17]

While proceeding through all three phases of this model, the interviewer should employ several cognitive techniques that will help to jog the witness's memory. By encouraging the witness to recreate the scene in her mind, visually picturing the event, you are helping her to recreate the context. This retrieval-enhancement cue conforms to the first model of memory encoding; it helps to increase the overlap between the event and the recall context, and it may also help the witness to recall hidden details of the event or episode.[18]

Once the witness has recreated the scene, question the witness about specific aspects of the image. You can ask her to describe specific details of the room, persons in the room, or physical sensations she feels. By probing the image for details, you may elicit further recalled images. At this stage, you should encourage the witness to report even partial information, regardless of how unimportant she perceives it to be. This may be effective both because the witness misperceives the importance of the information and because the act of remembering the seemingly inconsequential details triggers further recall.[19]

While guiding the witness through this recall process, explore other memory access routes. This technique exploits the multiple trace and schema models of memory retrieval and requires the witness to approach the event from an alternative perspective. Consider guiding the witness to rearrange the event temporally. For example, ask the witness to recall the event from the middle or some other nonchronological point. The reader should note that some research indicates that accessing the event in strict reverse-chronological order may be counterproductive with the context reconstruction technique. It is theorized that this is the case because the context reconstruction technique encourages the witness to recreate an exact image of the event in her head visually and temporally. By instructing the witness to access the memory in reverse-chronological order, the benefits of context reconstruction may be lost.[20]

As successful as these techniques may be, you should be aware that there is the increased possibility of error in recall.[21] It is inevitable that any technique that increases the amount of information recalled will necessarily also increase the number of errors in recollection. This is true of any interview technique that is designed to enhance a witness's ability to remember. It is the interviewer's responsibility, then, to lessen the impact of this phenomenon.[22]

One way to do this is to use this technique only as an investigative tool. As with any evidence developed during an investigation, the officer must make every effort to develop additional corroborating evidence. In the context of financial crime, corroboration can most likely be effected through the use of documentary evidence.

While discussing the topic of recall error, you should note that two types of error are generally associated with memory recall: errors in recall and confabulations. Errors in recall—simply called errors—are mistakes of fact about something that actually occurred. For example, if a witness reported that the vehicle was blue when in reality it was brown, it would be termed an error.

Conversely, a confabulation is an instance where the witness constructed a memory that did not exist in the first place. An example would be that of the witness who reported that the suspect carried a gun when in reality he did not. Confabulations are often seen, or suspected, in cases of repressed childhood sexual abuse reports. It is interesting to note that the research appears to indicate that cognitive interview techniques may increase errors as opposed to confabulations.

Research has also shown that the use of the cognitive interview on children under the age of eight may produce a higher rate of error.[23] In the context of financial crime investigation, the frequency of witnesses in that category providing relevant details in a case is small. However, as with any investigative technique, investigators should be aware of its potential for misapplication and govern themselves appropriately.

As we stated earlier, the most effective interview strategy is the combination of the cognitive interview with communication facilitation techniques. To a large degree, the free-report phase of this three-phase process is a communications facilitation technique. Because it transfers control to the witness, it empowers the witness and encourages her to participate in the process. More importantly it begins to establish a rapport.

Although often viewed as nothing more than idle "chit chat," or a luxurious nicety, preliminary questioning can be the key to building rapport and getting everything you need from a witness.

Often an interviewer's job can be likened to that of a clinical psychologist where an intimate bond must first be developed before intimate secrets can be shared. In the case of the interview, those intimate secrets might just be the details of the criminal enterprise you are seeking to uncover. Once the interviewer establishes rapport, barriers disappear, trust grows, and a free exchange of information follows.

During the rapport-building phase of the interview, the interviewer must build trust between himself and the witness. During this phase, two things must happen: (1) the interviewer must assess both the verbal and nonverbal cues to a witness's behavior patterns; and (2) the witness must become familiar with the investigator and develop a comfort level on which to build the tone of the conversation.[24] Often this may be accomplished through application of techniques from a communications model known as NeuroLinguistic Programming (NLP).

NeuroLinguistic Programming NeuroLinguistic Programming is a communications model that was developed by John Grinder, an assistant professor of linguistics at the University of California at Santa Cruz, and Richard Bandler, a student of psychology, in the early 1970s.[25] The technique is premised on the idea that all communication originates from the processes of seeing, hearing, tasting, feeling, and smelling. Our experiences are filtered through our sensory perceptions. However, because human beings are essentially verbal communicators, we must translate our thoughts and ideas into language—that is where linguistics enters the equation.[26]

According to Grinder and Bandler, each person uniquely decides how to organize ideas internally in order to access them and produce results. The main premise of NLP, therefore, is that people use their senses to perceive the world, and internally the filter of these senses determines how they will representationally access them. In essence, people can be classified as visual (seeing), auditory (hearing), or kinesthetic (feeling),[27] and, to a lesser degree, gustatory (tasting) and olfactory (smelling), based on how they perceive, store, and reaccess their thoughts and memories. Therefore, when people communicate, they access their thoughts by mentally accessing the sights, sounds, or feelings—and to a lesser degree tastes and smells—associated with the experience or memory. This is their representational system.[28]

We advocate the study and use of NLP models for building rapport and maintaining a productive informational flow during your interviews. By utilizing the information provided by NLP, an investigator can successfully create an environment where the witness or suspect feels much more inclined to speak freely.

The most effective approach to building rapport with an interviewee occurs on three levels: the kinesic, the language, and the paralanguage. The kinesic, perhaps the most obvious level, involves the mirroring of the person's body language. The language technique involves using words with bases in similar representational systems, and the paralanguage involves the mimicking of the interviewee's speech patterns.

KINESIC MIRRORING A person's kinesic[29] behavior includes things such as gestures, body posture, leg, hand, and arm position, and other subtle body movements. When an interviewer adopts similar body positions and subtly mirrors the interviewee's movements, a greater chance for rapport is realized.[30]

Please note the use of the term *subtle*. This technique, although quite powerful as a rapport-building tool, can, when overdone, lead to offense—exactly the opposite of the desired effect. There is a difference between matching a person's body language and mimicry. Matching involves very subtle adoption over a period of time. The process must be used cautiously and developed slowly. Otherwise, all hopes of a good rapport between the investigator and the subject are lost.

In kinesic mirroring, less is more. Small gestures, such as adopting a similar rate and depth of breathing pattern, and adopting a similar posture, head position, hand position, or seating arrangement all have a strong influence on the witness's subconscious defense system. Over time, like partners in an elaborate dance, the interviewer and interviewee will respond to each other's movements in unison. This mirroring of actions lays the foundation for building a strong rapport and ideal interview environment.

LANGUAGE MATCHING   People use language to communicate. They relate their thoughts and experiences through the veil of their individual sensory perceptions. This is the foundation of the entire structure of the NLP model. Language matching utilizes the knowledge that people's words provide in order to establish a subconscious connection.[31]

Language matching is not, however, simply the use of the same words as the interviewee. Although it may often involve using similar words, the theory is not meant to convey a notion that the interviewer is supposed to use street language if he is dealing with a person of that demographic. In fact, much like mimicry, if the investigator's use of slang terms and words is incongruous with her background, it will likely be interpreted as a mocking gesture—another definite killer of rapport.

Instead, language matching looks deeper into the theory of linguistic communication to the sensory processing that people undertake when storing memories. As we indicated earlier, people process information through a sensory filter: visual, auditory, kinesthetic, gustatory, and olfactory. It is this sensory filter that dictates the language people select in order to communicate. Visual people will communicate visually; kinesthetic people will communicate kinesthetically, and so on.[32]

These tendencies to communicate through the veil of sensory processing often exhibit themselves in subtle ways. For example, a person whose predominant representational system is auditory will speak in terms of auditory sensation. "I hear what you are saying," "that rings true," or "that sounds about right to me," are all examples of phrasings an auditory person may use.[33]

Visual people, on the other hand, speak in terms of sight. "Do you see what I mean?" "I can't see my way clear to speak to you now." Or "I get the picture," are probably much more likely to be used by visually centered people. Similar linguistic patterns are found in people centered in other processing paradigms.

In terms of rapport building, these linguistic cues into the person's representational system can be adopted. Respond to the interviewee's comments or questions with similarly centered answers. Phrase your questions in a way that the interviewee can relate to representationally. At first, this technique may be difficult. If you, as an interviewer, are predominantly an auditory person attempting to interview a visually representational person, you may have to carefully rephrase your questions in a visually centered form. It will take practice. Given the value of information to most investigations, however, the rewards are well worth it.[34]

In conjunction with the subject's choice of words, NLP provides other, non-linguistic cues to a person's representational orientation. According to Grinder and Bandler, eye movements, referred to in NLP parlance as "eye-accessing cues," reflect a person's data processing orientation. It follows from this tenet that people's eyes move to specific spatial areas when accessing information, dependent on their preferred mode of representation.[35]

These visual cues can be the key to unlock the subject's method of accessing information For example, people typically move their eyes up at an angle when remembering pictures, they typically look to the side when recalling past sounds, and they look down at an angle when recalling kinesthetic, or felt, sensations.

If your subject consistently looks up and to the left when accessing information, he is "seeing" a picture. If the witness is looking down and to the right, he is probably accessing information in a kinesthetic manner. Similarly, if he looks consistently to the side, he is probably an auditorily oriented thinker. These cues to the subject's preferred representational system can be used to the interviewer's benefit.[36]

When you ask questions of a subject who is visually oriented, attempt to stimulate the witness's visual recall by asking questions in that format. Ask for information based on how things appeared to the witness, how the scene looked, how the defendant appeared, or how things appear in her mind. By asking the witness to access the information in a manner that is internally consistent with her representational system, there is a much greater likelihood that her recall will be fruitful.[37]

Similarly, by asking a visually centered subject to recall things based on an auditory representational system, you are asking the witness to remember in a way that is both foreign and uncomfortable. That is not to say that a witness who is auditory cannot recall visual images. It simply means that by speaking with a witness in her "native language," a rapport is more likely to develop.

Claims have been made that interviewers can act as "human lie detectors" based on an advanced application of NLP. This technique has often been taught in kinesic interviewing seminars. However, it is widely disputed as a technique for detecting deception, and significant research has shown that factors other than deception often influence a subject's method of accessing information.[38]

The principle of this technique is based on an NLP model constructed in the late 1970s, which postulated that people access remembered and "constructed" (false) information from different spatial areas. For example, it is believed that a constructed cue is accessed with a rightward eye movement. Regardless of whether constructed cues are accessed in this manner, and whether this NLP model is predictably accurate regarding the spatial relationship of constructed cues, there are other difficulties associated with using this communications model as a predictor of deception.

People construct mental images and sounds for many reasons. For example, Grinder and Bandler explain that many people reconstruct their memories. This reconstruction would then show a "construct" eye-accessing cue, even though the information related was factual and not fabricated. When dealing with such critical matters as truth and deception correlating directly to guilt and innocence, this margin of error, in our opinion, is too great. There are much better nonverbal cues to deception that are more easily calibrated by the layperson. Therefore, we believe that this use of NLP is unreliable.[39]

PARALANGUAGE MATCHING Paralanguage refers to the optional vocal effects, such as rate, tone, and volume, which accompany or modify human speech patterns and often communicate subtle meaning. Although an investigator should be cognizant of changes in volume, tone, or inflection in a witness's voice, paralanguage matching goes beyond mere observation.

Paralanguage matching requires the interviewer to adopt speech patterns similar to those of the witness. If a witness speaks slowly in a low volume, an investigator should attempt to adopt a similarly slow and low pattern of speech. In this way, the investigator and the witness are allowed to get in "sync." This mirroring technique does not have to be an exact match. It should, however, closely resemble the speaker's cadence and volume to be effective. When done properly, it is perhaps the most powerful rapport-building technique available to the investigator.[40]

Ending the Interview: Bringing Closure to the Interview

Once you are confident that no further information will be developed during that interview, you then should continue the rapport building by ensuring that the witness feels like a stakeholder in the process and you should signify that the interview is being concluded.

When bringing the interview to a close, it is important to assure the witness that if he recalls anything else, he should feel free to contact you and relay the information.

In addition, it is important to establish that you may wish to speak to the witness again at a later time for further questioning. Clearly explain that this occurs frequently as new information surfaces and as various other witnesses provide their account of the incident. You should therefore reassure the witness that this happens all the time and is simply a matter of routine.

By closing the interview in this rapport mode, you will likely have a much easier time if you actually do need to reinterview that particular witness. Once the interview is closed, it is imperative to accurately document in your report the content of the witness's statement.

INTERVIEWING FINANCIALLY SOPHISTICATED WITNESSES

Although there is no methodological difference when interviewing a financially savvy witness, a language barrier is an added aspect of such an interview. Hopefully, you have carefully read the first section of this book and feel comfortable in your knowledge of the basic concepts of the accounting equation. If not, feel free to do so now. Understanding the language and reasoning used by accountants and other financial professionals will substantially reduce the communications barrier. Once this barrier is lessened, the interview becomes a matter of attention to details. The greatest difference between conducting an interview in financial crimes over other crimes, in our opinion, is the need for preparation. In other crimes, for example, murder, complication is seldom involved. Often, it is a smoking gun homicide, and you are questioning witnesses about personal observations.

Financial crimes are quite different. Many times complex corporate structures, nominee owners, and offshore transactions are involved that tend to blur or completely obliterate true ownership. There are complex financial transactions that, though perfectly legal, seem somehow illegitimate. Financial crime interviews are all about the details—unfortunately, as the saying goes, the devil is in the details. Because these types of witnesses will often recount complicated transactions, simple yes-and-no questioning, or "tell me what happened" open-ended questions will yield nothing. Therefore, preparation is of paramount importance.

When interviewing witnesses in financial crimes, the most critical time is before the interview even begins. Sometimes, the opportunity to interview a particular witness will present itself only once. This may be true in the case of a witness who later becomes a suspect; or, perhaps, the witness unfortunately passes away before the case can be completed. Because you may get only one shot, it is imperative that you plan carefully before you step into the interview room.

Use the background developed during the preliminary stages of the investigation. Begin by carefully studying the business operation that is the subject of the investigation (for more detail see Chapter 8, The Investigative Process). By understanding the day-to-day operations of the firm and knowing the normal flow of funds, you will be prepared to recognize answers that provide either keys to new lines of questioning or perhaps cues that the witness may be withholding information. It is important to understand the normal flow of funds within the firm. This is why you don't rush into interviewing the financially savvy witnesses first.

Know the specific language that your financial witness speaks (accounting-ese, SEC-speak, etc.). When preparing for the interview, conduct research on similar enterprises within that industry. For example, if you are preparing to interview the comptroller for a medium-sized import-export firm, know what a similar firm looks like. What sort of yearly revenue can you expect to see? Regardless of the industry, there are likely several journals and trade organizations that can provide detailed information about standard operating procedures and financial ratios within the industry. Often, a simple telephone call or Internet visit will yield enough information to keep you busy for several days.

Examining industry-specific information and making detailed notes allows you to assess the validity of the answers to your interview questions. For example, if the industry average for bad debt write-offs is 1 percent of gross sales, a figure wildly over that should signal that further inquiry should be made into accounts receivable.

Collect the documents that your witness will likely testify about. Nothing is worse than trying to understand a complicated trail of transactions at the same time you are trying to formulate a new question. If possible, request that the witness provide, in advance, copies of any documents that he will be referring to in his interview. This allows you time to study the documents and make detailed notes concerning what questions you wish to ask. Too often, an investigator examines the financial documents while also attempting to interview the witness. This poses two problems. First, because you are unfamiliar with the documents, you may not notice inconsistencies. Second, by dividing your attention between formulating your next question and examining a complex document, neither task receives its requisite attention. In short, do not force yourself to make up questions on the fly.

Stack the deck. Interview witnesses with general information first and specific information last. This way, you are learning more each time you interview, and are going from general to specific. For example, the comptroller has a great deal of knowledge regarding the overall operations of the business. However, it is unlikely, at least in a large operation, that he would be able to easily answer specific questions about any particular account within the company's receivables department. By interviewing this person first, you can often obtain a much broader picture of the operation, which may help you formalize a more specific tactical approach to the remainder of the investigation. Obviously, if you suspect the comptroller or other high-ranking financial officer as being complicit, you may wish to use an alternative strategy.

Build your knowledge as you go. By starting at the top and working your way down, you will be increasing your knowledge base about the business while you are narrowing the focus of your questions until you have reached the point where specific pointed questions will elicit the detailed evidence necessary.

Prepare an interview outline in advance. As we cautioned with witnesses in general, the best defense against the natural tendency to leave out questions is to make a general outline in advance. This is even more important when interviewing financially sophisticated witnesses because they will most likely be talking over your head. By formulating a list of general questions and planning out the interview in advance, you are much more likely to cover everything you need and stay on track.

Don't be afraid to take documents or visual aids into the interview room. Allow your witness to take you step by step through the process or flow of funds. Make him do it slowly, and several times if necessary. It is imperative that you understand the process, flow, or procedure you are interviewing the witness about. It might help to summarize the information. When time allows, you should create a summary, even if it's just a brief handwritten synopsis, of the financial information the witness will be expected to know based on your examination of the documents.

Draw a flowchart of funds, transactions, or deposits. Visual aids can be an indispensable part of your brainstorming session. If you can understand the information well enough to create a one-page summary or chart, you likely will have a strong enough grasp of the financial picture to thoroughly question the witness. In addition, if you have a chart or summary of the information with you while conducting the interview, staying on track is much easier—simply follow the summary.

Do not be afraid to ask the witness to look at your flowchart or diagram. Have the witness tell you exactly where you are mistaken. Let him make the corrections. Or ask the witness to draw a chart of his own. By following along visually as the witness explains the flow of transactions, what once was blurred in your mind may become clear.

Finally, be prepared to enlist help. Although you will have a much better handle on most financial crimes after reading this book, you will invariably run across scenarios that put you out of your league. Hopefully, these will be few and far between—and fewer as you expand your experience. They are inevitable nonetheless. When an unfamiliar scenario arises, set aside your pride and seek the assistance of an expert in that particular field. Whether you spend an hour trying to absorb as much information as possible, or whether you enlist experts' help in preparing your pre-interview analysis, don't be afraid to use them. Literally hundreds of financial professionals would be eager to assist in a little cloak-and-dagger work. Be careful though: Their assistance often comes at a price.

CONCLUSION

Although interviews with witnesses in financial crimes differ from interviews with witnesses in other types of crimes, certain key interview techniques can help you as an investigator develop as much information as possible. In this chapter we have introduced you to some techniques that can aid you in both types of interviews. Our goal has been that you take two things away.

First, remember that, in general, the interview process is a dynamic relationship. The interaction between the investigator and the witness is the key to success of the interview. By employing such techniques as the use of cognitive interview skills you can increase your chances of building a better rapport. These techniques, though designed to enhance the recall of eyewitnesses to crimes, can be used effectively to enhance the recall of witnesses in financial crimes as well.

Second, preparation is the key to properly and effectively interviewing a financially knowledgeable witness. Although there is no magical list of questions that an investigator must ask, the skills you have developed reading the first section of this book should suggest a logical sequence and some general questions to use in certain financial crime interviews. Beyond that, there is nothing magical about interviewing financially bright people. Preparation will give you the edge, which will allow you to elicit the most detailed and accurate statement possible. "Be prepared" should be the motto of the financial crime interviewer, not just that of the Boy Scouts.

SUGGESTED READINGS

Buckhout, R. "Eyewitness Testimony." *Scientific American*, 231, no. 6 (1974): 23–31.

Crombag, H.F., W.A. Wagenaar, and P.J. Van Koppen. "Crashing Memories and the Problem of 'Source Monitoring.'" *Applied Cognitive Psychology*, 10 (1996): 95–104.

Fisher, R. P., and R. E. Geiselman. *Memory-Enhancing Techniques for Investigative Interviewing*. Springfield, IL: Charles C. Thomas, 1992.

Geiselman R.E., R.P. Fisher, G. Cohen, H. Holland, and L. Surtes. "Eyewitness Responses to Leading and Misleading Questions Under the Cognitive Interview." *Journal of Police Science and Administration*, 14, no. 1 (1986): 31–39.

Gudjonsson, G.H. *The Psychology of Interrogations Confessions and Testimony*. Chichester, England: John Wiley & Sons, 1992.

Hall, J.A., and M.L. Knapp. "Nonverbal Communication." In *Human Interaction*. Fort Worth, TX: Harcourt Brace Jovanovich, 1992.

Kohnken, G., E. Scimossek, E. Aschermann, and E. Hofer. "The Cognitive Interview and the Assessment of the Credibility of Adults' Statements." *Journal of Applied Psychology*, 80 (1995): 671–684.

Laborde, G.Z. *Influencing with Integrity*. Palo Alto, CA: Syntory Publishing, 1987.

Mann, S., A. Vrij, and R. Bull. "Suspects, Lies and Videotape: An Analysis of Authentic High-Stakes Liars." *Law and Human Behavior*, 26, no. 3, 365–374.

Mantwill, M., G. Kohnken, and E. Aschermann. "Effects of the Cognitive Interview on the Recall of Familiar and Unfamiliar Events." *Journal of Applied Psychology*, 80 (1995): 68–78.

Memon, A., and D.B. Wright. "Eyewitness Testimony and the Oklahoma Bombing." *The Psychologist*, 12, no. 6 (1999): 292–295.

Memon, A., A. Vrij, and R. Bull, eds. *Psychology and Law: Truthfulness, Accuracy and Credibility*. New York: McGraw-Hill, 1998.

O'Connor, J., and J. Seymour. *Introducing Neuro-Linguistic Programming*. London, England: HarperCollins, 1990.

Parker, A.D., and J. Brown. "Detection of Deception: Statement Validity Analysis as a Means of Determining Truthfulness or Falsity of Rape Allegations." *Legal and Criminological Psychology*, 5 (2000): 239–259.

Rassin, E. "Criteria Based Content Analysis: The Less Scientific Road to Truth." *Expert Evidence* 7, no. 4 (2000): 265–278.

Sporer, S., R. Malpass, and G. Kohnken, eds. *Psychological Issues in Eyewitness Identification*. Mahwah, NJ: LEA, 1996.

United States Department of Justice, Office of Justice Programs. *Eyewitness Evidence: A Guide for Law Enforcement*. Washington, DC: National Institute of Justice, 1999.

Vrij, A. "Detective Deceit via Analysis of Verbal and Nonverbal Behavior." *Journal of Nonverbal Behavior*, 24, no. 4 (2000): 239–263.

Vrij, A. *Detective Lies and Deceit: The Psychology of Lying and the Implications for Professional Practice*. Chichester, England: John Wiley & Sons, 2000.

Vrij, A., and M. Baxter. "Accuracy and Confidence in Detecting Truths and Lies in Elaborations and Denials: Truth Bias, Lie Bias and Individual Differences." *Expert Evidence*, 7, no. 1 (1999): 25–36.

Vrij, A., and S.K. Lochun. "Neuro-Linguistic Programming and the Police: Worthwhile or Not?" *Journal of Police and Criminal Psychology*, 12, no. 1 (1997).

NOTES

1. B.L. Berg and J.J. Horgan, *Criminal Investigation*, 3rd ed. (Woodland Hills: Glencoe/McGraw-Hill, 1998), p. 122.
2. R. Milne and R. Bull, *Investigative Interviewing: Psychology and Practice* (Chichester, England: John Wiley & Sons, 1999), pp. 34–39.
3. C.L. Yeschke, *The Art of Investigative Interviewing*, 2nd ed. (Burlington, MA: Butterworth-Heinemann, 2003), pp. 15–21.
4. Berg and Horgan, *Criminal Investigation*, 3rd ed., p. 122. See also A.S. Aubry Jr. and R.R. Caputo, *Criminal Interrogation*, 2nd ed. (Springfield, IL: Charles C. Thomas, 1972), pp. 21–40. See also R.W. Shuy, *The Language of Confession, Interrogation and Deception* (Thousand Oaks, CA: Sage Publications, 1998), p. 12.
5. C.A. Meissner and S.M. Kassin, "'He's Guilty!' Investigator Bias in Judgments of Truth Deception," *Law and Human Behavior*, 26, no. 5 (2002): 469–480.
6. Shuy, *The Language of Confession*, p. 13.

7. Ibid.
8. D.E. Zulawski and D.E. Wicklander, *Practical Aspects of Interview and Interrogation* (Boca Raton, FL: CRC Press, 1993), pp. 7, 13–29. M.R. Kebbell and G.F. Wagstaff, "The Effectiveness of the Cognitive Interview," in D. Canter and L. Alison, eds., *Interviewing and Deception* (Aldershot, Hauts, England: Ashgate, 1999), pp. 26–30.
9. Ibid., p. 25.
10. Ibid., p. 25–26; see also Berg and Horgan, *Criminal Investigation*, 3rd ed., pp. 125–126.
11. Ibid., p. 25. See also Milne and Bull, *Investigative Interviewing*, pp. 33–34.
12. Milne and Bull, *Investigative Interviewing*, pp. 34–39.
13. Ibid., p. 36.
14. Ibid., p. 38.
15. Ibid., 33–34.
16. Kebbell and Wagstaff, "The Effectiveness of the Cognitive Interview," pp. 30–33.
17. Milne and Bull, *Investigative Interviewing*, pp. 39–47.
18. Ibid.
19. Ibid.
20. Ibid.
21. Ibid., pp. 184–187.
22. Ibid.
23. Ibid., pp. 136–139, 143.
24. Ibid., pp. 40–41.
25. S. B. Walter, *Principles of Kinesic Interview and Interrogation*, 2nd ed. (Boca Raton, FL: CRC Press, 2003), p. 139.
26. Ibid., pp. 139–140.
27. Ibid.
28. Ibid. See also R. Bandler and J. Grinder, *Frogs into Princes* (Moab, UT: Real People Press, 1979), pp. 5–8.
29. The terms *kinesic* and *kinesthetic*, while closely related, refer to two different areas of study. The term kinesic refers to the study of the relationship between body motions such as blushing or eye movement and human communication. Kinesthetics, on the other hand, refers to the relationship between human sensory experience and memory. When we discuss kinesics, we are referring to techniques for reading nonlinguistic cues in communications. When we are discussing kinesthetics, we are talking about the influence that human sensory experience has on the way in which people encode and access their memories.
30. Zulawski and Wicklander, *Practical Aspects of Interview and Interrogation*, pp. 143–146.
31. Ibid., pp. 146–147.
32. Ibid.

33. Ibid.
34. Ibid.
35. Walter, *Principles of Kinesic Interview and Interrogation*, pp. 140–142.
36. Ibid.
37. Zulawski and Wicklander, *Practical Aspects of Interview and Interrogation*, pp. 143–146.
38. Walter, *Principles of Kinesic Interview and Interrogation*, pp. 141–146.
39. Ibid.
40. Zulawski and Wicklander, *Practical Aspects of Interview and Interrogation*, pp. 147–149.

10

PROVING CASES THROUGH DOCUMENTARY EVIDENCE

INTRODUCTION

We prove all cases through evidence. In general, we divide evidence into two categories—direct and circumstantial. In addition to these two categories of evidence, we classify evidence according to its nature. For example, we classify actual witness testimony on the stand in open court as *testimonial evidence*. The statements that you obtained during your investigation are *documentary evidence*, as are canceled checks, bank statements, and photographs of suspect transactions. Additionally, since hundreds of canceled checks are often difficult to comprehend as they sit in piles, attorneys prepare charts and schedules to assist jurors in understanding the big picture. We call these schedules and charts *demonstrative evidence*. Finally, we refer to physical objects, like guns, knives, and fingerprints, as *real evidence*. It is through these different classes of evidence that attorneys prove that something did or did not occur.

The difference between financial crimes and nonfinancial crimes is the composition of the evidence. Prosecutors often use real evidence such as fingerprints and tool-mark comparisons to prove crimes such as murder and burglary. Sometimes, documentary evidence like pawn receipts and photographs become important in these cases, but generally, they are non-document-based cases. Conversely, financial crimes are very document heavy.

Because of this difference, investigators must often confront huge volumes of evidence. In the typical murder investigation, more than 500 pieces of evidence would be considered exceptionally high. Conversely, in major financial crimes, 500 individual pieces of evidence would be much more common. For example, the number of canceled checks belonging to a single account for a single year could easily exceed 500.

As we proceed through this chapter, we will prepare you to deal with this unique aspect of financial crime investigation. As we begin, we will focus on the basics of document collection. From consensual searches, to subpoenas, to search warrants, you will be exposed the various methods of securing documentary evidence. At the same time, we will offer some tips on what types of documents you might expect to encounter.

Next, we will offer some guidance on organizing your efforts. Because you are likely to encounter an unmanageable number of documents in your investigation, a system for organizing and collating them is very important. In the next section, we will offer a framework and some tips for creating an evidence tracking system that will serve you well regardless of the size of the investigation.

Finally, we will discuss how to prove your case. Using the framework of logic and inference, we will explain how you can apply the organizational techniques you developed in the first two sections to prove cases. Marshalling the evidence toward proving one ultimate thesis—guilt—is an art; becoming good at it requires you first understand the process of legal proof.

DOCUMENT COLLECTION

All cases require submission of the best evidence. The term *best evidence* does not refer to the most appropriate piece of evidence for a particular claim. Instead, it means that all evidence submitted to prove a claim must be the original.[1] Where the original is not available, the offering party must generally offer both evidence to show why it is unavailable and proof that the offered copy is accurate.[2] There are some exceptions to this rule; however, it is wise to view it as being inflexible.

This rule is of particular importance to financial crime investigators. When attempting to prove that suspect "A" killed the victim by shooting him, production and introduction of the actual gun is usually a given. Conversely, when seeking to prove that CFO "A" embezzled money from the pension fund, introducing copies of bank statements and other documents might appeal to prosecutors. While under certain circumstances courts will allow this, proper collection and submission of the original is of usually required.

Therefore, proper handling of documents from the very beginning is your primary concern. From the moment documents come into your possession, regardless of how they were obtained, you will be ultimately responsible for their safekeeping and for their production. If you take the necessary precautions beforehand, this responsibility should be a simple matter to fulfill.

Sources of Documents

Although you will probably find documentary evidence in a number of locations, we have decided to divide them into three categories. First, you will obtain documents from the victims of the financial crime. Whether it is an investor swindled out of his pension or the multinational conglomerate that lost a million dollars, this is usually the first place you will look for documentary evidence. Next, you will seek to obtain records and documentary evidence from third parties. Finally, you will probably attempt to collect evidence from the suspect herself.

Collecting your documentary evidence in that order is usually advisable. As with everything we have discussed up to this point, when and from whom you first seek to collect evidence may vary depending on the operational circumstances; however, we have found that this logical sequence usually works very well.

Documents from the Victim As soon as you receive the complaint or allegation, you should begin collecting documentary evidence. When you meet with the complainant, she will probably have some documentation available to substantiate her claim. If she does, collect it. While you may be tempted to instruct the complainant to hold onto the evidence until you make a more clear determination of viability, this could be problematic later on.

Although it is rare, documents sometimes get lost. If you allow the victim to hold on to the evidence and she misplaces, or worse, destroys it, the basis for your case may be gone. Likewise, there is the remote possibility that the original reporting party was complicit, but for some reason chose to initiate a complaint—perhaps to divert suspicion. If you allow the complaining witness to retain the evidence, destruction is possible if she later becomes a suspect. Finally, even if the complaining witness is not involved, the suspect may have accomplices in the company who have access to the documents. If so, removal, alteration or destruction is a real danger.

Make copies and issue receipts. Sometimes, the complainant may be reluctant to release the documents. This is often the case with sensitive financial data or trade secret information. Nonetheless, it is important that you explain to the victim the need for proper evidence handling procedures so that the court system can bring the guilty party to justice. Assure the victim that your evidence handling procedures are as secure as or better than his own; then make the appropriate copies for his files and issue him itemized receipts for everything you take.

Be meticulous in your paperwork. While we have seen cases in which the investigator who collected documents took shortcuts and got away with it, do not test the limits of your liability insurance coverage. When the task of collecting hundreds of documents at a time confronts you, the natural inclination is to list groups of documents in bulk and lump everything together. Not only does this make identification of specific documents difficult, it could trigger liability when the victim claims she released the company's most valuable trade secret to you and you cannot disprove it. The best advice is to take the time and list everything.

At the very minimum, you should leave with a statement. Even when the complainant has no documentary evidence to back the claim, you can still leave with something. Request that complaining witness complete a written, signed statement. By doing this, you are establishing a basis for investigation as well as protecting yourself from future confusion. If the complaining witness recants, for whatever reason, you have something to verify the nature of the original complaint. Likewise, if the original witness is unavailable in the future, the statement, while unlikely to be admissible in court, can serve as a reference in her absence. Finally, even if the witness does not recant, she may alter her story or forget pertinent details. If you have them in writing, from the beginning, you have lost no ground.

TYPES OF DOCUMENTS TO EXPECT

- *Signed statements.* Besides the original complainant, you should anticipate taking written statements from all witnesses at the victim business. These documents, while not substitutes for the actual testimonial evidence that the witnesses will offer later at trial, can serve as your outline of their likely trial testimony. In addition, the same cautions regarding complainant statements apply here.

- *Transactional paperwork.* This is another place where your preinvestigation planning will benefit you. Each business victim you encounter is likely to operate in a different manner. While most businesses have the same general flow of paper documents, there will be differences. Always be on the lookout for paperwork generated by the business that documents the various transactions that occur within its business cycle. Invoices, payment vouchers, and other original records of transactions are invaluable for tracking the flow of money.

- *Intranet sources.* In today's business world, more and more companies are establishing intranets that connect all employees and departments together. While this is a boon for productivity, it can also be a boon for you. Pay particular attention to chat facilities, weblogs, and other semipublic areas where suspects and witnesses may both lurk. While transactional information may not be available through these sources, they are often the unofficial communications channel in a firm. Background information, rumor, and gossip might prove to be a valuable place to begin looking for other clues.

- *E-mails.* Again, the rise of the company intranet and the growth of computer-based operations in business can be a boon to investigators. One area that has received considerable attention from the legal community recently is e-mail communications. Lawyers have quickly realized the value of e-mail communications, and more than one e-mail message has served as the smoking gun in civil cases. Many people treat e-mail correspondence with surprising flippancy considering the longevity of most messages on the corporate server. Their carelessness can be your windfall.

Even though this list is not exhaustive, it is a good place to begin. As we mentioned, the record-keeping systems and paper trails generated will differ from business to business. However, preplanning and intelligence gathering should serve as a guide to knowing exactly what you are looking for. Whether the suspect religiously uses e-mail, or simply sends out traditional paper memos, both can be valuable sources of evidence. The key is remaining flexible, and tailoring your search to the specific circumstances of each business.

Documents from Third Parties As a rule, in financial crime investigations the majority of documentary evidence you collect will come from third-party sources. In order for a financial criminal to be successful, he or she must interact with the traditional business world. They must deposit money into banks, secure the advice of financial and legal professionals, and generally, engage in the same type of conduct that noncriminals do. As a result, third parties become a very valuable source of information. Banks, accountants, and business and government organizations all have the potential to provide key pieces of evidence linking the suspect to the crime.

Remember, the diverse nature of business means that many different sources exist. Every business has a particular pattern of activity, and each has a circle of influence. In some cases, the contacts a business has may be limited to financial professionals. In other cases, their contacts will extend well beyond the financial sector into the community. Either way, keep in mind that the diversity of contacts the business has may dictate where you may find potentially incriminating documents.

Notwithstanding this diversity, we believe that a suspect's contacts can be broken down into five basic categories. First, the business or suspect will undoubtedly have contacts in the financial sector. These contacts can include banks, brokerage houses, and insurance professionals. Second, the suspect may have contacts within the professional community including lawyers and accountants. Third, the suspect will have industry contacts such as business organizations, associations, and networking groups. Fourth, there will be contact between the suspect and the government, and finally, every suspect will have personal contacts, which, while not necessarily integral to the suspect's illegal activities, may still be a valuable source of information.

Because of the diversity we discussed earlier, instead of discussing the various sources of documents individually, we will address them by category. We will offer you some basic guidance about what you may expect to find, and we may even offer some tips about particular documents that are available. However, in terms of tailoring your search, we will leave you to your own devices, since there are, as we mentioned, an endless number of permutations of the information that you are likely to find.

FINANCIAL CONTACTS   Banks are often a great place to begin. Most criminals, if not all, will need to have some contact with organized financial institutions. Whether they need a simple checking account, or utilize the full panoply of financial services most banks now provide, there will be paper trails from which you can construct a picture.

Access to some bank records may be restricted. For example, Currency Transaction Reports (CTRs) and other Bank Secrecy Act documents are strictly controlled through federal law.[3] As a result, civil investigators, and to a much lesser extent local and state criminal investigators, will be limited in their ability to use these powerful tools. On the other hand, there are many bank and bank-related documents that civil investigators can obtain through civil summons and pretrial discovery tools. Likewise local and state law enforcement investigators can obtain the majority of these documents through investigative and grand jury subpoenas and search warrants.

Do not overlook the non-obvious clues that banking records can reveal. Some inexperienced investigators may be tempted to focus immediately on the value that bank records have in proving income, or even documenting payments to business associates. As experience grows, an investigator will routinely find that bank records are valuable for many more things.

In addition to explicit information like amounts of cash flows, bank records hold metadata. Investigators loosely define metadata as a component of data that describes data: in other words, data about data.[4] The metadata of a bank record set then is the data surrounding the transactions and their origin. For example, an item deposited into the suspect's account is more than an increase in cash. On the contrary, we can extract much more than that. By examining the date, time, teller information, and format of the transaction, we can extrapolate many important clues.

Taken together, metadata can establish our pattern of activity. By analyzing, either digitally or manually, all the transactions, we can build patterns that can give direction to the investigations. These patterns may lead us to other associates, or other assets, or even allow us to make predictions about future illegal acts.

The metadata generated by each transaction can help reconstruct a suspect's movement. In addition to American Banking Association routing numbers, each check that goes through the clearing process collects additional clues. For example, during a counter transaction the teller will stamp the check with a unique transaction code, a time, date, and the teller's information. Each of these codes may differ from bank to bank, but the bottom line is that each transaction is uniquely identifiable to a particular point in time. Included among these numbers are clues to the disposition of the funds and, in the case of deposits, the source of the funds. Exhibit 10.1 shows an example of some of this metadata.

As you begin to evaluate banking transactions, it may be helpful to remember that there are essentially two categories of transactions. The first category, flow-through, is transactions that relate to the holder's account. For

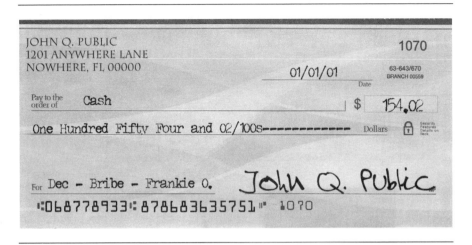

JOHN Q. PUBLIC
1201 ANYWHERE LANE
NOWHERE, FL 00000   **1070**

01/01/01   63-643/670
                 BRANCH 00559
                              Date

Pay to the   Cash $ 154.02
order of

One Hundred Fifty Four and 02/100s------------ Dollars

For Dec - Bribe - Frankie O.   John Q. Public

⑆068778933⑆ 878683635751⑈ 1070

EXHIBIT 10.1   Check Metadata

example, deposits, withdrawals, and debit/credit memos are all considered flow-through transactions. The second category encompasses the remainder of the banking transactions you are likely to encounter and we refer to them as nonaccount transactions, since they are not directly tied to a holder's account. Some of examples of common nonaccount transactions are loans, CD transactions (excluding conversions of CD proceeds into an account deposit), third-party transactions, and safety deposit box transactions.[5]

In order to extract the metadata necessary to formulate a hypothesis, it is also important to understand the basic progression of a flow-through transaction. Exhibit 10.2 shows the flow of an average transaction through the system.

Although you will often encounter loan files, securities statements, and other, nonaccount documentation, the greater portion of your analysis will involve flow-through transactions. Each transaction flows in generally the same way. First, there must be a transaction entry point. Usually, this is a window transaction where a suspect presents either an item for deposit or a draft for withdrawal, but it could just as easily take some other form such as an ATM or point of sale (POS) transaction. From the transaction entry point, the items proceed to the proof department where the teller's mathematical calculations are checked and the items are encoded with the bank's discrete identification numbers and the transaction-specific MICR information. From the proof department the transaction items are transferred to the microfilm department

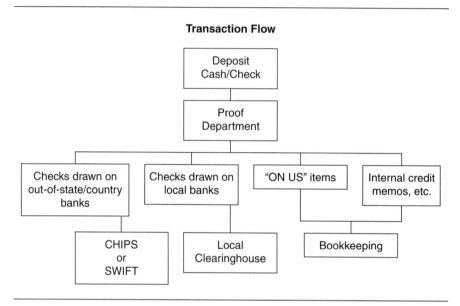

EXHIBIT 10.2   Transaction Flowchart

where all items are recorded and entered into the bank's computer system. From the microfilm department, the bank separates the transactions and then sends them to different departments for clearing.

Clearing is where the money changes hands. Depending on whether the transaction is an in-house transaction, meaning the item is presented against the institution on which the claim is held, or an outside transaction, the process may be more or less complicated. However, the general purpose of the clearing process is to ensure that at the end there is an exchange of claims between the payer and the payee. In the case of an in-house transaction, where the payer and payee institutions are the same, the transaction data are sent to the in-house clearing department, and then on to the bookkeeping department where the customer records are updated.[6]

If the transaction involves a local institution, the bank sends the transaction items to the local clearinghouse. When the parties to the transaction are local, usually within the same city, and the payer and payee institutions are not the same, the transaction items go to the local clearing department. These local checks are then usually cleared through the Fedwire funds transfer system or the Clearing House for Interbank Payments System (CHIPS).[7]

The transit department ensures the proper clearance of outside area transactions. The transactions that involve institutions outside the local area must be processed through alternative means. Depending on the origin of the issuing institution, this may be accomplished through either Fedwire, CHIPS or, for most international transactions, the Society for Worldwide Interbank Transfers (SWIFT).[8]

What is a clearinghouse? While a detailed explanation of the history and role of clearinghouses in banking is well beyond the scope of this text, a few key principles are worth understanding. Clearinghouses act as a means to settle payments between financial institutions. With the rise in popularity of checks and bank drafts by merchants in the mid-1850s, banks needed a system for rapid, accurate, and efficient settlement between themselves. This system of interbank settlements facilitates the reconciliation of transactions between unrelated banks, making it a simple matter for one bank to process the drafts of another bank with confidence.[9]

Lastly, the bank routes those items that require special processing to the special handling department. Items such as wire transfers or debit or credit memoranda that require special handling by the institution are sent to this department. In those cases, the bank forwards the items to an internal department, often called the special handling department, for processing and posting to the customer's account.[10]

Once you have obtained and examined the flow-through records, you must analyze them. Analysis can take many forms, from manual to computer. Regardless of its form, the underlying rationale is the same. You must tailor your analysis to the nature of the crime you are investigating. Different crimes will have different patterns. Thinking through the methodology of the particular crime you are investigating will help you visualize patterns and types of transactions that you are most likely to find.

While each investigation will present you with different operational concerns, there are a number of similarities among them. You should look for both patterns and missing data. Patterns occur in accounts for a number of reasons including legitimate things like paying monthly bills, and this is where the assistance of computer processing is helpful. By sorting the transactions by different criteria like payee, date, amount, and check number, you can more easily identify patterns and recurring transactions. Sorting is especially helpful in establishing the timing of transactions and may identify offense dates. For example, if your suspect's account, sorted by date, shows four months of steadily recurring biweekly deposits with the same non-whole-dollar amounts, it is highly possible the transaction is his paycheck. Suddenly, in the third month, on the first Monday, the suspect deposits a large whole-dollar amount. This should be a red flag based on the previous pattern of activity. While it is no guarantee, it may pinpoint the date of a bribe, kickback, or blackmail payment.

In short, we recommend careful scrutiny of the intimate details as well as the broad picture. As we stated earlier, a thorough explanation of bank record analysis is beyond the scope of this introductory text. For a detailed account, we highly recommend *A Guide to the Financial Analysis of Personal and Corporate Bank Records*, written by Marilyn B. Peterson, and published by the National White Collar Crime Center. It is highly instructive.

In addition to banks, insurance agents and stockbrokers are valuable sources of information. Insurance agents with whom the suspect has dealt are likely to have copies of insurance contracts and investment vehicles such as annuities and whole-life policies that can reveal additional sources of income. Likewise, brokerage firms can provide a wealth of information on the current and past financial status of the suspect. Activity in trading and margin accounts may reveal patterns or motives, and can help point you in the direction of other assets.

PROFESSIONAL CONTACTS You should always interview professionals with whom the suspect has dealt. Attorneys are not known for their liberality when it comes to discussing their clients. Even so, there are occasions when a lawyer may be both forthcoming and enlightening. Notwithstanding the attorney–client privilege and work product doctrines, there are matters within the knowledge of an attorney that they may in fact be able to tell you. While these times will be rare indeed, it is important to leave no stone unturned.

In addition, the attorney's fellow professional, the accountant, is often a much more fruitful target. In many jurisdictions, the accountant–client relationship falls outside the privileged information doctrine. Therefore, communications, both verbal and written, between a suspect and his accountant are both discoverable and admissible. As a result, you absolutely must question accountants, and if necessary compel them to produce all written documents pertaining to the client. The following is a list of a few of the documents that may be in the possession of your suspect's accountant:

- Working papers; these often identify sources of income, expenditures, hidden accounts, and loans.

- Notes and memoranda used to prepare the suspect's income tax return.
- Copies of income tax returns.
- Corporate minutes and other corporate documents leading to the identification of shell companies.

In short, nearly any financial document within the control of your suspect might also be available through his accountant. Rely on the meticulous record-keeping nature of most public accountants to provide a source of evidence.

Real estate professionals may also have records. Both real estate agents and title companies may have copies of contracts identifying real property that your suspect owns. Likewise, real estate and title companies commonly retain copies of insurance documents, settlement sheets, and copies of financial instruments used in consummating the transaction. These documents will show buyer/seller information as well as price, down payment, and the distribution of money at closing. Additionally, do not overlook the possibility that the real estate agent may be acting as a property manager. In the event the suspect retained the realtor in such a capacity, the realtor will have copies of items such as leases and tenant information.

INDUSTRY CONTACTS Industry organizations can provide information to which you may compare your suspect. Most industry-based organizations maintain vast amounts of marketing and sales information for their industry. While the data they have will not likely be specific to your suspect, it may be valuable in determining things such as actual sales, expenses, and COGS. By obtaining the proper industry information, you can arm yourself with a yardstick by which to measure both the timing and amount of cash flows in the suspect's account. For example, while an association of video retailers will not have the specific number of monthly rentals your suspect transacted, they can tell you what the industry average is. In some cases, their information is specific to each region or city. Armed with that information, you are prepared to spot overstated revenues when examining your suspect's books.

Persons with whom the suspect does business have records, too. Both suppliers and customers will have transaction records documenting their relationship with the suspect. The nature of the relationship, frequency of contact, and general cooperativeness of the third party may determine the value of the documentation to the investigation. Do not overlook it. In some instances, you must take care to avoid eliminating a vendor/customer as a suspect too early in the investigation. Assuming the business contact is legitimate, there are a number of documents of value in their possession. For example, purchase orders and invoices are a great way to disprove claimed sales figures or expenses. Likewise, unusual timing of invoices and unusually generous credit terms may tend to establish less-than-arm's-length transactions and sham asset transfers. Do not hesitate to seek support for the vendor's documentation. For example, just because the suspect's supplier produces a paid invoice for 3,000 pizza boxes does not mean the transaction actually occurred. Backup data should exist in the vendor's file as well, indicating the depletion of inventory, reorder, and similar activities.

Sometimes what you do not see is just as important as what you do. As we said, information from invoices and purchase orders could be great evidence; however, do not overlook the ramifications of no evidence. If the suspect's office supply account reflects $35,000 in purchases over the course of the year, and the supplier of record has no invoices reflecting such purchases, you have just proven that the suspect inflated the business expenses—a manipulation often used by local money launderers.[11]

GOVERNMENT CONTACTS Information that is useful to investigators fills government agencies. One of the purposes of government agencies and regulatory bodies is the collection of data. Agencies collect some of these data in the aggregate, such as census and accident data, but other portions of data are identifying. The number of documents that a single individual generates in his or her lifetime is practically immeasurable, from birth certificates, to marriage licenses, to corporate filings, to death certificates; some oversight authority is responsible for their collection and processing. Many of these documents are public records, meaning they are open to inspection by the public.

Recently, there has been a general call for restrictions, but many documents are still readily available. On October 26, 1993, Representative James Moran introduced House Resolution 3365, which proposed a severe restriction on access to driver's license information.[12] This resolution, later enacted and codified as Title 18, Section 2721, is known as the Driver's License Privacy Protection Act, and effectively limits access to driver's license information, with a few exceptions, to criminal justice agencies.[13] In the comments to the resolution, Representative Moran expressed considerable concern over invasions of privacy leading to identify theft, stalking, and insurance fraud.[14] Others have echoed Representative Moran's concerns. Even though this restriction does not affect law enforcement investigators, it does impinge on the investigative tools of the fraud examiner.

Notwithstanding this shift, there are a number of records that are still available. Aside from the limited class of records that fall within the purview of Section 2721, many public records are not only available but also easily accessible. As we mentioned earlier, the momentum of the Internet has swept up government no less than it has the public, and as a result, most public agencies are moving toward making public records available online. In addition to the vast number of individual records scattered across cyberspace, there are a number of subscription-based services that will scour the public databases for you—for a price.

Whether you invest in shoe leather, scour the cyberworld yourself, or pay a service to do it for you, do not exclude public records from your search. By this point in the investigation, you have likely identified the county in which your suspect lives and works. That should be a good starting place. Likewise, your analysis of bank records, accounting documents, and insurance policies may have uncovered other counties, states, or even countries in which records may lie. Using this information, conducting your search in ever-widening circles is usually a solid strategy. Beginning with the suspect's county records and moving out from there you should look for business, property, legal, and personal records:

- *Business records.* Businesses are highly regulated beginning at the local level. A minimum search would include looking for things such as occupational licenses, corporate registrations and filings, annual reports, state licenses from regulatory bodies such as real estate, mortuary, or banking commissions, and fictitious name registrations. In addition to licenses, regulatory agencies such as most state Departments of Agriculture record infractions and warnings for rule violations or failed inspections. Be sure to look at the names of all entities with which your suspect is associated. This process is one that you may have to repeat as more information about your suspect emerges linking him with new names and organizations.

- *Property records.* Depending on the jurisdiction, there are a number of names by which property records may be known. Likewise, some jurisdictions maintain separate files for recorded deeds and tax assessments. Both documents can be valuable as they might reflect nominee ownership of property or a fictitious transfer of property. Pay especially close attention to quit-claim deeds. While these instruments are both legitimate and common in real estate transactions, criminals can abuse them.

- *Legal records.* As with property records and other public documents, the rate at which individual jurisdictions make their systems available online is often related to their size and budget. However, in the past few years, even smaller jurisdictions have begun to place their court records on the Web. In some cases, there are efforts to consolidate the records systems from all jurisdictions across the state into a single searchable database system. On the federal level, the PACER system, as well as other commercially accessible search engines, can provide access to all civil and criminal case filings. As a minimum, your search should include queries on both the businesses and given names of all suspects. You can expect to find records of all civil litigation in which the suspect was involved—as either plaintiff or defendant. You may also find all criminal actions, both felony and misdemeanor, and in some cases traffic infractions. Of particular note to a financial crime investigator are bankruptcy filings, which can be the mother lode in terms of either proving a starting net worth or establishing ownership of assets, not to mention revealing a motive for a theft in the first place.

- *Personal records.* It is important to include a search for all personal records of the suspect in order to ensure that you can account for all identities by which she may have been known. Whether it is a name change, or perhaps just a typographical error, Suzanne Benson is quite different from Susan Benton. By locating birth records, name change petitions, or other documents linking the two individuals as the same person, you can provide new avenues of inquiry in your business entity search.

PERSONAL CONTACTS As we mentioned earlier, partners, spouses, and exes of both can be useful information sources. While we find that personal contacts with the suspect are generally more valuable as interview subjects than producers of documentary evidence, do not discount their value altogether. For instance, personal contacts are often privy to the personal thoughts and ruminations of the suspect, which may end up in e-mail or conventional correspondence. If an evidentiary privilege does not cover the relationship, there is nothing wrong with obtaining it as a lead. Likewise, personal contacts may be valuable in helping to identify additional bank accounts. For example, repayment of a personal debt with a check may lead to discovery of a personal checking account that previously slipped below the investigator's radar. Therefore, while not usually the most productive of the sources, personal contacts can be viable and might even provide the clues that tie up the loose ends.

Documents from the Suspect Suspects are usually the last people from whom you will seek documentary evidence. This is not always true, but in most cases, you will attempt to secure documentary evidence from your other sources before striking out on a fishing expedition with your suspect. For a number of reasons, it is advisable to learn as much as possible about the business and personal habits of the suspect first. Sometimes, lack of this knowledge will cause you to miss documents, or worse, mistake valuable evidence for irrelevant evidence, or in the worst case, prematurely tip your hand to your suspect. Any of these scenarios is undesirable, each for its own reasons.

However, once you decide that your suspect is the next target of your document search there are a few things to keep in mind. When you finally have the suspect in your sights in terms of document collection, you need to understand the limitations you may face. First, depending on the nature of your investigation, you may not have all the tools necessary. If the case is criminal, you have a full range of options including subpoenas and search warrants. Conversely, if you are pursuing a civil investigation your options may be somewhat more limited.

In a civil case, you are generally limited to civil process. While your criminal counterpart can rely on a court-issued search warrant (or in extreme cases a court-ordered wire intercept), you cannot. Although most third-party documents are available through civil process, documents in possession of the suspect may not be. In addition, due to the "voluntariness" of the civil discovery process, there is no guarantee that the suspect/defendant will produce the records, or even admit to their existence for that matter, upon your demand for production. Likewise, in many instances, the ability to invoke the civil process system is limited strictly to post-filing, meaning that the suspect must become a defendant before court jurisdiction will attach. Regardless of the nature of your investigation, whether civil or criminal, it is always advisable that you consult with counsel prior to proceeding down this path. While we can offer some general guidance and suggest what documents are available, we cannot offer specific advice concerning the particular legal peculiarities of your jurisdiction.

One last comment on sources of documents: Do not overlook consensual production. Even though we mention this last, do not assume that it is any small item. In fact, consensual production of records, in both civil and criminal cases, is a deceptively powerful tool. As we have stressed throughout this text, do not overlook the obvious. Ask the suspect for the necessary records. You would be surprised at the number of suspects who are eager to produce the records. Whether it is out of stupidity or misbelief that they can somehow talk their way out of the mess, we have encountered more than a few suspects who willingly turned over some of the most inculpatory evidence in their case. Nevertheless, if the suspect is not inclined in that way, then you may have to resort to more compelling means of getting what you want.

DOCUMENT ORGANIZATION

Now that we have introduced you to the nature of the records available, we need to talk about organizing them. Financial crime investigations result in more records and documents than perhaps any other type of case. The danger in this is the possibility of information overload. Coupled with this overload is the increased probability of loss and destruction. The existence of these dangers requires a very robust system of organization. Whereas some nonfinancial crime investigations can survive on a seat-of-the-pants approach, document-intensive cases cannot. Therefore, it is necessary to consider the organization and storage of your evidence long before you collect your first document.

Precollection

The key to any document organization system is a numbering and cross-reference system. When document counts run into the thousands of individual pieces of paper, perhaps the smoking-gun memo could get lost in the morass. Tracking them allows investigators, and later prosecutors and jurors, to locate them, even when they are literally one-in-a-million.

Ideally, the creation of your numbering system should occur before you begin your first investigation. As with all things in life, the ideal is rarely the norm. However, the minimum should be the creation of a workable numbering system before you collect the documents of this particular case. In order to ensure that this happens, we recommend a standard scheme of numbering that you can use in each case.

Create a numbering/identification system: As a minimum, your numbering system should have flexibility. Whether you are searching a one-bedroom apartment, or a ten-office suite, you should still be able to use the same system. The ability to expand the numbering and cataloging system means you can use the system repeatedly without having to redesign it.

While not essential, we find descriptive numbering systems helpful. Personal preferences aside, the ease with which an outsider can identify the nature of each particular item may determine the success of your case—especially when the outsider is a prosecutor to whom you are trying to demonstrate the merits of your case. With a descriptive system, the unique alphanumeric identifier assigned to each item of evidence immediately notifies the recipient of its nature. For example, in a descriptive system, the alpha character *W* before their numeric components might designate all witness statements. Then, as the case grows, investigators involved in the case will automatically know that any reference to an item designated with a *W* refers to a witness statement. It is important to consider carefully the ramifications of your alpha designations before implementation to ensure that each identifier is in fact unique. If you use the *W* for witnesses, and later also accidentally use the *W* for weapons, the uniqueness will be destroyed.

Have a plan of attack: A general plan of attack can help ease the difficulty in seizing a large number of records. How you will obtain the documents you are collecting may dictate how you will attack the problem. If the documents you need will be coming through the mail in response to a subpoena, you can sort, catalogue, and file them at your leisure. Conversely, if you are planning to execute a search warrant to obtain the records, often the chaos and time crunch associated with search warrant service will necessitate thorough planning to minimize errors.

Your plan will also vary depending on the nature of the target. If you are planning to search a small business with two employees housed in a two-room office suite, your search plan will vary considerably from that for a medical practice suspected of Medicaid fraud. For small offices and spaces where fewer documents and evidentiary items are expected, a standard search might be acceptable. However, high-volume or large-area spaces call for a coordinated search effort.

Sketch the search site and apply a grid. When dealing with a large area, it may be advisable to divide that area into sections using a grid overlay. You may either obtain a floor plan or sketch one yourself; the quality and scale of the drawing are relatively immaterial. Once you have sketched the floor plan, overlay it with a grid delineating a workable area. In lieu of the grid, assigning an identifying designation to each room may be sufficient. Generally, grids work well in large open spaces, and room designations work well in offices.

The area identifiers serve as collection guides. Regardless of whether you implement the grid method or room designation method, the unique identifier of each grid helps you in locating evidence later on. It also helps to promote an orderly canvass of the scene. Using the floor plan, you can search each individual grid, collecting evidence, and subsequently refer to its location relative to the room. For example, using the room designation, if a search of room "A" reveals an envelope of canceled checks in the first drawer of a lateral filing cabinet, the search warrant inventory and evidence/property receipt can identify its location as "Room A: Filing cabinet 1, drawer 1." Later, during the investigation, you can easily recall the exact location in which you found that item.

Once you have planned for your document collection you can move forward. Now that you have established a numbering system and planned how best to attack the search space, you can begin to focus on the actual search itself. While the rules of evidence are paramount, some considerations will make identification of potential evidence more efficient.

Collection

Searches require patience. Searches tend to take twice as long as anticipated, and never seem to go as planned; having said that, we should note that planning and preparation make these inevitabilities less frustrating. As you begin your search, you must consider how you will secure the evidence you seize in order to preserve its value for trial, and ensure that you can account for it later in case you must return it to the suspect. Careful inventory and attention to detail are helpful here.

Secure and package all evidence: At the scene, the evidence should be carefully packaged and secured to ensure that no damage or alterations occur during transport. Whether you use individual storage boxes, envelopes, or something else, ensure that you carefully protect the items.

While a cursory inspection of the documents is necessary, analysis that is more thorough will likely have to wait. As the magnitude of the search increases, so too does the time crunch. While you must inspect the documents that you are seizing to ensure that the warrant authorizes their seizure, a closer examination will have to wait until later. If you succumb to the temptation of beginning your analysis on-site, the length of the search operation will expand beyond acceptable limits. The goal of the search should be the safe and efficient collection of all the items authorized under the particular warrant.

Once you have concluded the search, and provided the proper return and receipts to the suspect, you can transport the evidence back to the office for further evaluation at your leisure.

Storage

As mentioned earlier, evidence integrity is the key to your case. Issues of both civil liability and evidentiary admissibility hinge on the ability to establish that the evidence presented to the jury is in fact the authentic evidence obtained from the defendant. To ensure that these issues do not arise, you must properly store and work with the evidence. As mentioned earlier, markings or alterations directly on the evidence can preclude their admission in court. However, it is often important to assign unique numbers to individual pieces of evidence for identification purposes.

If this is necessary, you have several options. The first and often the most preferable option is to make photocopies of the document. These documents are no longer the best evidence, and you can alter, manipulate, and mark them as needed. A second option is to encase the evidence in some sort of packaging. In most instances, this material is a plastic bag. For example, there are a number of commercial products manufactured specifically to hold checks. You can then put the identifying information on the outside of the bag. In the third option, suggested by Marilyn Peterson in *A Guide to the Financial Analysis of Personal and Corporate Bank Records*, you may place a self-stick label on the documents for identification. While all three are legally acceptable, your operational objectives might make one more attractive than another. Regardless of which method you choose, it is important to remember that the integrity of the evidence is the overriding factor.

As we have cautioned the reader throughout this text, financial crime investigations are unlike most any other type of criminal investigation. They are fraught with complexity and are by nature information intensive. Whether you are following the paper trail of a money-laundering organization or attempting to find the assets siphoned from the corporate bank account, you must follow the paper trail—a trail that often contains checks, bank statements, wire transfers, money orders, stock certificates, receipts, purchase orders, letters of credit, and possibly thousands more individual documents.

If you are lucky, your subpoenas, search warrants, and other documentary fishing expeditions will yield a plethora of information—so much so that the boxes of papers will fill your office (perhaps even the offices of your colleagues). This is, to put it mildly, a double-edged sword. Although everything you need to prove your case is contained in those boxes, they are worthless pieces of paper unless you can find exactly what you need when you need it. They are also worthless unless you can make them tell a compelling, persuasive story. Sitting in the boxes they offer nothing to your case.

The average nonfinancial crime probably has several hundred pieces of physical or documentary evidence (not considering major homicides, conspiracies, and organized crimes). However, many complex financial crimes have thousands of pieces of physical and documentary evidence.

The goal of any good investigation is to marshal the evidence in a way that tends to prove the ultimate theory of your case. In order to meet this goal, it is important to understand how you must arrive at the result. In order to understand that, it is first necessary to understand how to prove cases.

Investigators, as a rule, do not build their cases like lawyers; perhaps they should. If we can train investigators to think like lawyers (at least in terms of how to prepare and prosecute a case), we will help build a stronger case from the ground up. By investigating financial crime cases in this manner, you will not only present a more compelling case for prosecution, but you will also reduce the amount of superfluous work that tends to insinuate itself into the investigative process. The process of thinking like a lawyer begins with understanding how to build cases.

Everyone knows that in order to prove a case the lawyer must prove that the defendant committed certain acts. Codified law and legal precedent usually define these acts, or elements, with relative clarity. In the case of criminal accusations, statutory laws codify the elements of the offenses. In the case of civil accusations, the elements of the offenses are uncodified and generally based on common law principles of stare decisis and judicial precedent. However, knowing the elements of the offense is only half the battle: Knowing how to reach that burden is the other half.

THE PROCESS OF PROOF

We prove legal cases through inferences. These inferences, built in chains, must lead logically from point A to point B. It is the strength, or weakness, of these inferences that determines the strength or weakness of the case. In legal argument, inference is the persuasive effect of each individual piece of evidence. From the existence of the evidentiary item, jurors may infer that some ultimate fact exists. We may think of *proof*, then, as the total net effect of the

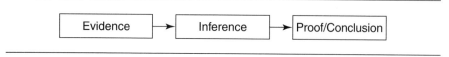

EXHIBIT 10.3   Role of Evidence

inferences that have been drawn. In other words, from evidence flow inferences, and from combined inferences flow conclusions. In the legal context, conclusions amount to proof.

As Exhibit 10.3 demonstrates, the ability to prove an ultimate fact rests solely on the strength of the inferences, not the evidence itself. This is true because regardless of the nature or volume of the evidence presented, if the inferences drawn are either incorrect or weak, we cannot reach the desired conclusion.

This notion may be new to some investigators. The difference is subtle, yet crucial. By bringing this critical distinction to your conscious thought, we hope to help you develop a better understanding of how to prove your case. The result will be better, more focused investigations.

Inference

Great lawyers (remember we are trying to teach investigators to think like lawyers), as distinguished from good ones, never forget that guilt is based on inference. Inference in turn relies on a chain of logic that must be forged one link at a time. Like proof of scientific theories, we must link together the inferences on which we base a finding of guilt in a logical, linear way. Unlike scientific discovery, however, legal proof must conform to a narrow framework of rigorously enforced rules. These rules, for the purpose of this text, revolve around relevance.

If this book were written for lawyers (real lawyers, not investigators thinking like lawyers), we would depart at this point and discuss the niceties of the rules of evidence and their admissibility. Because it is not, it will suffice to expound on the rules of evidence only far enough to say that we must confine our evidence to those things that are relevant. Of course, this does not mean that the investigator can totally disregard the bright line rules of admissibility. Collateral uncharged crimes evidence and other highly prejudicial facts, as well as illegally obtained evidence, are inadmissible (under most circumstances) and should not be the object of your pursuit. However, you should leave the finer details of these legal principles up to the prosecutor—a highly trained legal practitioner.

Relevance

In short, evidence is relevant if it tends to either prove or disprove an issue in contention. For example, if the question of whether the sun is shining were the ultimate question, the fact that it is ten o'clock in the morning would appear highly relevant. The fact that it is January 17, 2003, would not.

The confusion over relevance versus irrelevance arises because we rarely prove cases under a singular line of logic. What first appears to be a singular question—did the suspect take the money?—is ultimately misleading. Instead, each ultimate question contains subquestions. Collateral lines of logic can work together to blur the issue of relevance. A fact may not immediately appear to be relevant to the ultimate question at issue; however, when the ultimate question is broken down into its component subquestions, the relevance of the fact becomes clearer.

In our sun-is-shining hypothetical, the parenthetical reference to date at first may have appeared obtuse. However, if we reformulate the question into its subquestions, date might be more important. Implicit in this question is the assumption that we are referring to an observation at our current location. If our current geographic reference point is Nome, Alaska, date suddenly becomes important since Nome's hemispheric location limits the dates on which the sun is shining at ten o'clock in the morning: from irrelevant to relevant in one easy step. Clearly, this is a simplistic example. No doubt, many of our readers instinctively saw the relevance of the date fact; however, legal questions are rarely so transparent.

To understand fully how to effectively build this chain of logic, the investigator must grasp the nature of the logic underpinning the legal argument. There are several forms of logical argument; the two that we are most concerned with in the context of legal proof are deductive and inductive.

THE LOGIC OF ARGUMENT

Deductive Argument

Deductive reasoning is a form of argument that works from the general to the more specific; we often refer to this as "top-down" logic. Inductive reasoning, on the other hand, works from specific observations to the broader and more general; we sometimes call this "bottom-up" reasoning.[15]

An argument stated deductively offers two or more rules or assertions that lead automatically to a conclusion. This syllogistic form of argument, first propounded by Aristotle, is designed to produce mathematical certainty. The use of syllogisms, or mathematical statements, ensures that the lines of argument lead logically to the conclusion.[16]

A deductive argument has, at a minimum, three statements: the major premise, the minor premise, and the conclusion. The first statement, or the major premise, is a statement of general truth dealing with categories rather than finite objects. Contained within the major premise are two sections: the antecedent and the consequent.[17]

The antecedent phrase is the subject phrase, and the consequent phrase is the predicate. For example, the statement "all men are mortal" contains the antecedent phrase, "all men" (the general category), and the consequent phrase, "are mortal."

The second statement, the minor premise, is a statement about a specific instance encompassed by the major premise. For example, the phrase, "Socrates is a man," is a statement of truth dealing with a specific instance governed by the major premise.[18]

The third statement, the conclusion, must follow naturally from the relationship of the major and minor premises to one another. If no deductive fallacies exist, this statement will be the inescapable result of the first two statements. In the above example, "Socrates is mortal" is the natural and inescapable conclusion to the major and minor premise.[19]

In forming deductive arguments, we can relate the minor premise to the major premise in four different ways. Only two produce sound logical arguments; the other two produce deductive fallacies.

The structure in our illustration is an example of affirming the antecedent. In this form, the minor premise asserts that a particular instance is an example of the major premise's antecedent. In our example, we are asserting that Socrates is indeed a man. We are affirming that Socrates and the state of being a man are equal.

We refer to the converse of this form as denying the consequent. In order to construct a deductive syllogism in which we deny the consequent, we must assert that a particular instance does not equal the consequent. Our major premise, "all men are mortal," may remain the same. However, the minor premise must change.

If, instead of asserting that Socrates is a man, as we did in affirming the antecedent form, we deny that a specific object is mortal—"my car is not mortal"—we have constructed the second sound syllogistic argument. From this minor premise logically follows the conclusion that "my car is not a man."[20]

The strength, or soundness, of a deductive argument rests on the truth of the major and minor premise. If the first two statements are true, the conclusion must be correct. However, a sound argument does not necessarily guarantee the truth of the conclusion. If either the major or minor premise is false, we will still reach an incorrect conclusion using sound syllogistic logic.

Inductive Argument

In contrast to the mathematical precision of deductive reasoning, inductive reasoning is not designed to produce certainty. This form of logical argument uses a series of observations in order to reach a conclusion. We combine these observations, often referred to as a chain of observations, with previous observations to reach a defensible conclusion.[21]

Of the three basic forms of inductive reasoning, induction by enumeration, or generalization, is the most common.[22] In this form, you make a general statement regarding some predicted outcome based on observations of a specific instance of a class. For example, the statement, "all lawyers are sleazy," when based on your observation of the last three lawyers you have encountered, would be induction by enumeration.

Because inductive logic is less precise than deductive logic, fallacies are often less easily identified. The fallacy most commonly associated with inductive reasoning is the hasty generalization.[23] When an argument fails as a hasty generalization, the inductive leap that the proponent asks the decision maker to make is too remote. Sufficient evidence does not support it. The following statement suffers from the fallacy of hasty generalization:

XYZ Company is an import-export company operating from Miami, Florida. It is involved in money laundering.

This statement may or may not be true. There is insufficient evidence based on these statements to draw the conclusion. It is possible that the statement is true, but the leap from XYZ Company's existence as an import-export business in Miami to the conclusion that it is laundering money is much too broad to make with any certainty.

A second common fallacy associated with generalization is exclusion. Exclusion occurs when we omit important pieces of information from the chain.

Put simply, alternative explanations for reaching the conclusion have been excluded.[24] For example, consider the following argument:

> The police found a dead body with three bullet wounds.

It would be a safe, albeit not mathematically certain, conclusion that the person found by the police died because of his gunshot wounds—that is, unless we also knew that the body was missing its head.

Although it is still possible that the victim died of gunshot wounds and that the decapitation was inflicted postmortem, it is equally possible that the manner of his death was decapitation and someone administered the bullet wounds postmortem for some other purpose. The fallacy of exclusion forces the decision maker into reaching a false conclusion owing to lack of relevant alternative evidence.

Inductive versus Deductive in Case Proof

As you can see, inductive and deductive reasoning are very similar, the greatest difference being the manner in which we express the argument. When you argue from the general to the specific, deductive reasoning is in play. When you reason from the specific observation to broader generalizations, inductive logic is in play. It is important to note that we may recast all inductive arguments as deductive syllogisms and vice versa.

As an investigator, you will encounter both forms of logical reasoning. However, the offering of evidence in the legal system will most often expose you to inductive logic. In the process of proof, it is common to allege and prove specific isolated facts and build to a general conclusion. Therefore, the inductive process of moving from the specific observation to the general conclusion just seems to feel right.

We should note that some readers may argue that deductive reasoning, being the more mathematically certain, should be the more favored logical form in legal proceedings. Keep in mind that the law, and the system for legal resolution of disputes, is concerned with probabilities, not certainties. It is not absolute proof that we seek; it is proof beyond a reasonable doubt. Because inductive reasoning is ideally suited to reason from specific facts (evidence) toward broad generalizations (guilt or culpability), induction is the more natural form of legal argument. In truth, it does not matter greatly which form the argument takes. As stated earlier, we may form all arguments as either inductive or deductive premises.

That is not to say that deductive reasoning is useless in the legal context. Quite the opposite is true. When we choose the deductive over the inductive, the inferential focus shifts. There are still inferential leaps that you must make; we simply make them in a different location.

For example, we can formulate our argument regarding XYZ Company's activities either way. To state the argument inductively: XYZ Company is involved in money laundering since it is an import-export company operating in Miami, Florida.

Stated as syllogisms: (1) All import-export companies operating in Miami, Florida, are involved in money laundering. (2) XYZ Company is an import-export company located in Miami, Florida. (3) Therefore, XYZ, Company is involved in money laundering (deductive).

Obviously, these examples are oversimplified, exposing the fallacies of logic quite quickly. In reality, the inferential links in a logical chain will be much more subtle, and the facts often obscure the fallacies of logic that can cripple the argument.

Both arguments, as they stand, are legally indefensible. In the inductive example, the inferential leap may not be as evident as in the deductive, requiring the reader to infer that all import-export companies operating in Miami, Florida, are engaged in money laundering. Although the reader undoubtedly senses that something is not quite right, specifically pinpointing the source of the illogicality may be difficult.

In the deductive example, the breadth of the inferential leap required of the reader is much more apparent. By breaking the proposition down into deductive form, we more easily expose the fallacies of logic inherent in the inductive process.

Based on our previous discussion, and the fact that the process of legal determination revolves primarily around inductive logic, your job as investigator requires you to guard against the fallacies associated with its use. The danger of the two most common fallacies, hasty generalization and exclusion, can be reduced by carefully analyzing the line of argument and the inferences leading to proof of specific legal elements.

As noted above, we build all legal arguments on inference. However, it is rare for a legal argument to be based on one single inference. Instead, we pile many inferences one on the other until the ultimate proposition—usually guilt or innocence—is the inescapable conclusion. We refer to this chain of inferences as compound, or catenate, inferences.[25] The strength or weakness of the legal argument is determined by the granularity of this chain of inferences.

The finer the grain is (shorter inferential leap), the more powerful and per-suasive the argument becomes.

Understanding the complexities and dynamics of inferential logic is es-sential to properly investigating a case. During the investigative stage, the in-vestigator must remain cognizant of the intermediate inferential steps between the evidence that exists and the ultimate issue. Only by careful dissection of the intermediate inferences within the chain can we determine the location of the possibility of doubt. This explicit analysis of the catenate inferences is the greatest safeguard against fallacious reasoning an investigator possesses.

PROOF THROUGH INFERENCE

The inferential weight of evidence can range from weak to strong depending on how clearly we can draw the inference from the existence of the evidence. Weak inferences exist when the leap from evidence to conclusion is great. Conversely, strong inferences are generated when the leap from the evidence to the conclusion is short. A weak inferential relationship exists between the evidentiary statement, "The defendant and his ex-wife were hostile toward each other," and the conclusion that the defendant killed his ex-wife. A strong inferential relationship exists between the statement, "I saw the defendant stab his ex-wife," and the conclusion that the defendant killed his ex-wife.

In the first case, there is too great a leap between the statement and the con-clusion—there are too many intervening steps. In the second case, there are no, or at least very few, intervening steps between the evidentiary statement and the conclusion. The goal of the investigator is to reduce the distance be-tween intervening steps between the defendant and the conclusion.

We reduce this distance by creating a chain of inferences referred to as con-catenate inferences.[26] Concatenate inferences build one upon the other until ul-timately they reduce the chasm between the defendant and the conclusion to a manageable distance. We are not shortening the overall distance human rea-soning must travel; rather, we are merely breaking it up into smaller steps.

We can illustrate this process by concocting a hypothetical situation. As-sume we wish to link the defendant to the murder of his ex-wife. Initially, the connection—the inferential relationship—between the defendant and the vic-tim is weak, as shown in Exhibit 10.4.

We may argue for the inference that because the defendant and the victim knew each other and were divorced, the defendant had a motive to kill her. It

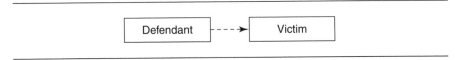

EXHIBIT 10.4   Initial Relationship of Defendant to Victim

is a plausible theory, yet not very strong—certainly not strong enough to proceed to trial. How can we strengthen this inferential relationship? We must build our chain.

Our investigation has uncovered a bloody glove at the crime scene. Immediately, there is an inference that the glove is somehow involved in the murder. If we later learn that the DNA from the blood on the glove matches that of the victim, the inferential relationship between the glove and the murder becomes very strong, as shown in Exhibit 10.5.

Although the connection between the defendant and the victim is still tenuous (as indicated by the dashed line in Exhibit 10.5), the connection between the victim and the glove is strong. Obviously, we are not satisfied. Our investigation continues.

The forensic examiners at the crime lab have determined that the gloves are in fact a very expensive brand sold only in exclusive upscale department stores. They are so exclusive that the store has sold only 25 pairs in the past year. This information alone does not necessarily strengthen the inferential relationship to the defendant. However, taken in combination with the fact that department store records show that the defendant purchased a pair of these gloves using his credit card two months earlier, we are slowly strengthening our chain.

Exhibit 10.6 illustrates the evolving inferential relationship. We have still depicted the link between the gloves and the defendant in a dashed line. Although there is a good connection between the two, 24 other people have a connection to the gloves, at least hypothetically.

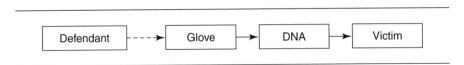

EXHIBIT 10.5   Building the Inference Chain

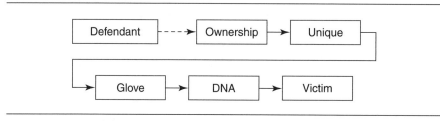

EXHIBIT 10.6   Strengthening the Chain

Finally, our forensic experts compare the DNA from skin cells found in the glove's lining with those of the defendant and they match. This final piece of evidence is the link we have been waiting for. Up until now, we could link the defendant inferentially as an owner of similar gloves. Now, we can link him as the owner of these gloves. Exhibit 10.7 illustrates the completed inferential chain.

We can now depict the relationship between the defendant and the victim with solid lines. Does this mean that we have proven that the defendant murdered the victim? Of course not; all it proves is there is a strong inference that a pair of gloves owned by the defendant were found at the scene of the murder with the victim's blood on them. Such is the nature of inferential proof. Is this chain of inferences strong enough to convict the defendant of murder? Only the jury can answer that question.

As you can see by this simplistic example, the job of the investigator is not to prove that the defendant committed the crime. The investigator's job is to construct a chain of inferences sufficiently strong enough to convince a fact finder that the desired conclusion is the most plausible sequence of events. In order to do that, you must internalize the distinction between evidence and inference.

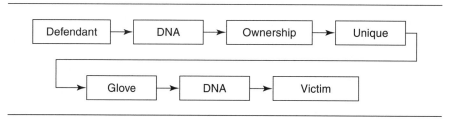

EXHIBIT 10.7   Completed Inferential Chain

Hidden Inferences

Until now, we have been discussing only explicit inferences—those inferences that the investigator directly urges. For example, the inference that the gloves were involved in the murder is an explicit inference because the investigator has asserted the fact that we found DNA belonging to the victim on the gloves. There are, however, other inferences that are of concern to the criminal investigator; they are hidden, or implicit, inferences.

The evidence does not directly urge an implicit inference; instead, implicit inferences tag along as baggage. An example of an implicit inference that the investigator expects the jury to draw involves the ownership of the gloves. Before introducing evidence that we found the defendant's DNA inside the gloves, we drew an ownership inference based on the credit card purchase.

The inference was a reasonable one. However, implicit in that inference was the assumption that the defendant, not someone using his credit card, had purchased the gloves. If we lay bare this implicit inference, a weakness in our inferential chain becomes apparent. Our link between the defendant and the murder, absent the DNA-glove evidence, weakens when we consider the alternative possibility that someone using the defendant's credit card purchased the gloves. By ignoring the implicit inference, we leave the flank of our logical line of argument open for counterattack.

Generalizations

Closely related to the implicit inference is the generalization. A generalization is merely an implicit inference that most people generally recognize. For example, most people accept the generalization that dropped objects fall. Therefore, an eyewitness account of the victim being pushed from a tall building, coupled with the recovery of the body at the base of the building, will urge the jury to conclude that the defendant died as the result of the fall. Implicit in this conclusion are the hidden inference that there were no intervening causes of death (no one shot the victim on the way down) and the generalization that gravity acted upon the body, propelling it downward. Both implicit inferences in this scenario are quite reasonable and in fact relatively safe from attack; not all generalizations are so bulletproof.

Generalizations become especially dangerous when trained investigators make them. This is true because investigators draw very specific conclusions from random facts based on their experience and training. Juries in general do not possess the same training and experience and may not draw the same generalized conclusion. The nature of generalizations makes them so dangerous.

We might also call a generalization an assumption based on experience. The key, then, is the fact that people have a broad range of experiences and may or may not make the same assumption given the facts. As Lawrence Lessig put it, facts derive their meanings from "frameworks of understanding within which individuals live."[27] It is this diversity of experience that makes ignorance of the existence of implicit generalization, or reliance on common sense, so dangerous to the process of logical proof.

Like it or not, common sense plays an integral role in judicial determination. The legal rules guide the formation of our original legal hypothesis. Our common-sense understanding of the world ultimately grounds these. Common sense, however, may be problematic. Not all common-sense assumptions are legitimate grounds for the interpretation of evidence.

Common sense, though implicit in any legal context, can cause inferential errors. For example, common sense can be culturally specific. Assumptions, based on culturally specific common-sense principles, can cause grave inferential errors. One result of common sense inferential logic is tunnel vision in police investigations.

This does not necessarily mean that a single generalization in your line of argument will doom it to failure. It does mean that broad generalizations may leave your otherwise airtight logical chain vulnerable. As an investigator, it is imperative that you guard against assuming that the jury will draw implicit inferences and generalizations. The only way to guard against them is to recognize them. The only way to recognize them is to analyze carefully the entire logic of the case.

CONCLUSION

Evidence proves the case. How you collect evidence and what you recover has a direct relationship to whether you will prove your case. Likewise, the logical underpinning of your case dictates whether the jury reaches the same conclusion you want them to. In this chapter, we first discussed the evidence you are likely to encounter in a financial crime investigation, then we offered some practical advice on how to collect the evidence in an organized and defensible way. Finally, we offered some insight into how we prove cases through inference, and demonstrated that the evidence we have collected must build the chain of inferences. In doing this we hope to have provided you with a stronger foundation in the process of legal proof.

SUGGESTED READINGS

Abimbola, K. "Abductive Reasoning in Law: Taxonomy and Inference to the Best Explanation." *Cardozo Law Review*, 22 (2001): 1683–1689.

Abimbola, K. "The Logic of Preliminary Fact Investigation." *The Journal of Law and Society*, 29 (2002): 533–559.

Allen, R.J. "The Nature of Juridical Proof." *Cardozo Law Review*, 13 (1991): 373–401.

Allen, R.J., and A. Carriquiry. "Factual Ambiguity and a Theory of Evidence Reconsidered: A Dialogue between a Statistician and a Law Professor." *Israel Law Review*, 31, nos. 1–3 (1997): 464.

Arthur, W.B. "Inductive Reasoning and Bounded Reality." *American Economic Review*, 84 (1994): 406–411.

Binder, D., and P. Bergman. *Fact Investigation: From Hypothesis to Proof.* St. Paul, MN: West Publishing, 1999.

Cohen, L.J. *The Introduction to the Philosophy of Induction and Probability.* New York: Oxford University Press, 1989.

Eco, U. *Semiotics and the Philosophy of Language.* Bloomington: Indiana University Press, 1984.

Eco, U. *A Theory of Semiotics.* Bloomington: Indiana University Press, 1976.

Eco, U., and T. Sebok, eds. *The Sign of Three: Dupin, Holmes & Pierce.* Bloomington: Indiana University Press, 1983.

Finkelstein, M., and W. Fairly. "A Bayesian Approach to Identification Evidence." *Harvard Law Review*, 83 (1970): 489–517.

Franklin, J. *The Science of Conjecture: Evidence and Probability before Pascal.* Baltimore, MD: Johns Hopkins University Press, 2001.

Hastie, R., and N. Pennington. "The O.J. Simpson Stories: Behavioral Scientists' Reflections on *The People of the State of California v. Orenthal James Simpson.*" *University of Colorado Law Review*, 67 (1996): 957–976.

Huygen, P.E.M. "Use of Bayesian Belief Networks in Legal Reasoning." Presented at *Seventeenth BILETA Annual Conference.* Amsterdam: Computer Law Institute, 2002.

"In Praise of Bayes." Retrieved March 25, 2003, from the University of California, Berkeley, Computer Science Division website, September 30, 2000; www.ai.mit.edu/~murphyk/Bayes/economist.html.

Josephson, J., and S.G. Josephson. *Abductive Inference Computation, Philosophy, and Technology.* New York: Cambridge University Press, 1994.

Kadane, J., and D.A. Schum. *A Probabilistic Analysis of the Sacco and Vanzetti Evidence*. New York: John Wiley & Sons, 1996.

Kaye, D.H. "Bayes, Burdens and Base Rates." *International Journal of Evidence and Proof*, 4, no. 4 (2000): 260–267.

Kaye, D.H., and J.J. Koehler. "Can Jurors Understand Probabilistic Evidence?" *Journal of the Royal Statistical Society*, Series A, 154, part 1 (1991): 75–81.

Ketner, K.L., ed. *Pierce and Contemporary Thought: Philosophical Inquiries*. New York: Fordham University Press, 1995.

Koehler, J.J. "The Base Rate Fallacy Myth." *Psycoloquy*, 4, Article 93.4.49. Retrieved March 13, 2003, from www.monash.edu.au/journals/psycoloquy/volume_4/psyc.93.4.49.base-rate.1.koehler.

Lempert, R., S. Gross, and J. Liebman. *A Modern Approach to Evidence*. St. Paul, Minn.: West Publishing, 2000.

Leonhardt, D. "Adding Art to the Rigor of Statistical Science." *New York Times* (electronic version), April 28, 2001.

MacCrimmon, M. "What Is 'Common' about Common Sense?: Cautionary Tales for Travelers Crossing Disciplinary Boundaries." *Cardozo Law Review*, 22 (2001): 1433–1460.

Oldroyd, D.R. *The Arch of Knowledge: An Introductory Study of the History of the Philosophy and Methodology of Science*. London: Routledge Kegan &Paul, 1986.

Pennington, N., and R. Hastie. "A Cognitive Theory of Juror Decision Making: The Story Model." *Cardozo Law Review*, 13 (1991): 519–530.

Pierce, C.S. "Reasoning and Logic of Things." In K.L. Ketner, ed., *Reasoning and Logic of Things: The Cambridge Conference Lectures of 1898*. Cambridge, MA: Harvard University Press, 1993.

Robertson, B., and G. A. Vignaux. *Interpreting Evidence: Evaluating Forensic Science in the Courtroom*. New York: John Wiley & Sons, 1995.

Saks, M.J., and R.F. Kidd. "Human Information Processing and Adjudication: Trial by Heuristics." *Law and Society Review*, 15 (1980): 123–160.

Schafer, G. *The Art of Causal Conjecture*. Cambridge, MA: MIT Press, 1996.

Schum, D.A. "Alternative Views of Argument Construction from a Mass of Evidence." *Cardozo Law Review*, 22 (2001): 1461–1502.

Schum, D.A. *Evidential Foundations of Probabilistic Reasoning*. New York: John Wiley & Sons, 1994.

Schum, D.A. *The Evidential Foundations of Probabilistic Reasoning*. Evanston, IL: Northwestern University Press, 2001.

Schum, D.A. "Marshaling Thoughts and Evidence During Fact Investigation." *Southern Texas Law Review*, 40 (2001): 401–454.

Schum, D.A. "Species of Abductive Reasoning in Fact Investigation." *Cardozo Law Review*, 22 (2001): 1645–1681.

Schum, D.A., and P. Tillers. "Marshaling Evidence for Adversary Litigation." *Cardozo Law Review*, 12 (1991): 657–704.

Thagard, P. "Probabilistic Networks and Explanatory Coherence." In P. O'Rourke and J. Josephson, eds., *Automated Abduction: Inference to the Best Explanation*. Menlo Park: AAAI Press, 1997.

Thagard, P. *Computational Philosophy of Science*. Cambridge, MA: MIT Press, 1993.

Thagard, P., and C. Shelley. "Abductive Reasoning: Logic, Visual Thinking, and Coherence." In M.D. Chiara, K. Doets, D. Mundici, and J. van Benthem, eds., *Logic and Scientific Methods*. Volume 1 of the *Tenth International Congress of Logic, Methodology and Philosophy of Science*, Florence. Dordrecht: Kluwer Academic Publishers, 1997, pp. 413–427.

Tillers, P. "Webs of Things in the Mind: A New Science of Evidence." *Michigan Law Review*, 87 (1989): 1225–1226.

Tillers, P., and D. Schum. "Charting New Territory in Judicial Proof beyond Wigmore." *Cardozo Law Review*, 9 (1993): 907–950.

Wagenaar, W.A. "The Proper Seat: A Bayesian Discussion of the Position of Expert Witnesses." *Law and Human Behavior*, 12 (1988): 499–510.

Walker, V. R. "Theories of Uncertainty: Explaining the Possible Sources of Error in Inferences." *Cardozo Law Review*, 22 (2001): 1523–1570.

NOTES

1. C.P. Nemeth, *Law and Evidence: A Primer for Criminal Justice, Criminology, Law and Legal Studies* (Upper Saddle River, NJ: Prentice Hall, 2001), p. 124; see also T.J. Gardner and T.M. Anderson, *Criminal Evidence: Principals and Cases* (Belmont, CA: Thomson-Wadsworth, 2004), p. 334–335.

2. Nemeth, *Law and Evidence*, p. 124.

3. See generally,Title 31 USC Chp. 53, sub. 11.

4. *PC* magazine. "Definition of Metadata," Encyclopedia, PCMAG.com, www.pcmag.com/encyclopedia_term/0,2542,t=metadata&i=46858,00.asp.

5. See generally, C.H. Morely, *Asset Forfeiture: Tracing Money Flows through Financial Institutions* (Washington, DC: Police Executive Research Forum, 1989).

6. M.B. Peterson, *A Guide to the Financial Analysis of Personal and Corporate Bank Records* (Richmond, VA: National White Collar Crime Center, 2002), p. 4.

7. Ibid.

8. Ibid.; see also Morley, *Asset Forfeiture*.

9. Federal Reserve Bank, *Fedwire Funds Transfer System: Self-Assessment of Compliance with the Core Principles for Systemically Important Payment Systems* (San Francisco, CA: Federal Reserve Board of Governors, 2001), pp. 2–3. See also The Clearing House Interbank Payment System, "What is CHIPS?" The Clearing House Interbank Payment System, www.chips.org/home.php.

10. Peterson, *A Guide to the Financial Analysis*, p. 4.

11. See generally, Morley, *Asset Forfeiture*.

12. Driver's Privacy Protection Act of 1993, HR 3365, 103rd Cong., 1st sess., *Congressional Record* (November 3, 1993): E2747.

13. Driver's Privacy Protection Act of 1993, U.S. Code (2005) Sec. 2721 et seq.

14. Representative James P. Moran, speaking for the Legislation to Protect Privacy and Safety of Drivers, on November 3, 1993, to the House of Representatives, HR 3365, 103rd Cong., 1st sess., *Congressional Record* (November 3, 1993): E2747-48.

15. D. Kuhn, *The Skills of Argument* (Cambridge, MA: Cambridge University Press, 1991), pp. 7–9.

16. W. Schaeken, G. De Vooght, A. Vandierendonck, and G. d'Ydewalle, eds., *Deductive Reasoning and Strategies* (Mahwah, NJ: Lawrence Erlbaum, 2000), pp. 9–15.

17. Ibid.

18. R.M. Johnson, *Fundamentals of Reasoning*, 4th ed. (Belmont, CA: Wadsworth/ Thomas Learning, 2002), pp. 37–41.

19. Ibid.

20. Ibid.

21. T. Anderson, and W. Twining, *Analysis of Evidence: How to Do Things with Facts Based on Wigmore's Science of Judicial Proof* (Evanston, IL: Northwestern University Press, 1991), pp. 63–65.

22. Ibid. See also "Deductive and Inductive Arguments" (February 8, 2003). Retrieved February 8, 2003, from Shepherd College, Rhetoric Department website: http://webpages.shepherd.edu/maustin/rhetoric/deductiv.htm.

23. Ibid.

24. Ibid.

25. Anderson and Twining, *Analysis of Evidence*, pp. 57–59.

26. Ibid., pp. 57–59, 89–91.

27. L. Lessig, "The Regulation of Social Meaning," University of Chicago Law Review 62(1995): 952.

11

ANALYSIS TOOLS FOR
INVESTIGATORS

INTRODUCTION

In this chapter we will introduce you to a series of analysis tools to aid you in conducting your investigation. These tools are valuable to all sorts of investigators, but they are especially useful when dealing with a lot of information and difficult cases. In this chapter we will examine tools that are helpful in revealing relationships and visualizing time-based data. Later, in Chapter 12, we will take a look at investigative inference networks, a powerful tool for following the logic of your case.

Although we have broken these tools into two categories, there is some overlap. The associational tools that we cover in this chapter are well suited to identifying relationships among people, places, and organizations—practically anything. The temporal analysis tools you will learn can also prove valuable in analyzing relationships; however, they are most powerful in analyzing time-based relationships. We have chosen the categories based on the strengths of each tool. As new types of investigations arise, we urge you to be creative in how you apply them.

WHY USE ANALYSIS TOOLS AT ALL?

For years, criminal intelligence analysts have recognized the value of graphic tools in helping to visualize relationships. Whether the relationship under observation is between people, businesses, or transactions, analysts have been using some form of associational analysis for a long time.

What began as simple link diagramming has expanded. In the early 1970s, Anacapa Sciences, Inc., a company in California, began advocating the use of graphical tools[1] known as link diagrams to assist law enforcement in visualizing complex relationships. While this was one of the first recorded times that such tools were used by investigators, it was not the first time researchers were examining relationships though graphical analysis. In fact, the study of relationships between people and among groups has been going on for many years.

As John Scott points out in *Social Network Analysis: A Handbook*, Jacob Moreno was a pioneer in this area as early as the 1930s.[2] Moreno, a social psychologist, began studying human relationships and the structural and social dynamics of interpersonal relationships.[3] It was through this study, and his interaction with a number of other leading researchers in this area, that he developed a graphical tool called the Sociogram, an early predecessor of the link diagram.[4] Moreno's rudimentary method of depicting human relationships as sets of nodes and lines in two-dimensional space transformed many of the ways in which we thought about social structure.

Meanwhile, other advances were being made. Elsewhere, scientists were examining human relationships using purely mathematical principles grounded in a field known as graph theory.[5] Two researchers, Frank Harary and Dorwin Cartwright, began to apply the mathematical properties of graphs to Moreno's sociograms in an effort to provide more interpretive results.[6] These early investigations became the basis for today's Social Network Analysis.[7] However, it would not be until the mid-1950s that true social network analysis would evolve.

The result of all this scientific study was a formal set of rules to describe human relationships. Based in an advanced area of mathematics known as graph theory and matrix algebra, modern social network analysis provides researchers and investigators with tools through which networks of relationships can be both modeled and studied. By using these mathematical foundations, researchers are able to identify people within the structure who are both powerful and influential. In network analysis, the terms *powerful* and *influential* may not necessarily mirror the common understanding. For example, power may merely mean the ability to control the actions of others within the group.

Eventually, researchers made the connection between the theoretical research and practical application. Although the idea that the field of social network analysis might prove valuable in evaluating criminal enterprises may seem evident today, it was not until much later its value became evident. Researchers such as Dr. Malcolm Sparrow, Wayne Baker, and Robert Faulkner began to suggest that, although illegal networks pose some practical problems for study, their behavior could be reliably studied using social network analysis.[8]

Today, the value of network analysis tools is clear. From first-generation tools like simple link diagrams, to second-generation measures such as centrality, betweenness, and degreedness, to third-generation tools like dynamic network analysis, these investigative aids are crucial and gaining popularity. In addition, the emergence of powerful software packages such as Analyst's Notebook, Visual Links, and Netmap has made the analyst's and investigator's job much easier in this area.[9]

A staple of organized crime investigations, these tools have equal value in financial crime investigations. Notwithstanding our earlier discussion of the relationships between organized crime and financial crime and the obvious value of network analysis in these investigations, they can help the financial crime investigator in other ways. As we move forward in this chapter, we will offer an introduction to the science behind the tools, and offer some suggestions for ways in which you can incorporate them into your investigative repertoire to increase productivity and success rates.

ASSOCIATIONAL ANALYSIS

As stated, link diagrams and social network analysis are related concepts. In fact, they are essentially the same process, just different degrees of study. As such, we will introduce you first to the basic ideas behind diagramming relationships. Then, we will use that basic knowledge to build a stronger understanding of the capabilities that advances in social network analysis have brought to the investigative sciences.

Matrices and Link Diagrams

Matrices and link diagrams are valuable tools for visualizing relationships. Both are two-dimensional representations of a three-dimensional relationship among objects. It is possible to construct a link diagram without using an association matrix, but the more complicated the diagram, the more difficult it becomes. That is where the association matrix comes into play.

An association matrix is a way to represent relationships among things in an orderly manner. A matrix can show relationships between people, between organizations, between people and organizations, or practically anything. Advanced mathematical principles are the basis for matrices and in the proper hands can be manipulated and transformed into highly sophisticated predictive tools. Although we will discuss some of these mathematical principles and their potential later, you don't need to be a math wizard to use matrices and link diagrams. You simply need to understand the relationship between them in order to take advantage of their power.

The Matrix There are many forms of matrices, but all are essentially a collection of rows and columns. Sometimes called tables, matrices consist of an ordered number of columns and rows. Exhibit 11.1 shows an example of a simple four-by-four matrix.

We can use this square matrix to represent a single object under study. For example, we can represent the relationship between people in an organization.

Along the left axis we list the names of all the people among whom we wish to show a relationship. Then, along the top of the matrix, we re-list everyone in the same order. To represent a relationship, we simply place an X in the cell where the row vector for A and the column vector for B intersect. Exhibit 11.2 illustrates this.

EXHIBIT 11.1   Four-by-Four Matrix

	A	B	C	D
A	x	x		
B	x	x		
C				
D				

EXHIBIT 11.2   Four-by-Four Matrix Showing Relationship

Even though square matrices are very powerful tools, to model relationships between different types of objects, we need to expand our vocabulary. To represent a relationship between more than one type of object (for example, people and corporations), we need to use a rectangular matrix. Using the same concept as the square matrix, we list the people we are studying, for example, CEOs, along the left axis. The companies to which we are trying show CEO relationships then go along the top axis. Similar to square matrices, we place X's in the cells at the intersection of each CEO with his or her company. Exhibit 11.3 illustrates this.

Although the concept is identical, the difference between a square and a rectangular matrix is the ability to relate unmatched items.

	A	B	C	D	E	F	G
Jones	x		x			x	
Franks	x	x		x		x	
Brown			x		x	x	
Green							x

EXHIBIT 11.3   Rectangular Matrix of Officers

We can extend the power of our matrix through link diagrams. While matrices are powerful modeling tools in their own right, they are often used by analysts as preliminary steps in the analysis process. As you can see, hidden relationships among objects can become clearer when we show them through a matrix. However, for power of visual representation, link diagrams are often a better choice.

The Link Diagram   As you will learn later, analysis of organizations can be done on a much greater scale. For now, however, we need to introduce you to the foundation. Often referred to as first-generation analysis tools, associational matrices and simple link diagrams are very close relatives to Moreno's sociograms.[10] For example, we can easily represent the relationship between five friends in a link diagram through five dots, called nodes, connected by four lines, known as edges (see Exhibit 11.4).

Simple to construct, and relatively easy to interpret, the value of this diagram is belied by the simplicity of our exemplar social network.

Were we to expand our circle of friends to include many more members, the value of link diagrams would become clearer. Instead of five members in our network, assume that each member has five friends, and each of these friends has five friends. As we expand our social network exponentially, the complexity of keeping the basic relationships clear in our mind becomes more difficult.

Adding to the inherent difficulty created by sheer numbers is the complication that few social networks that occur in the wild will be variations on the simple network depicted by Exhibit 11.5. Most, if not all, members of the network will have relationships with more than one other member. These cross-links can logarithmically increase the number of associations we must track.

Keeping relationship data in your head is difficult. Given the size and structure of even the smallest of criminal organizations, it is unrealistic to

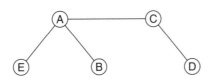

EXHIBIT 11.4   Five-Person Link Diagram

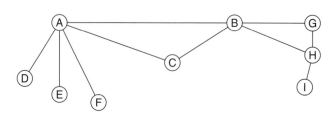

EXHIBIT 11.5   Large Network

expect to keep them straight. By using link diagrams, the basic structure is visually comprehensible. Often, by studying the intersecting lines and existence of multiple connections, you can even identify more and less important members of the organization and hidden relationships become clearer.

Combining diagrams with the power of the matrix to handle vast amounts of data we can model very complicated scenarios. Sometimes, plotting a diagram from scratch is possible. A simple four-member group would likely plot out quite easily. Conversely, tracking the relationships among 150 board members is tougher. Putting the members into a matrix simplifies that. Then, using the matrix, we can plot the chart in a systematic and orderly way.

THE SYMBOLS The basic symbols of link diagrams are the circle and the line. While these basic symbols can be adapted to individual needs, they are often all that are necessary. In conventional link diagrams, circles represent people and the lines represent their relationship to one another. Sometimes, we can even depict value judgments about the relationships.

This can be easily done through line characteristics. When a relationship is confirmed, whether through surveillance, telephone toll analysis, or perhaps informant testimony, we commonly use a solid line. Conversely, when we add a new member to our organization, yet are not sure of his role, we may show our hesitance through a dotted line. Further, by varying the thicknesses of lines we can denote ties of varying strengths. Your imagination is the only limit to the variety with which you can depict relationships; however, consistency is crucial for readability.

We can add more symbols as the need arises. While we can model a surprising level of sophistication through the basic lines and circles of the rudi-

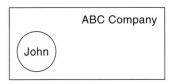

EXHIBIT 11.6   ABC Company Ownership

mentary link diagram, we may occasionally need to add to our repertoire. For example, a common addition to the link diagramming toolbox is the rectangle.

The rectangle is often used to symbolize a group or organization. Groups and people often share associations. Sometimes groups are defined by their members, and other times members are defined by the groups to which they belong. In criminal investigations, we sometimes need to visualize the web of organizations to which our network of suspects belongs. This is especially valuable when trying to visualize things such as interlocking directorates, or when analyzing terrorist networks.

Rectangles add to—they do not replace—the circles of link diagramming. We continue to represent our people through circles. However, as memberships in organizations or ownership of companies become established, we can place the circles within squares that represent the organization. For example, if we identify John as the CEO of ABC company, we will place John's circle inside the rectangle depicting ABC Company (see Exhibit 11.6).

If the companies under study share directors, demonstrating the relationship through lines can become confusing. Instead, interlock the two rectangles representing each company around the common director. For example, if John is the President of ABC Company, place John's circle inside the ABC rectangle. If he is also the Treasurer of XYZ Corp., draw XYZ Corp.'s rectangle so that it interlocks with ABC, and John's circle is inside (see Exhibit 11.7).

Aliases sometimes arise. Occasionally, criminals adopt either pseudonyms or dual identities. For ease of readability and to avoid clutter, instead of using two separate circles to represent the dual identity, simply depict the relationship through two interlocking circles with each name in the respective portion of the individual circles (see Exhibit 11.8).

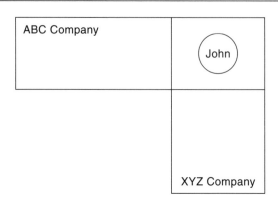

EXHIBIT 11.7   Interlocking Directorate

The Basics of Link Analysis Now that we have introduced you to the basic principles of matrices and diagrams it is time to put it all together. Matrices and diagrams, as we have said, are very powerful tools. When used in conjunction with each other, they offer investigators the ability to visualize complicated relationships. In order to get the most from these tools, we recommend that you try and proceed through the following steps: Collect the data, construct a matrix or matrices, plot the graph, and analyze the relationships.

COLLECTING THE DATA Any analysis is only as valuable and accurate as the quality of the underlying intelligence data on which it is based. If your intelligence is flawed, then your associations will be flawed. For that reason, everything must begin with your intelligence gathering. Whether you are simply searching corporate records, occupational licenses, and other public records filings to establish relationships, or conducting content analysis of wiretaps, you must ensure that the relationships are verifiable. Of course, what consti-

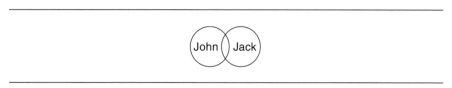

EXHIBIT 11.8   Representation of Aliases

tutes verifiable relationships will vary from case to case and even from day to day, but the need for accuracy will not. Once you have collected your intelligence, you are ready to move to the next phase, matrix construction.

CONSTRUCTING THE MATRIX Using the data that you have collected in phase one, you can now simply plug the names, companies, groups, terrorist cells, or whatever it is you are concerned with into the matrix and note the relationships among the entities. Although a bit more complicated than it sounds, the essential process is straightforward. Where associations are verifiable, you simply place an association point in the intersecting row and column. As we will discuss later, a variety of systems exist for signifying a confirmed relationship; however, for a simple link diagram we use an *X* for confirmed, a *zero* for no relationship, and a *dash* for a suspected, but unconfirmed relationship. After you have constructed all the relationships, you can move on to the diagramming phase (see Exhibit 11.9).

DIAGRAMMING THE NETWORK Before we put pen to paper, we need to evaluate and analyze the matrices themselves. We are looking for organizational cues to help us more efficiently plot the diagram. To begin with, you need to determine the number of associations each member has. You must count across the rows for each individual. This provides a total number of associations for that person. You can do the same for each column (this would only result in a different figure for rectangular matrices as square matrices have a symmetrical relationship; more about that later). Now, starting with the member with the largest number of associations, begin to draft your chart.

	A	B	C	D	E	F	G
Jones	x		x			x	
Franks	x	x		x		x	
Brown			x		x	x	
Green							x

EXHIBIT 11.9   Completed Matrix

Work from most active to least active trying to group members together by association. *Draft* is an apt choice of words here, since your chart will evolve through several drafts before the final chart is drawn.

ANALYZING THE RELATIONSHIPS Once the final draft is complete, examine the relationships that appear. What are the characteristics of the groups? Who are the most active members in terms of membership in organizations or contacts among members? After reviewing the relationships, you can make some predictions and draw some conclusions about questions such as: Who is central to the organization? Who is crucial to communications? Who are the best candidates for future surveillance or interviews? Answers to these questions can provide valuable direction to your investigation.

Social Network Diagrams

Social network diagrams add a dimension of complexity. Although the underlying theory is the same, social network analysis begins to take into consideration the dynamics of the social relationship. This adds a certain degree of complexity. However, with the complexity also comes increased value through better modeling tools. In simple link diagrams there are no convenient means to depict strength of relationship or directionality. In real life, these characteristics are crucial in understanding the true structure of the organization.

Social network diagrams provide a more accurate picture of human relationships. In most relationships there are inequities. For example, in a relationship between Alice and Bob, Alice may like Bob; however, Bob does not necessarily like Alice. In a more crime-like environment, Al may give orders or sell drugs to Bruce, but Bruce cannot give orders or sell drugs to Al. Conventional link analysis would be able to show us that a relationship exists, but not the true dynamics of that relationship. You should be able see the inherent value in adding this dimension to our analysis.

Likewise, strengths of relationships can be displayed. As with our Alice and Bob example, Alice's affection is not reciprocal. It is easy to imagine a scenario in which Alice loves Bob, yet Bob only likes Alice as a friend. Again, depiction of this complicated dynamic between two individuals is impossible in our simple link diagram. In social network diagrams, we can easily and accurately model both of these real-world problems.

The Tools of Social Network Analysis Taken from the basics of graph theory, nodes and edges are the foundational building blocks of all network diagrams.[11] The term *graph* in this case does not refer to the typical graph with which most readers are familiar. We are not talking about the bar charts or line graphs that permeate the business world. Instead, we are referring to the specialized area of mathematics known as graph theory that relies on rigid mathematical formulas and complicated algorithms for modeling problems. While the mathematics that support this area of study are very complex and far beyond the scope of this book, their scientific acceptance and universal application make social network analysis the valuable tool it is. As we move forward, we will present you with the theoretical foundation; however, rest assured we would not expect you to grasp the underlying mathematical principles. Much like computers are powerful tools regardless of whether you understand binary math, social network analysis can be a valuable tool without the need to understand matrix algebra. To begin, we must examine the building blocks: nodes and edges.

Nodes represent your primary object of study. Nodes, interchangeably referred to as vertices, are how we represent our object of study. Each node represents a single entity. Whether that entity is a person, an organization, or in some cases, a transaction, the node acts as its place holder in our graph.

Edges represent relationships. Since the purpose of our study is to model the relationships between entities (in graphical terms, our vertices), we must connect them where appropriate. We do this through edges. As noted earlier, there are several kinds of relationships that we may wish to model. In our first example, Alice likes Bob, but Bob does not return her sentiments. In graph theory, we call this an unreciprocated relationship, and we depict it with a directed edge (a line with a directional arrowhead; see Exhibit 11.10).

Conversely, if Bob did like Alice, we could depict the relationship using a bidirectional line with arrowheads at both ends (see Exhibit 11.11).

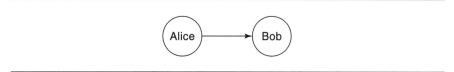

EXHIBIT 11.10   Directed Relationship

EXHIBIT 11.11   Reciprocated Relationship

Weighted relationships are also possible. In the case where Alice loves Bob, but Alice only likes Carol, a dilemma confronts us. The differentiation between the strength of affection Alice has for Bob, versus that for Carol, might be a key issue in our case. For example, it may be of great importance that our suspect Al has called associate Bruce 42 times during our period of interest, and yet called Charles only three times. In terms of establishing Al's importance in the organization, frequency of contacts might prove a key factor. Luckily graph theory offers us the ability to weight the strength of our edge. In our Al-Bruce-Charles organization, the strength of Al's connection to Bruce is much greater than Al's connection to Charles. Exhibit 11.12 graphically depicts this scenario.

Through these tools all networks can be modeled. You can model any social network, from a simple five-person star network to a highly complex and cellular terrorist network, using these two fundamental objects. However, as the network grows, extracting valuable information can become more difficult. Larger, more complex organizations can be more efficiently analyzed using matrix theory.

For example, the network depicted in Exhibit 11.13 is simple to analyze.

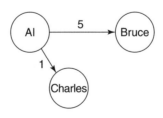

EXHIBIT 11.12   Weighted Relationships

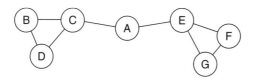

EXHIBIT 11.13   **Link Diagram of Seven-Person Network**

This graph models a seven-person organization. We have labeled the vertices A through G. As you can see, the organization is essentially two individual cells connected together by a common link with individual A. The identification of a key point of information exchange in this network, A, is easy. However, more complex networks may tend to obscure the visibility of such links, and make identification of points of vulnerability difficult. The matrices that we introduced you to earlier can help.

Matrices come in many forms. As noted previously, *matrix* is merely another term used to describe a collection of objects. Sometime we call them arrays. These rectangular arrangements of elements show the relationships among members. In our case, this matrix will be a collection of relationships.

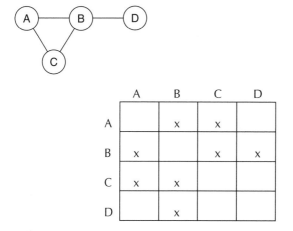

EXHIBIT 11.14   **Link Diagram with Association Matrix**

The beauty that underlies social network analysis is that we can represent all graphs as matrices. Then, using the principles of matrix algebra, characteristics of the graph can be identified using mathematical precision. Exhibit 11.14 illustrates both a graph and matrix representation of a simple organization.

In Exhibit 11.14, which is an undirected, also known as a simple, graph, there are four members of our group, A through D. A is associated with B and C but not D. B is associated with C and D (in addition to A). As noted, there is reciprocity among the relationships so there are no arrowheads necessary. A graph such as this might occur when we merely want to show association without concern for who is directing whom. Exhibit 11.14 depicts this relationship. For every relationship between members, an X is placed in the corresponding cell in the matrix. For example, in our group, A is associated with B, therefore in the cell A,B, there is an X.

We call these adjacency matrices and they are the simplest form of matrix you will encounter. Because our relationship disregards both the strength of the relationship and its direction, you will note that the upper-right portion of the matrix is a mirror image of the lower-left portion. The symmetrical nature of the matrix allows us to discard the upper-right portion along the main diagonal (the line of cells extending from the cell labeled A,A down and to the right to the cell labeled D,D). You will note that the main diagonal has no X's. That is because there is no need to represent A's relationship with A. While there are occasions in which you may need to represent this relationship, most matrices you will encounter will have no entry in these cells.

As powerful as these matrices are, there are times in which you will need to expand their capabilities. The relationships in the matrix are binary in the

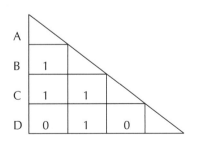

	A	B	C	D
A	0	1	1	0
B	1	0	1	1
C	1	1	0	0
D	0	1	0	0

A			
B	1		
C	1	1	
D	0	1	0

EXHIBIT 11.15   Binary Matrices

sense that they either exist or they do not. Because of this we can substitute zeros and ones for our blanks and X's. Exhibit 11.15 represents this new matrix.

This is the standard way of noting a binary matrix. Additionally, as noted earlier, there will be many times in which you want to represent directionality in the relationship. We can use the same matrix; however, it will no longer be symmetrical.

Exhibit 11.16 shows an asymmetrical matrix and its resulting graph.

Modeling the following is now possible: A talks to B and C, but B only talks to C and D. D talks to A, and C only talks to B. You will note that our matrix is no longer symmetrical; therefore, we must depict the full square. We can further expand our matrix's capability by adding strength of relationship to the mix.

If our operational requirement is to model how strongly our players are connected, as stated earlier we can use interval level elements. If the relationship between A and B is twice as strong as that between A and C, we can easily represent that through intervals. The matrix shown in Exhibit 11.17 illustrates that the tie between A and B is twice as strong as that between A and C. For example, this might be valuable when analyzing telephone toll records. Suspect A calls suspect B 100 times, whereas he only calls suspect C 50 times. This information, when trying to determine the key players in the organization, might be important.

	A	B	C	D
A	0	1	1	0
B	0	0	1	1
C	0	1	0	0
D	1	0	0	0

EXHIBIT 11.16   Asymmetrical Matrix and Related Link Diagram

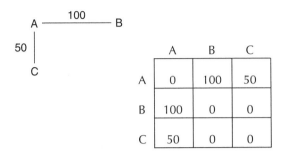

EXHIBIT 11.17   Relationship Strength Representation

As we indicated earlier, these square matrices are very useful for depicting relationships among like objects. When we are comparing relationships between the same type object, whether people to people, organizations to organizations, or transactions to transactions, there will be an equal number of rows to columns, hence the square matrix. These matrices are called single-mode, since they represent only a single type of object. There are times, however, when we want to depict relationships among two different types of objects. These are called two-mode matrices and further extend our analytical power.

Two-mode matrices are rectangular. Unlike their square relatives, rectangular matrices can represent unmatched pairs. For example, while the set of similar objects will always match up, in a rectangular matrix we may have seven

	A	B	C	D	E	F	G
1	x		x			x	
2	x	x		x		x	
3			x		x	x	
4							x

EXHIBIT 11.18   Two-Mode Matrix

suspects whom we want to relate to four organizations. The resulting matrix will have more rows than columns (assuming suspects are depicted using rows and organizations are depicted in the columns). This is shown in Exhibit 11.18.

It is from these very humble beginnings and the tremendous power of mathematics that all social network analysis flows.

Depicting simple relationships is easily done manually. We can organize our nodes in matrices, determine their relationships, and then plot our graph very simply when we have a manageable number of modes. As the complexity of our network expands, so too does our reliance on the underlying mathematical theory. In theory, all the mathematical analysis that needs to be done can be done manually. However, manual manipulations of matrices, even simple ones, can be a very complicated undertaking. Additionally, solid understanding of the algorithms involved is essential. Luckily, investigators do not need to master these mathematics skills. There are a number of computer programs available to conduct the necessary manipulations and render a final verdict. We are not going to, assuming we even could, explain the math. Instead, we will identify and explain the social network measures that are most often of concern to investigators in financial investigations. When you understand these measures, you can enlist the assistance of the readily available software programs to perform the analysis. The important measures are centrality, degree, and closeness.

Analyzing Networks According to Robert A. Hanneman, a Professor of Sociology at University of California Riverside, well-connected individuals within organizations are the most influential.[12] Besides intuitively feeling right, Hanneman's research indicates that social network analysis empirically supports this notion. Hanneman finds that well-connected people within an organization have greater access to information, have greater reach among their peers, and as a result have a greater ability to influence and direct an organization's movement.[13] As a result of this principle, information regarding how connected each individual within our criminal organization is with each other member can help us identify key players, and perhaps points of vulnerability.

DENSITY Overall network density is a key concept. One measure of overall organizational strength is the speed with which information can diffuse across it.[14] The more rapidly information can spread, the more rapidly an organization can adapt and overcome hurdles. Density is determined by identifying the total number of connections present, then finding the ratio of those connections to the total number of possible connections. The closer this ratio approaches one, the better connected (i.e., dense) the network is. A dense network is a flexible network. A dense network by definition contains redundancy of connections.

CONNECTIVITY An extremely important concept in assessing overall strength of the network is connectivity. Connectivity is the ability of each actor within the network to reach other actors. Relying heavily on the concept of paths, walks, and trails, connectivity allows you to calculate vulnerability to disruption. Disruption refers to the condition in which the remaining members of the network are unable to communicate among themselves.[15] For example, it is possible to disrupt networks with low connectivity, where few individuals are well connected, by removing only a few key individuals. Conversely, in networks where many individuals are well connected, you must remove many more key individuals before the entire network will be disrupted. Closely related to density, the connectivity measure can be valuable in attempts to target an organization. Perhaps your investigation identifies a consortium of businesspeople who are conspiring to artificially set the price of widgets. If this organization has high connectivity, disruption by removing one or two key players will be unlikely. However, if it has low connectivity, disruption will be much easier.

CLOSENESS Distance can also be an important indicator of overall organizational strength.[16] Distance measures the closeness between members of the organization in steps. For example, two nodes that are directed connected to one another by an edge are called adjacent. Adjacent nodes are one step apart. Likewise, if A is connected to B, who is connected to C, then A and C are two steps apart. Logically, nodes that are a great distance from each other are more vulnerable to disruption than those that are close. The overall coefficient of distance across members of the network likewise signals the strength of the organization as a whole.[17] This becomes even more important when key actors are separated from one another by numerous steps. In that case, communications are both unreliable and slow. Flexibility and adaptability are reduced. Further, greater distances between nodes can create a susceptibility to stratification. In directed graphs (where communications channels flow in only one direction) these distances can be even more crucial.

DEGREE In evaluating an individual actor's role within the organization, degree is a very important measurement.[18] Degree refers to the total number of ties one actor has within the organization. For example, if A is tied to B and A is tied to C, A has two total connections whereas both B and C only have one each. A, therefore, has a higher degree than either B or C. Degree becomes important because actors with higher degrees tend to have more power within the organizations. Intuitively this makes sense, but it makes even more sense if we examine it logically.

Looking at a star network as our model, we see that this is true. In the star, actor A is connected to every other member of the network (see Exhibit 11.19).

In order for B to contact C, or any other member for that matter, C must go through A. Because of A's number of connections relative to the total connections in the overall network (i.e., the existence of alternative channels linking B, C, D, etc.), he is in a position of influence and therefore powerful.

CLOSENESS Closely related to the concept of degree is closeness. Direct connections are more powerful than indirect connections.[19] These structural advantages can translate into power. In terms of efficiency, shorter path lengths translate into greater speed of communication and hence more influence.

BETWEENNESS Another measure of the possible power of an actor within a network is betweenness.[20] Betweenness refers to the number of relationships that lie between other actors and a particular actor. This sounds complicated, but in reality is a simple concept to grasp if we return to our star network depicted in Exhibit 11.19. Person A lies between all possible pairs of actors. Any

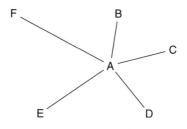

EXHIBIT 11.19   Star Network

communication between B-C, C-E must go through A. While sounding nearly identical to our illustration of degree, this measure of potential power is slightly different as network size tends to increase. In our simple star network, there are no communications in which A does not participate. However, as the network grows the total number of connections will grow, and the ability for A to be involved in all of them becomes, as a practical reality, limited. Therefore, while A may have a very high degree in relation to other actors, comparatively few communications must use him as an intermediary.

Now that we have discussed the three main measures, let us return for a moment to degree. As we mentioned earlier, a strong indication of actor strength within the organization is degree. This simple statement assumes an undirected graph (undirected graphs do not account for the direction of relationships). In directed graphs, however, another concept must be examined; the notion of indegree versus outdegree.

Indegrees refer to edges terminating with an actor.[21] When a directed edge connects two nodes, assuming it is not bidirectional, it will originate in one node and terminate in the other. If A and B are connected by an edge originating with A and terminating in B, then B has a single indegree (the communication is coming in to B). Likewise, in relation to that same communication, A has a single outdegree, meaning one line of communication is flowing out of A. Indegree and outdegree can be important in relation to the power structure of an organization.

Generally, actors who have a high number of indegrees are usually prominent within the organization. An actor characterized by a large number of communications coming into him from many other actors signifies someone with whom many other actors are seeking a tie; they are seeking out that actor. Conversely, actors with high numbers of outdegrees are able to exchange information with many others and impress upon others their views. This results in a strong ability to influence.

Putting it all Together   As we explained earlier, manually analyzing networks is possible, and for those times where the number of nodes and connections make visual and manual analysis too complicated, there are a number of software programs available.

These programs range from academic freeware to expensive commercial packages costing thousands of dollars. Each has its advantages, and depending on your level of computer skill may be easier or harder to learn. Many of the academic packages have been developed by university researchers in the area of social network analysis and are not criminal investigative tools per se. However, since the measures that we have discussed are central to all social network analysis, their output will be equally valuable to you. The commercial applications that have been developed specifically for investigations tend to be more user friendly, often balanced against their versatility, but compute essentially the same measurements as their academic counterparts. Regardless of which package you consider, you should resign yourself to spending a considerable amount of time learning the nuances of the software.

Interpreting the results is often the hardest part. Whether you use computer-based tools, or simply manually count connections and apply the ratios, you will end up with some form of the measures we have previously discussed. As with all investigative tools, you must use them with both caution and reason.

These are investigative tools, not exact measures. When you begin using social network analysis, you must understand that, while very helpful in some circumstances, these tools are limited. Measures of degree and centrality can be strong indicators of organizational actors who have a high potential to influence. Conversely, they should be looked at as nothing more than guides. Likewise, nodes within the organization that your analysis indicates may be points of vulnerability may in fact be peripheral nodes with little real connection to the organization. Remember, these are tools. We encourage you to use them often, but recognize their limitations and the fact that they are poor substitutes for good solid investigative work and intelligence gathering.

TEMPORAL ANALYSIS

Temporal analysis tools help organize the flow of events or data over time. Unlike associational analysis tools that help us model relationships among people, organizations, or groups, temporal analysis tools allow us to model the relationship between time and some other entity. For example, a simple timeline is a temporal analysis tool that allows us to order the events in a sequence that we can visually comprehend.

This group includes a variety of tools. Some tools, like the time-event chart (TEC), are obviously temporal analysis tools, while others, like the transaction flow diagram, are less obviously temporal analysis tools. The characteristic common to all the tools that we have grouped in this category is their ability to help the investigator order things within a frame of reference.

The most common frame of reference is often chronological time. We have chosen to include in this category of tools time-event charts and simple timelines, PERT and VIA charts, and transaction/process flow diagrams.

TEC

Timelines are the traditional tools for ordering events. Whether trying to order criminal acts or investigative steps, investigators have traditionally relied on the standard timeline. The left edge of the graph begins at a predetermined date/time and each succeeding material event is charted along the horizontal axis moving toward the right. In this type of arrangement, the passage of time is denoted by movement to the right on the horizontal scale. Negative time concepts, for example, two days before the theft, are denoted by movement to the left of the zero point on the horizontal axis. These are very simple concepts that are practically universal.

While they are universal, they are often cumbersome. Over time, your timeline can become unwieldy in both length and detail. Most of us who have used timelines have wrestled with the situation in which we need to add more and more events to our timeline until there is no more room. Likewise, sometimes making written entries on the timeline is inefficient. For example, when charting the sequence of events in embezzlement we must note each suspect transaction on the timeline. Being forced to write out the description of each transaction can ultimately make the timeline confusing and cluttered. Lastly, as the investigation progresses, the timeline will inevitably grow as well, resulting in two, three, or even four pages of data strung together. Time event charts aim to correct these shortcomings.

While none of the problems that we have cited with timelines are overly critical, they can be frustrating. Likewise, there is nothing magical about a time-event chart that will assure you that you won't end up with more than a single page of information. However, time-event charts rely on the same psychological basis as our associational tools—the power of graphic representation and visual cues.

The key to time-event charting is visual clarity. Similar to our link diagrams, time-event charts use symbols and visual place holders to simplify and unclutter the timeline. Just as graphical user interfaces and traffic signs recognize the fact that humans can infer a great deal of information from a sim-

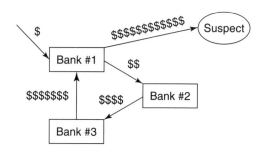

EXHIBIT 11.20   Check-Kiting Scheme

ple picture, time-event charts harness our ability to quickly process a set of pictures and form a relationship between them.

For example, a picture of a cigarette with a crossed circle superimposed on it is a near-universal symbol. Independent of reading level and native language, most people will instantly recognize the symbol as one prohibiting smoking. The ability of symbols to communicate concepts, not simply single words, makes them an ideal investigative aid.

Time-event charts combine symbols with logical flow. While neither new nor particularly revolutionary, the idea of using symbols to represent discrete events on a timeline feels logically coherent. Moving from left to right on a timeline, "reading" the pictures is very intuitive. By carefully selecting our symbols, their shapes can convey double the information. Exhibit 11.20 shows a simple yet effective TEC that depicts a check-kiting scheme.

Transaction and Process Flow Diagrams

Also closely related to the timeline are flow diagrams. Like timelines, flow diagrams often graphically represent events and slices of time. However, the difference is that flow diagrams are usually used to depict a single incident that may or may not act as a representative of other events. For example, in an investigation of a complicated embezzlement, the suspect may accomplish the crime through a number of individual account manipulations. A timeline (or TEC) shows the overall picture of the embezzlement. Conversely, the flow diagram depicts a single incident of account manipulation.

Flow diagrams are valuable in understanding complicated processes. When confronted with a complicated scheme or a process that is unfamiliar, flow diagrams allow you to picture the event. For example, when first studying accounting, many students are confused by the flow of the accounting cycle; it is common for instructors to use a flow diagram to illustrate how the cycle operates. Likewise, investigators can use flow diagrams to break down both accounting and computer processes into bite-size pieces that become easier to digest.

Flow charts used by computer programmers are also forms of flow diagrams. When a programmer first tackles a particularly difficult programming problem, instead of setting off half-cocked, he will usually walk through each step of the problem, charting what must occur and what product will result using special symbols, until the end of the process is reached. This visual step-through process breaks down the complicated algorithm into manageable steps. Likewise, the flow diagram can do the same thing for investigators. Exhibit 11.21 shows a simple flow diagram.

The key to good flow diagrams is the selection of the graphic symbols. Like TECs, the graphic symbols that you use to act as informational place holders in the flow diagram must convey lots of information. For example, using a picture of a stack of dollar bills to represent the flow of money is a common and

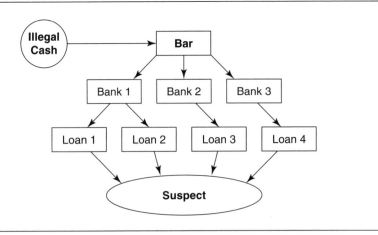

EXHIBIT 11.21   Simple Flow Diagram

logical choice in a money laundering flow diagram. Careful selection of your symbols can greatly improve the readability of your diagram.

PERT and VIA Charts

Program Evaluation Review Technique (PERT) charts are a common sight in business and construction managers' offices. A traditional tool of project managers and computer programmers, PERT tools like Microsoft Project harness the power of graphics to organize the flow of events in any critical task. Also similar to timelines, PERT charts are a temporal ordering tool, but with a difference.

PERT tools are more forward looking than historical. Where we tend to construct timelines and TECs to examine events that have occurred in the past, we construct PERT charts to plan how events must occur in the future. Managing mission-critical processes requires tight coordination of personnel and strict attention to deadlines. The larger these projects become, the harder management becomes. With PERT tools graphic place holders on our timeline of critical events help managers stay organized.

Applying PERT charts can help you stay organized among the chaos of the financial crime investigator's office. One of the values of PERT is its ability to break down complicated tasks and events into their component parts. These sub-parts are then charted out as a series of discrete yet related and interconnected tasks. Breaking each task down helps to identify critical tasks that must be accomplished before subsequent events can occur. For example, we all take pouring a cup of coffee for granted; however, using PERT, we can see that there are a number of critical subtasks that must occur in exact sequence before we can pour our first cup.

You cannot pour the cup until the pot stops brewing. Likewise, the pot cannot brew until the water is poured in and the filter is in place. We cannot put the filter in place until we measure and pour the grounds. Thinking of such a simple routine task in relation to its component steps clearly illustrates the complications that might arise in a financial crime investigation involving multiple investigators, thousands of documents, and dozens of interviews.

Visual Investigative Analysis (VIA) is the PERT chart's brother. PERT is a tool that is often used to plan an investigation. Conversely, VIA is used to deconstruct a criminal episode. First used by the Los Angeles Police Department to aid in the investigation of the assassination of Robert Kennedy, VIA is an adaptation of PERT.[22] It was later used in such famous investigations as the Zodiac and Slasher killers in California.[23]

PERT and VIA are valuable because they are flexible. Like many investigative tools, PERT and VIA can be adapted to many different situations. As evidenced by their varied use from the Kennedy assassination to the Zodiac Killer investigation they can be molded to fit the facts of the case. The key to their success in that regard is their foundation on a core set of symbols and rules. There are four main categories of symbols: activities, events, bursts, and merges.

Activities These are processes that take up time, and on which the remainder of the process or investigation depend. For example, an activity might be an interview with the comptroller of ABC Company. Clearly, this particular task dictates the outcome of the remainder of the investigation. In VIA and PERT, lines and arrows frequently represent activities.

Events These are milestones in the process. Unlike activities, events are the intermediate goals within the overall process. For example, an event might be the execution of a search warrant at the headquarters of ABC Company. Events can be further broken down.

Using our search warrant example we can see how this might work. Search warrant execution is the event. Within that larger event there are other sub-events that must occur in a particular order. We must arrive at the premises, knock and announce, enter, serve the warrant, collect the evidence, and so on. There are generally two symbols used to depict events. Triangles frequently represent starting and ending events within the process and circles represent processes within the event. In our search warrant example, we use a triangle to depict our arrival, circles represent the knock-and-announce, entry and execution, and a triangle would signify the deposit of the evidence into the evidence storage facility.

Bursts A burst is an event that kicks off a series of simultaneous events. We commonly depict bursts using a circle with three activity lines growing from it. Bursts are critical phases of an investigation or criminal act that, although simultaneous, are undertaken independently. For example, the CEO of ABC Company places a call to the accounting firm ordering them to begin destroying all working papers related to the most recent audit. Three different branches of the firm then begin carrying out the CEO's request. While the

CEO's action triggered the events, they were independent and carried out simultaneously.

Merges Merges are similar to bursts with the difference that multiple simultaneous activities culminate in one event. While bursts are activities that must begin simultaneously, merges are the events in which several critical activities end. A merge must occur in order for subsequent events to occur. A merge is often depicted using multiple activity lines converging in an event circle. An example of a merge event would be structured purchases of large shares of XYZ stock by three executives of ABC in a silent hostile takeover attempt. In this scenario the takeover of XYZ, which would be the merge event, cannot occur prior to the executives of ABC covertly acquiring a combined controlling interest in XYZ.

Labeling the Chart

Labeling the chart will depend on its complexity. For simple VIA or PERT charts, labels might be appropriate within the event circles or on the activity lines. With more complicated charts, however, you may need to identify each event circle and activity line by number and list a legend or key alongside the chart as an identifier. Regardless of the method of labeling events you choose, you should work to follow some simple rules. Exhibit 11.22 illustrates a VIA chart and its symbols.

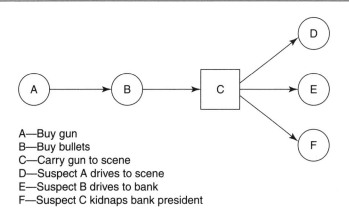

A—Buy gun
B—Buy bullets
C—Carry gun to scene
D—Suspect A drives to scene
E—Suspect B drives to bank
F—Suspect C kidnaps bank president

EXHIBIT 11.22   Simple VIA Chart

Strive for Clarity Cluttered and crowded charts are often more confusing than no charts at all. Having that in mind, you should work to produce clean, clear, and precise charts. Generally, similar to link diagrams, your VIA activity lines should not overlap. Charts should logically flow from left to right, and labels, identifiers, and key symbols should be consistent and unique.

Strive for Accuracy Before charting, it is important to identify the key events in your case. Regardless of whether you are using a PERT chart to plan an investigation, or using a VIA chart to deconstruct a criminal incident, you must answer some simple questions first: What events happened simultaneously? What events must finish before others can begin? How much detail must I achieve in my chart? These are all valid and important questions.

Once you have answered these questions, you are in a much better place to begin charting. The remainder of the charting process should be more mechanical than anything. In fact, the act of thinking through and actually charting the events will help you internalize a stronger understanding of the crime, independent of the chart itself.

CONCLUSION

In this chapter, we have introduced you to a number of powerful tools to help in analyzing your case. While no tool can take the place of solid investigative work, they can aid you in staying organized and understanding difficult topics.

Whether you are trying to visualize the structure of an interlocking directorate in an unfair competition case, or simply trying to understand the path a particular invoice took through the victim company, these tools can help you reach your goal. While these tools are different, they all share the common element of visualization. As we have said repeatedly, visualizing difficult concepts through graphic representation is often the only way to make them clear. As you move on to the next chapter, we hope that you will add these tools to your investigative repertoire and use them frequently.

In the next chapter, we will expand on the concept of visual analysis and introduce you to another visual tool with a slightly different approach. While the tools from this chapter examine relationships among organizations, people, and events, the tools introduced in Chapter 12 will help you visualize relationships between pieces of evidence.

SUGGESTED READINGS

Carley, K.M. *Dynamic Network Analysis for Counter-Terrorism*. Pittsburgh, PA: Carnegie Mellon University, 2001.

Chen, H., W. Chung, Y. Qin, M. Chau, J. Jie Xu, G. Want, R. Zheng, and H. Atabakhsh. *Crime Data Mining: An Overview and Case Studies*. Tuscon, AZ: University of Arizona, Department of Management Information Systems, 2003.

Klerks, P. "The Network Paradigm Applied to Criminal Organizations: Theoretical Nitpicking or a Relevant Doctrine for Investigators? Recent Developments in the Netherlands." *Connections*, 24, no. 3 (September 1999): 53–65.

Milward, H.B., and J. Raab. "Dark Networks: The Structure, Operation, and Performance of International Drug, Terror, and Arms Trafficking Networks." Paper presented at the *International Conference on the Empirical Study of Governance, Management, and Performance*, Barcelona, Spain, October 4–5, 2002.

Muir, H. "Email Traffic Patterns can Reveal Ringleaders." *New Scientist* (March 27, 2003); http://newscientist.com/article/.ns?id=3550&print=true (accessed on January 12, 2006).

Nagaraja, S., and R. Anderson. "The Topology of Covert Conflict." *Technical Report* (Cambridge, UK: University of Cambridge Computer Laboratory, July 2005), no. 637.

Wasserman, S., and K. Faust. *Social Network Analysis: Methods and Applications* (New York: Cambridge University Press, 1994).

Williams, Phil. "Transnational Criminal Networks." In John Arquilla and David Ronfeldt, eds., *Networks and Netwars: The Future of Terror, Crime, and Militancy*. Santa Monica, CA: RAND National Security Research Division, 2001, pp. 61–97.

NOTES

1. M.B. Peterson, *Applications in Criminal Analysis: A Sourcebook* (Westport, CT: Greenwood Press, 1994), pp. 2–4.
2. J.P. Scott, *Social Network Analysis: A Handbook*, 2nd ed. (Thousand Oaks, CA: Sage Publications, 2000), pp. 10–11.
3. Ibid.
4. Ibid., pp. 17–18.
5. Ibid., pp. 10–13.
6. Ibid., p. 6.
7. See generally, Scott, *Social Network Analysis*, pp. 10–22.
8. See generally, W.E. Baker and R.R. Faulkner, "The Social Organization of Conspiracy: Illegal Networks in the Heavy Electrical Equipment Industry," *American Sociological Review*, 58, no. 6 (December 1993): 837–860; B.H.

Erickson,"Secret Societies and Social Structure," *Social Forces*, 60, no. 1 (September 1981): 188–210; M. Sparrow, "Network Vulnerabilities and Strategic Intelligence in Law Enforcement," *International Journal of Intelligence and Counter Intelligence*, 5, no. 3 (1986): 255–274.

9. You can find out information about these products at the following Web sites: Analyst's notebook, www.i2.co.uk/Products/Analysts_Notebook/default.asp; Visual analytics, www.visualanalytics.com/; Netmap, http://netmap.sourceforge .net/.

10. See generally, Scott, *Social Network Analysis*; see also Peterson, *Applications in Criminal Analysis*.

11. R. Hanneman and M. Riddle, *Introduction to Social Network Methods* (Riverside, CA: University of California, Riverside, 2005); http://faculty.ucr.edu/~hanneman/ nettext/ (accessed January 3, 2006); see also Scott, *Social Network Analysis*.

12. Ibid., Chapter 7; http://faculty.ucr.edu/~hanneman/nettext/c7_connection.html.

13. Ibid.

14. Ibid.

15. Ibid, Chapter 10; http://faculty.ucr.edu/~hanneman/nettext/c10_centrality.html.

16. Ibid.

17. Ibid.

18. Ibid.; see also Hanneman, *Introduction to Social*, Chapter 7.

19. Hanneman, *Introduction to Social*, Chapter 10.

20. Ibid.

21. Ibid.

22. Peterson, *Applications in Criminal Analysis*, p. 3.

23. Ibid. See also GlobalSecurity.org, "Counterterrorism Analysis Court: Defense Intelligence College: Introduction to Terrorist Intelligence Analysis," www.global security.org/intell/library/policy/dod/part5_ct_analysis_course.htm (accessed January 3, 2006).

12

INFERENTIAL ANALYSIS

INTRODUCTION

In Chapter 10 we introduced you to a simple hypothetical in which we were attempting to prove that the defendant killed his wife. In that rudimentary example, the line of logic was simple. We found the defendant's glove at the scene with the victim's blood on it. The logic of the argument seems to compel the conclusion that the defendant committed the murder. It is rare that the logic of a case is so simple. It is even rarer that the logic of a financial crime case is that simple. On the contrary, most financial crime cases suffer from a double curse. First, the sheer mass of evidence is incomprehensible. Second, the logic necessary to prove the case is often composed of several interlocking and conjunctive lines of argument formed in a proposition of alternatives.

This form of allegation can confound the investigator and can bog down an investigation that lacks a strong focus. To avoid this miring effect, you must organize your investigation and construct it from the simplest logic possible. The tools in this chapter will help you do that.

HOW INFERENTIAL ANALYSIS HELPS

Deconstructing the legal theory of the case into the ultimate probandum and penultimate probanda is the first step. In legal terms, a probandum is simply the proposition we want to prove. Therefore, the ultimate probandum is that final proposition we are trying to prove. In most cases, the ultimate proban-dum will be that the defendant committed the criminal act. The penultimate probanda (plural of probandum) then become all the intermediate propositions that we must prove on our way to proving the ultimate probandum.

When we talk about deconstructing the case we simply mean that we ana-lyze what we intend on proving. The crime that we believe the suspect has committed will ultimately dictate what the ultimate probandum and penulti-mate probanda are. Once we have defined these propositions, we may move on to the second step.

The second step focuses the efforts of the investigative team by establish-ing the lines of argument leading up to the ultimate probandum. These lines of argument should always dictate and focus our investigative effort. If your lines of argument are weak, so is your focus.

By organizing the lines of argument of your case into coherent discrete lines leading up to your ultimate probandum, you can analyze both the explicit and implicit inferences that jurors must draw in order to reach the ultimate con-clusion (guilt). As a graphic representation of both the lines of logic and how the evidence fits within them, an inference network visually alerts the inves-tigative team to areas in need of support, areas that lack logical basis, and areas of potential attack. The third step is to create an inference network.

WHAT IS AN INFERENCE NETWORK?

Inference networks make implicit inferences more obvious and allow you to see those sneaky generalizations we mentioned in Chapter 10 more clearly. The hope and purpose of the inference network are to point out your folly and allow you to react before the prosecutor (or defendant) does. After you have recognized the weakness, you can reorganize your efforts in a more directed, purposeful way.

An inference network is a graphic representation of an inferential relation-ship. Graphical models provide a natural tool for dealing with uncertainty and complexity. They provide us with an intuitively appealing interface by which we can understand highly interactive sets of variables. Often used for prob-lems in applied mathematics and engineering, graphical models provide a nat-ural framework with which to examine the multivariate nature of legal proof and logical argument.

Bayesian Networks

Graphical models offer us a way to view all the variables in our reasoning problem, express assumptions, and facilitate making inferences from observed data. In the context of legal investigation, an inference model can allow us simultaneously to assess all our variables—evidence—and follow the flow of our argument in a logical fashion.[1]

Many forms of graphical models for representing inference networks exist, from Bayesian networks[2] to Markov networks.[3] Generally, however, all inference networks consist of nodes, often called vertices, and links known as edges (these terms should be familiar to readers from Chapter 11). In a traditional Bayesian inference network, the vertices in the graph will correspond to variables within the problem we are modeling. Similarly, the edges correspond to relationships that exist between pairs of variables.

In Exhibit 12.1, the nodes A, B, C, and D represent variables in a causal relationship. For example, if D represents an event—my car will not start—the vertices A, B, and C may represent possible causes for the event. Like most real-world situations, the event "my car won't start" is not a binary relationship.

Instead, more than one variable may be the cause of the event D. If we allow B to represent the condition "I am out of gas" and C to represent the condition "my battery is dead," our model becomes a more accurate representation of a real-life problem. Our model tells us, graphically, that there are two possible causes of our event—either B or C. Bayesian networks of this type are helpful both in diagnostic reasoning, known as "bottom up" since it works from event to causation, and in causal or "top-down" reasoning because it

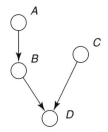

EXHIBIT 12.1   Variables in a Causal Relationship

helps compute the probability that an event will occur given a predecessor event.

Diagnostic Models

Diagnostic models often incorporate Bayesian techniques to help choose from among several competing hypotheses. For example, using Bayesian decision-making techniques, Microsoft has created its infamous anthropomorphic Office Assistant™ paperclip. Using Bayesian decision-making techniques, the paperclip offers context-sensitive advice to users based on the program in use and other real-time data.[4] Similarly, Microsoft's new Mobile Manager takes a vast amount of information about the nature and content of incoming e-mail into account in order to sort, filter, and forward the message based on Bayesian decision theory.[5]

In much the same way that Bayesian diagrams and inference networks can be used to reason through statistically difficult and voluminous problems, we can use them, with some adaptation, to reason through complex legal and investigative problems. This adaptation entails revision of the terminology of Bayesian theory, as well as elimination of the theory of probability and statistics that accompanies its use in mathematic and scientific problems. This leaves us with a skeleton framework on which we can build an inference network. John Henry Wigmore developed one such device, which bears his namesake—the Wigmorean Chart.[6]

Wigmorean Charts

John Henry Wigmore, an early twentieth-century legal scholar in the field of evidence and proof, devised a graphical model for proceeding from point A to point B in terms of legal proof. Based loosely on probability theory combined with notions of the science of judicial proof, Wigmore's method was a study in exposing the underlying logic of each thread of legal argument.[7] His approach and perspective, and the approach of those who have followed, were decidedly lawyerly. To the extent that his method has received notice in terms of investigative potential, it has been from the standpoint of a lawyer conducting fact investigation during the pre-trial discovery process.

Admittedly, lawyers in trial preparation and criminal investigators have divergent methods and differing roles, but at its heart, their goal is very similar.

Both the criminal investigator and the lawyer in the pre-trial discovery, fact investigation phase must uncover as much evidence, both inculpatory and exculpatory, as possible and marshal it into a working hypothesis that supports their theory of what happened. Often, these are a decidedly parallel set of tasks. Wigmore's method, with some adaptation, is very well suited to this task.

As with all graphical models, Wigmore's chart method of analysis presents a structured approach to a complex problem. In Wigmore's case, the problem we face is reasoning from a mixed mass of evidence to some ultimate fact in issue. In other words, a mixture of evidence, which varies in both type and probative force, confronts us, and we must organize that mass into a coherent, hopefully forceful, explanation of a real-world event. In broad terms, our graphical inference network is a communication medium—it allows us to convey meaning. Underlying this communication medium, like all forms of communication, is a language. Although Wigmore's method is well suited to visualize the legal arguments necessary to prove a case in court, there are some minor limitations to its application and effectiveness in analyzing a complex investigative process. For that reason, we have borrowed Wigmore's theory underlying his method and adapted it slightly to reflect more accurately the investigative process. This investigative inference model will aid criminal and civil investigators in their pursuit of legal proof much like Wigmore's chart method, but using a slightly different perspective.

INVESTIGATIVE INFERENCE ANALYSIS

The Language

The first task in designing our inference model is the definition and explication of language. In this case, the "language" derives from a palette of standard graphic symbols, combined with syntax for ordering them. In a way no different from traditional language systems, our inference network language must provide the words as well as the punctuation that gives them meaning. Also in a way only slightly different from traditional language, our system can benefit from some broad general rules as a starting point. In this case, we may begin by discussing the nature of a mixed mass of evidence.

The term mixed mass of evidence refers to the notion that we prove cases through evidence that is heterogeneous, not homogeneous.[8] In other words, a case is built on evidence of different types and probative value. Though not a difficult concept to understand, it is important to define for the reader exactly the distinction between type and probative value in the context of this system.

In general, we shall use the term *type* to refer to the extrinsic quality of evidence. For example, fingerprints, documentary evidence, trace fibers, and DNA evidence are all different types of evidence for our purposes. We will use the term *probative value*, on the other hand, to discuss the inferential weight of an item of evidence.

In the legal context, probative force refers to cogency, or the weight and impact the evidence will exert on the jury. Although our definition of probative force is nearly identical, since we are after all ultimately trying to convince the jury of the defendant's guilt, we shall think of it in a slightly different way. We will think of it in terms of its inductive and deductive qualities. We will think of probative force in terms of how strongly it supports or defeats the logical steps in our inferential chain. We should think of probative value, then in terms of the mode in which the evidence tends to prove the ultimate fact. For practical purposes, we are speaking of the difference between direct and circumstantial evidence.

We use the term *direct evidence* to describe evidence that directly proves the ultimate fact in issue, with no intervening inferential steps in between.[9] Because direct evidence usually comes in the form of testimony from an eyewitness who actually heard, saw, or touched some thing or event, its probative value is high. If an eyewitness takes the stand and testifies that on Friday morning he observed the defendant take out a gun and shoot the victim, he has given direct testimonial evidence, which, if believed, directly proves that the defendant did in fact kill the victim. As such, the inferential value is high and we should accord it appropriate weight within our system of analysis.

Conversely, *circumstantial evidence* is evidence that indirectly proves the ultimate fact in question.[10] Circumstantial evidence consists of evidence that builds up inferences tending to show that the ultimate fact occurred. It is evidence from which the finder of fact can infer other facts based on the circumstances. Clearly, then, circumstantial evidence requires more inferential steps between subordinate facts and the ultimate fact in question. It is important to caution the reader at this point not to confuse issues of credibility and corroboration with the probative value of evidence in this context.

Normally, probative value is the sum of both credibility and the nature of the evidence, either circumstantial or direct. However, for the purposes of constructing our graphical inference, we will address issues of credibility separately. For now, we want the reader to focus on the differences inherent in the two forms of evidence. If, for the sake of argument, we assume that the credibility and reliability of both witnesses—the one providing testimony regarding the ultimate fact and the other providing testimony regarding circumstances from which inferences about the ultimate fact may be drawn—is equal, the probative value of their testimony becomes easier to evaluate. In turn, the discrete inferential steps between our evidence and our ultimate probandum become more easily definable.

Introduction to the Symbols

The first symbols in our language palette, then, must represent the difference between circumstantial and direct evidence. This is true because the key to organizing our argument is in being able graphically to see where the weakest and strongest links are being made. Circumstantial arguments, which are by definition weaker, must be readily distinguishable from direct arguments.

Exhibit 12.2 introduces the first two symbols our system uses: the circle, to represent circumstantial evidence, and the square, to represent direct evidence. To this limited palette, we must add a few more symbols that are basic.

First, in order to represent real evidence, evidence that the fact-finder will physically perceive, we will use the symbol for infinity: ∞. We can use this symbol to represent both testimonial assertions and tangible physical evidence. For example, we can represent either eyewitness testimony regarding the location of a weapon, or the actual weapon itself using this symbol.

Next, we must assign a symbol to represent propositions that will be either stipulated to by the defense or taken as judicially noticed by the fact-finder. For example, in a divorce case it is necessary to prove that a legal marriage exists at the time of the action. If this fact were uncontested, it would be

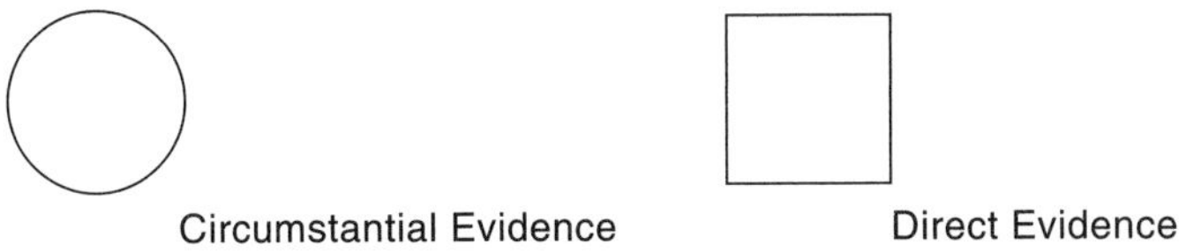

　　Circumstantial Evidence　　　　　　Direct Evidence

EXHIBIT 12.2　Symbols for Circumstantial and Direct Evidence

helpful to have a way to represent this in the chart. Similarly, in the criminal arena, certain facts may be subject to judicial notice without extensive proof. Scientific facts, foreign laws, and other uncontroversial matters are often subject to such notice. By providing a symbol to depict this condition, we graphically identify areas of the investigation where we need to do no further investigation. We will use the proofreader's paragraph symbol to represent this condition—¶.

As we discussed earlier in reference to the need for graphic analysis, generalizations often play crucial roles in the proof process. As we stated, they are often hidden and sometimes the center of uncertainty in our investigative logic. Because we base our generalizations on common-sense assumptions, they are often not supported by evidential proof, so representation by other evidentiary symbols would lead to confusion. However, they are clearly circumstantial arguments by their very definition, and it is imperative that we identify them so that their role in our investigation becomes clear. We will depict generalizations within the chart using the symbol ¥.

This rudimentary set of symbols will allow us to depict certain nodes within the investigative chain—in other words, individual propositions within the overall flow of proof. These nodes of evidence are worthless, in terms of the overall picture, unless we can represent their interrelationship to one another. After all, the power of Bayesian networks and their offspring is in their ability to make visually clear the influence each node has upon the others within the problem space. Enter the simple directional arrow (see Exhibit 12.3).

Using directionally oriented arrows, we can clearly represent the flow of the theory of proof from one proposition to another. These symbols give us the ability to order logically and graphically the propositions within our investigative chain. Finally, to our growing basic palette of symbols we will add the two signs shown in Exhibit 12.4.

EXHIBIT 12.3   Directional Arrow

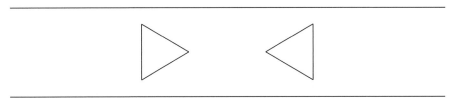

EXHIBIT 12.4   Right/Left Vertical Triangles

We will use the right- and left-facing vertical triangles to represent lines of logic that detract from our main theory and corroborating lines of logic, respectively. We will discuss the use and flexibility of these final two symbols in more detail later, but for now, their introduction to the reader will suffice. Exhibit 12.5 is a summary of our basic symbol palette.

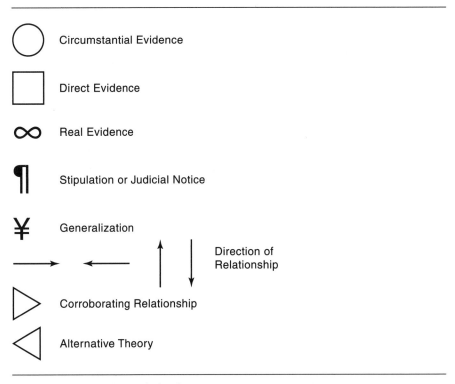

EXHIBIT 12.5   Basic Symbol Palette

A Word about Supplemental Symbols

One of the most powerful aspects of inferential models is their ability to deal with a variety of different situations. As such, our basic inferential model with its basic symbol palette should be more than adequate to deal with any investigative situation that arises. However, inferential models in general lend themselves well to adaptability. This intrinsic adaptability provides even more flexibility because you can modify the basic system so that you can illustrate new or unique relationships, and graphically plot their cause, effect, and influence.

Given that unique situations might arise in the course of real-world application of investigative inference models, you can make additions and modifications to the basic palette of symbols at any time. For example, certain applications may call for a more well-defined, or specialized, way of representing an alternative theory or explanation. In that case, we can create a new symbol to represent succinctly perhaps an alibi, a defendant's argument or affirmative defense, or any other condition that needs greater clarity.

The introduction of the new symbol gives the model more visual impact because it allows the users to immediately recognize lines of argument or investigative flows that relate to that particular condition. A new symbol must meet three requirements: (1) The symbol must be well defined; (2) the symbol must be unique; and (3) its use must be consistent.

If a symbol is introduced without a universally agreed-upon definition, confusion instead of clarity will ensue. Similarly, if each symbol represents more than one condition, say circumstantial corroborating evidence and alibi evidence, its visual impact and logical clarity will be lost. Finally, related to uniqueness is consistency.

Consistency allows the user to recognize immediately, from argument to argument, that certain logical propositions are being pursued. By representing each similar logical investigative proposition with the same symbol, immediate recognition will result. Otherwise, the user of the chart will spend needless time examining definitions and symbols trying to internalize a labyrinthine set of variables with no coherent similarity.

Finally, although not a requirement, we highly recommend that any adaptation or expansion of inference models strive for simplicity. The beauty of the graphical representation of complex relationships is lost when the model becomes nearly as complicated as the relationship itself. For that reason, the fewer symbols your system contains, the easier it will be to clearly see the relationships and evaluate their influence on each other. The goal then, as we see it, should be to represent accurately each unique fact pattern with as few symbols as possible. Avoid superfluity.

THE KEY LIST

As we have said, the beauty of graphic models lies in their simplicity. This simplicity is lost when the model contains more information than is necessary. For this reason, the key to effective investigative management with inference models is the "key list." The key list is a list or database, depending on the complexity of the case, that contains a numerically indexed list of propositions and evidence. Each entry in the key list, therefore, corresponds to an individual node in the model.

By using the key list and model in tandem, every proposition is cross-referenced and represented on the chart. Later, you can use the key list to organize and order your evidence for presentation to whomever you want to persuade.

Although we have introduced the concept of the key list after introducing the model, in reality, key list preparation comes first. It is from the key list that the actual model is constructed and from which we chart the propositions.

The process of developing the key list and organizing its elements is both reflexive and somewhat intuitive. It is reflexive in that it requires constant revision. It is intuitive in that each element in the key list should be relevant to the ultimate proposition we are trying to prove. This task is not always easy; what is relevant is sometimes the product of inductive and deductive reasoning. Because these are the very processes we are striving to pin down, there is the constant risk that your key list will be either overly inclusive or overly restrictive.

Given the choice between the two, it is preferred that, at least during the initial phases of the investigation, you err on the side of overinclusiveness. It is much easier to remove references from the key list later when they become irrelevant than it is follow nonexistent lines of logic that your underinclusive key list has eliminated too early on. An underinclusive key list will obscure productive lines of inquiry and is the graphic equivalent of tunnel vision in investigations.

What then do we include on our key list? We include anything that tends to prove or disprove the ultimate fact in issue. This is precisely where the ultimate and penultimate probanda we introduced earlier become crucial. Our key list has a direct relationship between the ultimate probandum and the investigation. Using the ultimate probandum, we examine the evidence that is in existence and organize it into lines of argument leading up to the final proposition. Let us examine the creation of a key list using a hypothetical crime as follows.

CONSTRUCTING AN INVESTIGATIVE INFERENCE CHART

A Hypothetical

Frank's landlady entered Frank's apartment to collect the rent and found him lying in a pool of blood on the floor of his bathroom with a single gunshot wound to the head. A .38-caliber revolver was lying three feet from Frank's body. A neighbor observed Frank's girlfriend, JoAnn, enter Frank's apartment at 4:00 P.M. on the day of the murder. The UPS driver observed a woman matching JoAnn's description leave his apartment at 5:30 P.M. that same day. A witness heard a gun shot in the area of Frank's apartment at 5:10 P.M. JoAnn's best friend stated that JoAnn was planning to break up with Frank after she found out that Frank had slept with another woman. Responding officers located an apparent handwritten suicide note, covered in blood and signed in Frank's name.

As discussed previously, our ultimate probandum is the ultimate fact that we are attempting to prove. The penultimate probanda are, therefore, the component sub-facts that we must prove in order to prove the ultimate fact. As an example, we will construct our ultimate probandum as follows: "JoAnn murdered Frank." We must break this ultimate fact down further, however. The penultimate probanda for this scenario could be stated as three sub-propositions as follows: "Frank is dead"; "Frank did not die of natural causes"; and "it was JoAnn who killed him." Now, using our first four statements, we can begin to assemble our key list.

Beginning the Construction of Our Key List

The first statement in our key list is "JoAnn murdered Frank." We assign this statement number 1, since it is the starting point of our inquiry. We follow this statement with one of our penultimate probanda, "Frank is dead," "Frank was murdered," and "it was JoAnn who killed him," numbers 2, 3, and 4, respectively. Next, our intuitive abilities and our deductive and inductive reasoning skills get a workout.

It will most likely be easiest to begin by analyzing the supporting propositions underlying probandum number 2. (We have syntactically switched the structure of the sentence to place "Frank is dead," grammatically before "JoAnn murdered him," since arguably[11] it will be easier to prove that Frank is in fact dead than to prove that JoAnn killed him. This allows us to logically assign Frank's death to proposition 2 in our key list—not a requirement but as a matter of housekeeping, more orderly.) Using this proposition, we must look for the supporting evidence to prove it.

Since there is a body, we will likely have a wealth of evidence from which we can support our proposition. It is likely that the medical examiner responded, or at least conducted a subsequent postmortem examination of Frank. Given that, she will be in a position to testify regarding Frank's state of health. We now have proposition number 5, "Medical examiner Jones reports that Frank is dead." In creating our key list, it is important that we do not overlook trivial steps such as making explicit the medical examiner's testimony. Similarly, it is important to make distinctions between various forms of evidentiary support. For example, although the medical examiner will undoubtedly testify at trial, the basis for her testimony will be her report on the autopsy. Therefore, it is imperative that we include in our key list an entry for the autopsy report. Attention to detail in this regard can make the difference between productive analysis and time-wasting exercises.

After making this adjustment, we renumber our key list (an example of the reflexive nature of this type of analysis). Medical examiner Jones's testimony is now number 6, and the autopsy report is number 5. Given this simple scenario, the line of logic is easy to visualize in our heads. If all cases were this simple, an investigative inference would be unnecessary. After all, we prove that "Frank is dead" by the autopsy report, which is authenticated by Dr. Jones's testimonial evidence. This is a short, straight—as opposed to a bifurcated—line of logic, with very little room for inferential error. You will learn through experience that not all lines of exploration will be so straightforward.

Having "proven" or at least built a chain of inferences that lead us to believe that Frank is dead, we can turn our attention to the more difficult task of

#1	-	JoAnn murdered Frank.
#2	-	Frank is dead.
#3	-	Frank was murdered.
#4	-	JoAnn did it.
#5	-	Autopsy report—Frank is dead.
#6	-	Dr. Jones's testimony "Frank is dead."

EXHIBIT 12.6   Initial Key List

proving that he was both murdered and that JoAnn did it. First, Exhibit 12.6 presents our key list, as it looks now.

Because we have phrased proposition 3, "he did not die of natural causes," proposition 7 becomes "Frank died of a gunshot wound."

Again, given the evidence that confronts us, we may or may not be more certain than not that Frank was murdered. If there is uncertainty, as here, then we must chart both propositions in order to avoid tunnel vision and false conclusions. The problem with this is that the propositions "Frank was shot by someone else" and "Frank committed suicide" appear to be irreconcilable propositions; they cannot coexist in a logical world. How, then, do we represent them in our key list?

At this stage, we do not have to worry about dealing with this polemic. We simply list both opposing propositions in the key list and address it later during the charting phase. The two propositions become number 8, "Frank was shot," and number 9, "The gunshot wound was self-inflicted."

Expanding Our Key List

We have now listed the ultimate and penultimate probanda in our scenario. Next, we must scour the hypothetical, or in the real world evaluate our evidence, and extract from it the remaining evidentiary propositions that naturally flow from the facts—including generalizations. In compiling our key list, the remaining order, or the initial order for that matter, is not of great consequence. However, for cosmetic purposes and for purposes of readability, deconstructing the ultimate and penultimate probanda and assigning them numbers first is usually best.

From the remaining facts of our hypothetical, we can cull the following additional evidentiary points:

10. Landlady discovered body in bathroom.
11. Body was in bathroom.
12. Landlady's testimony.
13. Frank was killed in the bathroom.
14. Frank was killed with a gun.
15. Witness no. 1 saw JoAnn enter the apartment at 4:00 P.M. on day of murder.
16. Witness no. 1's testimony.
17. Witness no. 2 heard a gunshot in the area at about 5:10 P.M.
18. Witness no. 2's testimony.
19. Witness no. 3 saw a woman matching JoAnn's description leave Frank's apartment around 5:30 P.M.
20. Witness no. 3's testimony.
21. JoAnn was at Frank's apartment at 5:10 P.M.
22. Frank died at 5:10 P.M.
23. People who have strong motives act on them.
24. Jealousy is a strong motive.
25. JoAnn was jealous.
26. Frank was cheating on JoAnn.
27. Witness no. 4's testimony about Frank's cheating and plans to break it off with JoAnn.
28. Frank was planning to break up with JoAnn.

Invariably, the reader has picked out some propositions and generalizations that we may have overlooked or excluded from this list. Although thoroughness is important, at this stage an exhaustive listing is not necessary. As you will see, there is room for addition, refinement, and deletion as we test our hypothesis during our investigation.

Speaking of hypothesis, it is clear from the facts that a hypothesis emerges that may explain the sequence of events that led up to Frank's untimely demise. In fact, two competing hypotheses emerge with relatively equal strength. The first implicates JoAnn, and the second exonerates her.

The Role of the Key List in Hypothesis Formulation

All experienced investigators formulate working hypotheses at very early stages of the investigation. The formation of a hypothesis allows us to explain observations, test theories, and propose cause-and-effect relationships based on the two forms of reasoning. For example, in our scenario our primary hypothesis is probably that on the date in question, JoAnn came to Frank's apartment to confront him about his philandering ways. Unhappy with his infidelity and in a fit of jealous rage, she shot him with a .38-caliber revolver. Realizing the consequences of her action, she hastily scribbled a suicide note and fled the apartment shortly thereafter. This is a believable theory, fully supported by the evidence. Our job during the investigative process will be to test this hypothesis using the reasoning process and our inference model. First, we must construct our model using the evidence we have gathered so far.

PLOTTING THE CHART

If you have carefully defined your ultimate and penultimate probanda, and diligently constructed your key list, the plotting of the inference chart should be largely a straightforward matter. However, if you have not carefully considered the formulation of your penultimate probanda, or you have slighted the compilation of your key list, plotting the chart will become very tedious and cumbersome.

Because in our example we have carefully considered our ultimate and penultimate probanda, we can chart at least the top level with relative ease. It is here that we combine the language of our system with the logic of our hypothesis.

Plotting the Ultimate and Penultimate Probanda

Using our symbols, we must represent each numbered item in our key list and connect them, logically, with each other in order to form a logical chain proceeding to the conclusion that JoAnn murdered Frank.

We start with our ultimate probandum—"JoAnn murdered Frank." We must prove this circumstantially since there is no eyewitness that links JoAnn to the actual act of killing Frank. Therefore, we represent the ultimate probanda, number 1 on our key list, with a circle from our symbol palette (see Exhibit 12.7).

EXHIBIT 12.7   Circle

Next, we plot the relationship between the ultimate probanda and the penultimate probandum—numbers 2, 3, and 4—as shown in Exhibit 12.8.

Ultimately, if we can prove numbers 2, 3, and 4, we can prove number 1.

Plotting Supporting Probanda As we discussed earlier, proving number 2 depends on testimony from Dr. Jones relating to her autopsy of Frank and the resulting autopsy report. The underlying propositions for this node of the chart would look like the illustration in Exhibit 12.9.

In Exhibit 12.9, nodes 5 and 6 represent Dr. Jones's autopsy report and her testimony, respectively. As such, we place the symbol depicting real evidence inside the nodes. This makes it clear that some physical evidence exists that supports that inference. In node 5, it is the actual autopsy report. In node 6, it is Dr. Jones's testimony. Similarly, we can show Dr. Jones's testimony using the direct evidence symbol. Although Dr. Jones is not a witness to the murder itself, she is a direct witness who will testify to the ultimate fact relative to Frank's state of health, that is, his death. Inasmuch as the analysis of our case reveals that no further decomposition of this line of argument is necessary, our charting for node 2 is complete.

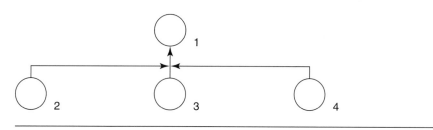

EXHIBIT 12.8   Relationship of Ultimate and Penultimate Probanda

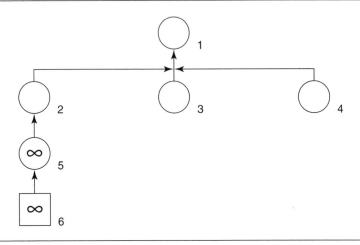

EXHIBIT 12.9   Underlying Propositions

Charting Alternative Theories Charting the relationship of the sub-facts to probandum number 3 is very similar. The reader should note the use of the alternative theory symbol (>) in Exhibit 12.10. As we stated earlier, Frank could have killed himself.

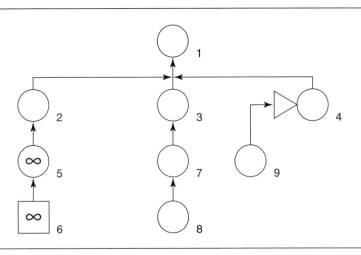

EXHIBIT 12.10   Relationship of Sub-Facts

Since proposition number 4 stands for the assertion that JoAnn caused Frank's death, we need to represent the competing hypotheses that would explain the origin of the gunshot wound as self-inflicted. Proposition 9 (Frank's wound was self-inflicted) offers an alternative theory, as such. We can chart this possibility using the ">" sign to denote an alternative cause of the gunshot wound. As we uncover new evidence and test new hypotheses, we can add nodes onto either chain until one or the other appears the more likely of the two explanations.

Charting the Remainder of Our Hypothetical

Charting the relationships between the evidence and our hypothesis continues until we have worked all the remaining items in our key list into our inference model. As we proceed down the key list, we determine which probandum the evidence tends to support—which ultimate fact in question is most relevant to proving or disproving—and then plot it in the logical chain leading up to that fact.

We urge the reader to chart the rest of the case for him- or herself. Pay particular attention to lines of logic originating with generalizations. Note that some propositions at first might appear overly simplistic, such as "Frank was killed with a gun" and "Frank died of other than natural causes." These two statements seem redundant and an almost simpleton-like statement of the obvious. In our example, these two statements are so naturally obvious that charting them seems somehow obsessive. It is precisely this type of attention to detail and deconstruction of the logic of argument and reasoning that makes inference models effective tools for investigative tasks. Because the proposition "Frank died of other than natural causes" is a natural inference flowing from the proof that he was killed with a gun, our example seems obvious. If the logic was faulty, or the premise was not so universally accepted, our chart would point it out.

We see an example of this when we begin to examine the underlying generalizations in our key list. When we examine the underlying logic of proposition 4 (JoAnn killed Frank), we see that inferences 21, 22, and 13 are straightforward—JoAnn was at Frank's apartment at 5:10 P.M., someone killed Frank at 5:10 P.M., and Frank was killed in his bathroom (which is in his apartment), respectively. Inference number 23, however, is less obvious but just as necessary to prove in order to develop probable cause to believe that JoAnn did it.

We have stated number 23 as the proposition that "People who have a strong motive to act, usually act." This proposition goes directly to JoAnn's motive for killing Frank (jealousy) and, though not an element of the crime, certainly constitutes relevant evidence. Wouldn't it have been just as easy, and required two fewer inferential steps, to simply state JoAnn killed Frank out of jealousy? This is easier, but not as accurate.

Simply stated, the beauty of the inference model is contained in its ability to help identify fallacies of logic. This requires recognition of all underlying generalizations—systematically. Propositions 23 and 24 are broad generalizations regarding jealousy and their effect on human behavior. If either generalization in this case does not hold true, the force of our evidentiary chain leading up to JoAnn is destroyed. If the generalization that jealousy is strong enough motive to make someone murder is not universally accepted—at least by the universe that comprises our jury—then all propositions and inferences that flow from it crumble.

When we conflate the logical steps into one overgeneralization such as JoAnn killed Frank out of jealousy, we are stating what we wish to prove. We are glossing over what we must ultimately convince the jury of—the fact that human jealousy is a sufficient motive for murder—in order to make our larger proposition believable.

In obvious arguments such as this one, the damage may be minimal. In this case, fortunately, there are several remaining inferences that seem to point equally toward JoAnn as the guilty party. The reader, however, could easily imagine a situation in which this is not the case. Getting into the habit of carefully deconstructing each proposition into its component generalizations is good practice and can serve you, the investigator, well when you encounter truly tenuous leaps of logic.

Ultimately, you will face a situation where an item in the key list may tend to support or disprove more than one penultimate probanda. For example, number 5, the autopsy report, would logically be valuable in both establishing that Frank was dead as well as the cause of Frank's death. Similarly, Dr. Jones will likely be a necessary witness to both elements of our penultimate probanda. This is not a problem. The flexibility of our model allows for this type of redundancy. In fact, the ability for a proposition to appear in more than one place is a crucial element in this model's flexibility. To accomplish this we simply re-plot that item in its proper place within the inferential chain in which it is a support element. It is acceptable to have some repetition within the chart, as with Dr. Jones's testimony appearing in two separate lines of argument.

As such, individual investigators will often develop charts with different lines of logic reaching the same conclusion. Neither investigator is necessarily more correct. Nor does one more accurately describe the investigative effort than the other does. It is simply a matter of approaching the same problem from different perspectives.

In fact, as long as the logic that underlies the inferential steps within each segment of the chart is sound, there are a large number of "correct" charts.

SOME TIPS FOR CHARTING SUCCESS

Charting the model is an inherently personal process exhibiting a great deal about the reasoning process of each individual investigator. As we stated above, you can reach a successful conclusion via any number of routes. However, we need to consider a few key notions when charting the investigation—especially where the investigation is complex.

Top Down

First, try to chart from the top down. Although there is no hard-and-fast rule governing the best pattern to use, top-down charting offers some advantages. It has a more intuitive feel because you are thinking from general to specific. You are working from the general statement about who killed Frank, down to the minutest detail such as that the gun was found three feet from the body.

Top-down charting also allows you to plan the chart more efficiently. By using top-down methodology, your physical layout of the chart becomes more apparent. Invariably, you will end up squeezing new probanda into tight spaces in the end, but using the top-down paradigm tends to reduce this inevitability.

Modular Charting

Second, plot the chart in segments. When you use a modular approach to plotting, it makes organization and layout easier. Modularity makes for a less crowded, simpler-looking chart. After all, simplicity and ease of visual reference are our goals.

Finally, as we have seen in our example, charting complex investigative problems often requires duplication of nodes. In our hypothetical, Dr. Jones's autopsy report is valuable to proving more than one proposition. Similarly, a responding officer's observations and crime scene search are necessary to prove some physical aspects of the scene. As such, these items will necessarily appear in more than one area of the chart. It is, therefore, imperative that a common number apply to all instances of that witness's testimony appearing on the chart. In other words, do not switch numbers on the same witness in the middle of the chart. If Dr. Jones appears under number 6 in segment 1 of the chart, she must remain number 6 for the remainder of the chart.

APPLYING THE CHART TO THE INVESTIGATIVE PROCESS

Once the chart is completed, or at least the initial chart is completed, the focus turns to how we synthesize it into the overall investigative process. As a reasoning tool, you can use the chart to help clarify where your case is and where it needs to go.

Using this model, we can test our assumptions about how the events unfolded. For example, in our hypothetical, if we wish to explore the possibility that Frank committed suicide, we could examine the inferences leading up to node 9 in order to test our logic. The self-inflicted gunshot wound and the evidence of a suicide note logically lead us to deduce that Frank may have killed himself. Reasoning from the evidence to the conclusion is common in investigating a crime. Abductively, however, our model can offer us other avenues of assistance—avenues that may help us uncover more clues or eliminate one of several competing hypotheses.

Instead of following the logic from the bottom to the top, we select a proposition or inference and we propose underlying logic to support it. For example, in inference number 9 we propose that Frank's death was suicide. In this mode we ask ourselves, if in fact Frank committed suicide, what we would expect to find. Our example already identifies a fair number of evidentiary facts that support suicide. However, if it did not, we would be forced to think about what should have been found.

One such undiscovered item might be gunshot residue (GSR). Under normal conditions, any person who fires a handgun deposits trace amounts of metals on his or her hands and clothing. The explosive nature of a bullet's discharge causes burning particles to embed themselves in the surrounding soft tissue and cloth. These deposits are often undetectable with the human eye and the shooter is rarely ever cognizant of their existence. Nonetheless, chemical tests can conclusively demonstrate the existence of GSR.[12]

In our hypothetical, if Frank had inflicted his own gunshot wound, logically we should find GSR on his hands, his clothing, or both. Taking this process one step further would also force us to examine and propose an evidentiary proposition concerning Frank's "handedness." Was Frank left- or right-handed?

Depending on the trajectory and entry angle of the bullet, Frank's natural proclivity to one hand or the other could prove significant. If we lack evidence regarding this line of logic, the reasoning process, assisted by our inference model, will urge us into an evidence search and recovery mode. If we find evidence to support this proposition, we chart the outcome as a corroborating factor—or at least as an additional supporting inference.

Conversely, if we fail to find evidence where logic tells us we should, we can chart that either as an alternative proposition (suicide as an alternative explanation for Frank's unnatural death) or as a corroborating factor supporting an alternative proposition.

Either way, we have laid bare the underlying logic of our case, examined what we know critically, and tested the hypothesis. In the process, we have discovered new evidence and moved the case forward drastically.

In the investigative stages of a case, the inference model proves an invaluable tool in directing and organizing the efforts of one or more investigators. Its assistance does not end there. The usefulness of inferential analysis does not end once you have solved the case and made an arrest; it is quite the opposite in fact.

As we have said repeatedly—and the reader is no doubt tired of hearing— the power of graphic inferences lies in their ability to organize large volumes of mixed evidence. As indispensable as this characteristic is during an investigation, it is even more so while documenting the investigation.

As we proceed to Chapter 13, which deals with documenting the investigation, we hope that the value of the inference model as a reference tool, demonstrative exhibit, and debriefing tool will become more obvious. For now, we trust that the reader's curiosity and appetite have been piqued.

CONCLUSION

As we have seen in this chapter, our first task, definition of our language, must necessarily set the tone for the analysis process that follows. Simplicity is the watchword. As we delved deeper into the investigation of inference models as tools for investigators, we asked the reader to bear in mind that the purpose of our newly acquired language is simplification. However, with simplification comes compression. After all, we are trying to construct a model of a complex, real-world event with eight or nine "words." This is equivalent to attempting to paint a sunset in black and white.

Capturing nuance and subtlety will be difficult, but like anything in life, this is a trade-off. We are trading verbosity for clarification of logic. Because our vocabulary is intentionally limited, we must pay careful attention to what we wish to say with our words. A man of limited vocabulary, as long as it includes some key, carefully chosen words, can communicate very effectively, albeit less eloquently, as long as he thinks logically and plans his speech carefully. Clarification of logic depends on how well we can deconstruct our phrases. As we encounter complex causal theories and long chains of inference, we must strive to decompose them into simple statements capable of expression with our limited vocabulary. The process of deconstruction and restatement enables us both to think critically about the legitimacy of our logical propositions and visualize the natural flow of the investigative process. These by-products of the investigative inference model alone make the investment of time worthwhile.

The concept of the key list underpins the implementation process. By carefully constructing a key list comprised of simple propositions and inferences broken down into their most rudimentary elements, the actual charting phase becomes simply a matter of plotting symbols following the defined syntax of our new language. It is the mechanical translation of simple phrases into our new language. The analysis therefore predominantly occurs during the key list preparation phase since the task of preparation necessarily forces the investigator to completely digest the premise of the case and think through exactly what is being said.

SUGGESTED READINGS

Allen, R.J. "The Nature of Juridical Proof." *Cardozo Law Review*, 13 (1991): 373–401.

Allen, R.J., and A. Carriquiry. "Factual Ambiguity and a Theory of Evidence Reconsidered: A Dialogue Between a Statistician and a Law Professor." *Israel Law Review*, 31, nos. 1–3 (1997): 464.

Binder, D., and P. Bergman. *Fact Investigation: From Hypothesis to Proof.* St. Paul, MN: West Publishing, 1999.

Cohen, L.J. *The Introduction to the Philosophy of Induction and Probability*. New York: Oxford University Press, 1989.

Finkelstein, M., and W. Fairly. "A Bayesian Approach to Identification Evidence." *Harvard Law Review*, 83 (1970): 489–517.

Franklin, J. *The Science of Conjecture: Evidence and Probability Before Pascal*. Baltimore, MD: Johns Hopkins University Press, 2001.

Hastie, R., and N. Pennington. "The O.J. Simpson Stories: Behavioral Scientists' Reflections on *The People of the State of California v. Orenthal James Simpson*." *University of Colorado Law Review*, 67 (1996): 957–976.

Huygen, P.E.M. "Use of Bayesian Belief Networks in Legal Reasoning." Presented at *Seventeenth BILETA Annual Conference*. Amsterdam: Computer Law Institute, 2002.

"In Praise of Bayes." Retrieved March 25, 2003, from the University of California, Berkeley, Computer Science Division website, September 30, 2000: www.ai.mit .edu/murphyk/Bayes/economist.html.

Josephson, J., and S.G. Josephson. *Abductive Inference Computation, Philosophy, and Technology*. New York: Cambridge University Press, 1994.

Kadane, J., and D.A. Schum. *A Probabilistic Analysis of the Sacco and Vanzetti Evidence*. New York: John Wiley & Sons, 1996.

Kaye, D.H. "Bayes, Burdens and Base Rates." *International Journal of Evidence and Proof*, 4, no. 4 (2000): 260–267.

Kaye, D.H., and J.J. Koehler. "Can Jurors Understand Probabilistic Evidence?" *Journal of the Royal Statistical Society*, Series A, 154, part 1 (1991): 75–81.

Koehler, J.J. "The Base Rate Fallacy Myth." *Psycoloquy*, 4, article 93.4.49. Retrieved March 13, 2003, from www.monash.edu.au/journals/psycoloquy/volume_4/ psyc.93.4.49.base-rate.1.koehler.

Lempert, R., S. Gross, and J. Liebman. *A Modern Approach to Evidence*. St. Paul, MN: West Publishing, 2000.

Leonhardt, D. "Adding Art to the Rigor of Statistical Science." *New York Times* (electronic version), April 28, 2001.

MacCrimmon, M. "What Is 'Common' About Common Sense?: Cautionary Tales for Travelers Crossing Disciplinary Boundaries." *Cardozo Law Review*, 22 (2001): 1433–1460.

Pennington, N., and R. Hastie. "A Cognitive Theory of Juror Decision Making: The Story Model." *Cardozo Law Review*, 13 (1991): 519–530.

Robertson, B., and G.A. Vignaux. *Interpreting Evidence: Evaluating Forensic Science in the Courtroom*. New York: John Wiley & Sons, 1995.

Saks, M.J., and R.F. Kidd. "Human Information Processing and Adjudication: Trial by Heuristics." *Law and Society Review*, 15 (1980): 123–160.

Schafer, G. *The Art of Causal Conjecture*. Cambridge, MA: MIT Press, 1996.

Schum, D.A. "Alternative Views of Argument Construction from a Mass of Evidence." *Cardozo Law Review*, 22 (2001): 1461–1502.

Schum, D.A. *Evidential Foundations of Probabilistic Reasoning*. New York: John Wiley & Sons, 1994.

Schum, D.A. *The Evidential Foundations of Probabilistic Reasoning*. Evanston, IL: Northwestern University Press, 2001.

Schum, D.A. "Marshaling Thoughts and Evidence During Fact Investigation." *Southern Texas Law Review*, 40 (2001): 401–454.

Schum, D.A. "Species of Abductive Reasoning in Fact Investigation." *Cardozo Law Review*, 22 (2001): 1645–1681.

Schum, D.A., and P. Tillers. "Marshaling Evidence for Adversary Litigation." *Cardozo Law Review*, 12 (1991): 657–704.

Thagard, P. "Probabilistic Networks and Explanatory Coherence." In P. O'Rourke and J. Josephson, eds., *Automated Abduction: Inference to the Best Explanation*. Menlo Park: AAAI Press, 1997.

Tillers, P. "Webs of Things in the Mind: A New Science of Evidence." *Michigan Law Review*, 87 (1989): 1225–1265.

Tillers, P., and D. Schum. "Charting New Territory in Judicial Proof Beyond Wigmore." *Cardozo Law Review*, 9 (1988): 907–950.

Wagenaar, W.A. "The Proper Seat: A Bayesian Discussion of the Position of Expert Witnesses." *Law and Human Behavior*, 12 (1988): 499–510.

Walker, V. R. "Theories of Uncertainty: Explaining the Possible Sources of Error in Inferences." *Cardozo Law Review*, 22 (2001): 1523–1570.

NOTES

1. K. Murphy, "A Brief Introduction to Graphical Models and Bayesian Networks." Retrieved January 1, 2005, from the University of California, Berkeley, Computer Science Division website: www.cs.ubc.ca/~murphyk/Bayes/bintro.html.

2. Despite the name, not all Bayesian networks necessarily adhere strictly to the principles of Bayes's theory. Bayes's theory is a mathematical technique that allows scientists to combine and test data with prior hypotheses and observations to arrive at a new probabilistic prediction of cause and effect. It was first propounded by Thomas Bayes, an eighteenth-century Presbyterian minister.

3. Murphy, "A Brief Introduction to Graphical Models and Bayesian Networks."

4. Unfortunately for users, the decision-making framework for when the paperclip appears is not based upon Bayesian theory, but instead upon a relaxed, non-Bayesian algorithm that allows the paperclip to pop up with more frequency—and concomitant annoyance to most users.

5. "Son of Paperclip," *The Economist* (electronic version), March 22, 2001.

6. See generally, J.H. Wigmore, *The Principles of Judicial Proof: As Given by Logic, Psychology, and General Experience and Illustrated in Judicial Trials* (Littleton, CO: Fred B. Rothman & Co., 1988).

7. T. Anderson and W. Twining, *Analysis of Evidence: How to Do Things with Facts Based on Wigmore's Science of Judicial Proof* (Evanston, IL: Northwestern University Press, 1991), pp. 47–48.

8. Ibid., pp. 50–51.

9. Ibid., pp. 56–57.

10. Ibid., p. 57.

11. We say "arguably" because prosecutions for murder have been known to proceed, more or less successfully, lacking a corpus delicti. In that case, proving Frank's death would be a matter of proving, largely through circumstantial evidence, that he is in fact deceased, which might be difficult to do without a body.

12. S.H. James and J.J. Norby, eds., *Forensic Science: An Introduction to Scientific and Investigative Techniques* (Boca Raton, FL: CRC Press, 2003), pp. 272–273, 344–347.

13

DOCUMENTING AND PRESENTING THE CASE

INTRODUCTION

This chapter will explain how to pull everything together into a coherent report, and then, using the report, how to prepare a concise flexible filing system that you can use and incorporate into the analytical aids previously discussed.

CREATING A SYSTEM

In the last few chapters, we introduced the reader to some powerful organization and analysis tools. Their utility, however, is limited by the investigator's ability to quickly and accurately retrieve the underlying facts and data on which they are based. Without the ability to put your hands on the evidence supporting the conclusion, or to identify the witness who will testify for a particular fact, the models are nothing more than elaborate flowcharts. To be effective, they must be related directly to the process of prosecution. The most efficient model in the world will be useless to us if we have to wade through several stacks of paper on our desk in order to find the specific document necessary to prove a particular proposition. We must have ease of retrieval.

To achieve this ease of retrieval, we must integrate our organizational system with our analysis tools. The organizational system must fulfill some basic requirements. First, the system must have a direct correlation between the underlying data and the models. In other words, we must be able to directly reference each item in our models from our system and vice versa. Second, the system must be easy to implement. With ease of implementation, consistent use of an organization tool becomes more likely. Third, the system must be flexible—it must be able to expand or contract in complexity according to the nature of the case at hand. Rigidity limits the application of the system to only those particular types of cases for which it was originally designed. It is important that the system be just as applicable to drug investigations as it is to financial crime investigations. And fourth, the system must be scalable.

Scalability, much like flexibility, allows our system some degree of portability. What flexibility is to various *types* of cases, scalability is to the size and complexity of cases. Implementation of our system must be as easy for a complicated racketeering scheme as it is for a small employee theft. Keeping these four primary requirements in mind, we have borrowed from the tool-kit of experienced trial lawyers and adapted the casebook system to the investigative arena.

THE CASEBOOK SYSTEM

Like investigation, trial preparation is fluid, often complicated, and always a time-consuming endeavor. For this reason, lawyers have searched for tools in order to minimize the time necessary to prepare for trial and prosecute a case. Behind this search has always been the principle that coherence must be assembled from chaos, and immediate access to coherent information must be maintained. The transition from trial preparation to prosecution must be seamless. The product of this search is the trial book, sometimes referred to as the casebook.[1]

The casebook is nothing more than an organizational tool. It is a central repository for everything that is known about your case. From preliminary reports through final disposition, the casebook catalogues and organizes everything in the life cycle of the investigation. It is both the index to, and the body of work resulting from, your ongoing investigative efforts.

In practice, the trial book[2] is often prepared during the final stage of pre-trial preparation. It is often seen as a way to pull everything together into a coherent unit and organize the evidence in a logical way, given the anticipated needs of a trial. As such, it may be introduced relatively late in the life cycle of the case (that is not to say that the experienced litigator ignores the trial book until the last minute, but simply that the book itself is often compiled late in the case).

From an investigative standpoint, this approach is inefficient. Instead, initiating the casebook system at the time the initial case report is received will organize your investigation into a much more efficient and focused undertaking. Every investigation could benefit from a greater focus at the outset. If nothing else, beginning your casebook preparation at the outset forces you to examine the case closely and helps identify goals early on.

Direct Correlation

As we have stated, the first requirement of our organization system is relatedness. In other words, we must have a direct, easily identifiable link between our model and our information. At the heart of this correlative capacity is a robust cross-reference capability. We index and cross-reference everything in the case in a way that allows immediate and intuitive access to it.

For example, if a witness appears on our inference chart, it is imperative that the casebook contain an entry that both summarizes the witness's involvement and directs the investigator to additional contributions or follow-up requirements. Therefore, we must develop a consistent system of indexing and cross-reference.

Ease of Implementation

From the beginning, the casebook is a filing system. Implementation of the filing system will occur immediately. Once you recognize that your case has the potential to benefit from greater organization, you should establish the casebook as the main source of investigative documentation. Because this method is essentially nothing more than a filing system, implementing it should be fairly straightforward. The most difficult facet of implementation will probably be to discipline oneself constantly to maintain the system.

The casebook system does not contain any complicated strategies, nor does it require a lengthy "learning curve" in order to comprehend the method behind the madness. Instead, it is quite straightforward and requires no more effort than any other system for maintaining a group of files.

Flexibility Flexibility is built into the system. Because it is nothing more than a filing system that is diligently indexed, it may contain any number of different types of evidentiary matter. From a filing and indexing standpoint, there is no material difference between a murder weapon and a canceled check. Both must be indexed, and both qualify as evidentiary items. The only difference is what they tend to prove—or disprove—and what relevance they may have within our investigative framework.

For this reason, the casebook system contains all the flexibility necessary for application to any type case. Whether you are investigating traditional organized crime network activity, or a phantom employee payroll scam, the casebook system will efficiently track and organize all the evidence necessary to plan and complete your investigation.

Scalability The casebook system of investigative organization is not a commercial product. Nor is it the brainchild of any particular individual or group. It is really nothing more than the application of a concept to the process of problem solution. In this case, the problem is concise organization of a large mass of evidence and information. Because we are not advocating a particular product or device, scalability is inherent in the method.

Our system scales from one defendant to 100 simply by expanding the size and method of file maintenance. There are no additional "modules" to buy, nor are there more user licenses to acquire. Simply expand the filing system to include a larger number of participants—suspects, victims, or witnesses.

Because the system is merely the implementation of a concept, it is effective on many scales. The casebook system has been used effectively in situations as simple as an indexed notebook and as complex as several filing cabinets. The difference between the two is in volume, not in additional effort to adapt the system. An inherent beauty in the system is its innate ability to grow with the investigation.[3]

Having said all this, we would like to note that what follows is nothing more than an illustration of the casebook concept. As such, it is no more or less correct than any other filing system that the reader may develop or currently use. In addition, we make no claim as to the originality of the concept, nor do we hope to inspire a revolution in investigative technique.

What we do hope to accomplish is to illustrate how the concept can add greater value to the investigative models that are such valuable tools in the investigative arsenal. We encourage the reader to digest the information, reformulate it, and apply it to whichever situation he or she desires. There is nothing particularly special surrounding our method; it is simply something that the test of time has validated. We hope that the reader will also benefit from the insight that clear organization can provide.

The Components of the System

Typically, a casebook will contain a number of documents and checklists ranging from initial reports to probable-cause affidavits and to-do lists. What you choose to include in your casebook will largely be dictated by the nature of your case, combined with personal preference.

Generally speaking, however, every casebook should contain certain basic elements. First, regardless of the scale of your investigation, every casebook should have an actual book. This consists of a three-ring binder ranging in thickness from 1 inch to 3 or more inches, depending on the size of your investigation. In small investigations, the book might in fact comprise the entirety of the system. In larger, more complicated cases, the book will act as the index and cross-reference system between the reports, charts and models, and evidence, logically linking the three.

The role of the book is to coordinate those three elements. The casebook, then, will have a many-to-many relationship (to borrow from relational database parlance) between the inference chart and the supporting evidentiary material. In other words, each piece of evidence will point to an entry in the book, which will in turn point to each individual item of proof in the allegation.

Exhibit 13.1 illustrates the relational quality between the elements of the allegation, the book, and the supporting evidentiary documents. As you can see, a relationship also exists between the underlying documentation, the book, and the elements of proof in the allegation. In other words, given a specific item of evidentiary support, by using the book it should be possible to locate the proposition it supports in the allegation. The existence of this two-way relationship gives the casebook system its robustness. The book is composed of three sections: administrative, investigative, and evidentiary.

The Administrative Section The administrative section contains important documentation about the case itself, such as the underlying legal premise on which the case is based. If the investigation is based on an allegation of racketeering, a restatement of the racketeering law and the elements underlying it

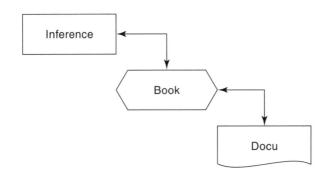

EXHIBIT 13.1   Relational Quality between Inference Model, Book, and Documentation

must be made. By restating the crime alleged in terms of specific elements relative to the actual facts of your case, you can ground the investigation in the reality of the situation. For example, our initial report accuses JoAnn of first-degree murder in the death of Frank. In most jurisdictions, the essential elements of criminal homicide are act, intent, concurrence, causation, and harm. Therefore, we must prove that JoAnn committed a voluntary act (*actus reus*), which was coupled with the criminal intent or purpose of killing Frank (*mens rea* and concurrence), and that her act was both the legal and factual cause of Frank's death (causation), and there was the resulting harm. Additionally, since the state is alleging first-degree murder, they must prove the existence the attendant circumstances or premeditation.[4] Your casebook should reflect a restatement of these elements in relation to our particular case.

Eventually, this statement, to the extent that your investigation supports it, will become the basis for the probable-cause affidavit and subsequent charges.

The administrative section should also contain a synopsis of the facts being alleged in the original complaint. The synopsis should be written based solely on what is being alleged, not on what you believe you can prove. If it were done the other way around, there would be a danger that tunnel vision might occur. In other words, if you limit the synopsis of the facts to what seems easily provable at the time, you will begin to foreclose lines of inquiry and limit your creativity with regard to alternative explanations of factual events.

If there is no allegation, perhaps this case is self-initiated based on suspicion of wrongdoing you observed; then create a synopsis of the facts based on what you believe has occurred. You should be mindful that narrowing the field of inquiry too quickly might result in a similarly over-narrow view of the facts, precluding the ability to quickly recognize alternative explanations. In short, this section of the casebook should contain basic documentation of an administrative nature.

The Investigative Section   The investigative section should contain all paperwork that pertains directly to the investigation. Items such as the original initiating report, all supplemental reports, and all investigative narratives should be filed in this section.

This section of the book should also contain a master chronology, which, as noted earlier, is invaluable in clarifying the chain of events under investigation. The chronology is an evolving document that expands as new facts are added and contracts as old facts are eliminated. It is always in flux, and it helps to anchor the event in a reference system that is familiar to us.

A detailed list of witnesses will appear in this section. With this portion of the section we begin to realize the full power of the casebook system. Each witness is assigned a unique identifying number, such as W1, and gets his or her own individually tabbed section. Included behind each tab should be the full identification of the witness, including address, phone number, and the full contact information that might be necessary in order to locate the witness quickly. It might also be helpful to include a photograph of the witness, especially in the event the witness suddenly becomes "difficult to locate," and canvassing needs to begin.

Then each witness's anticipated testimony should be summarized and included with that witness's entry. This facilitates recall of what each witness can bring to the case. Similarly, an exact listing of each piece of evidence or proposition to which the witness will testify is kept. For example, our medical examiner in the JoAnn and Frank hypothetical, Dr. Jones, would be listed as witness W1, with an attendant summary of her involvement. Following that summary, we would compile a list of propositions that Dr. Jones will be responsible for substantiating. Each entry in this fact list will correspond to an entry on our key list (and subsequently on our inference model).

If the witness provides physical evidence, such as a document or other tangible item, that item will be listed here in the witness section, and you will file the item in the evidence section of the casebook. (A detailed explanation of how the evidence section is organized follows this section.)

Finally, any unfavorable information about this witness must be included. Information that reflects on the witness's credibility such as prior arrests, previous misconduct, or perhaps inducements to testify is important. By listing this information here, the investigator can assess the potential weight that the witness's testimony can be expected to have on the jury in light of potential defense impeachment.

Following the witness portion of the investigative section is a serialized listing of all the evidence collected to this point, with a reference to its location within the inference model. For example, we will list the suicide note in the hypothetical with a corresponding reference to the inference chart. In addition, this item of evidence will have a reference to which witness will authenticate and testify regarding its importance. In this case, the responding officer who discovered the note would testify to its discovery; therefore, his corresponding witness number would appear in the evidence list next to the note.

Other witnesses, however, may need to testify regarding this item. Crime lab technicians tested the blood, and handwriting experts analyzed the signature. Although each of those witnesses would have individual documents from which they would testify, they will also testify to the note itself. Therefore, each of these witnesses will also be listed adjacent to the evidentiary item.

By using these three portions of the investigative section, the investigator can move seamlessly from model to witness to evidence and back without losing his mind. If we want to understand a proposition in our allegation better, we simply look it up in our allegation section and find out what it stands for, who provided us with the information, and what physical evidence supports it. From here, we can delve further into the system by looking up the witness using the witness number and finding out the entirety of the witness's testimony and all pertinent facts surrounding his involvement.[5]

Evidentiary Section The last section of the book, the evidentiary section, can take on a number of forms. For smaller cases, it is possible that nothing more than photocopies of papers will comprise the entirety of the section. Conversely, in larger cases, it is possible that this section of the book will itself be an index to folders within a file box or filing cabinet.

As evidence is collected, it must be assigned a unique number within the case. Whether the item is a document or a gun, it is imperative that we be able to discretely reference each item by a unique number.

There are probably as many acceptable ways of identifying evidentiary items as there are investigators. Whatever system you choose, it may be helpful to include within the numbering system some way of immediately recognizing the tangible quality of the evidence. For example, it could be helpful, from an organizational standpoint, to be able to immediately recognize that the particular item in question is a piece of narcotics evidence as opposed to a document. With that in mind, an alpha character followed by a serial number may be helpful. For example, the alpha character *D* could be used to designate all documentary evidence such as bank records or other documents. A *W* might be used to preface the serial number for all weapons, and so forth. The specificity with which you assign prefixes to the serial number is entirely within your discretion, provided you maintain both consistency and uniqueness.

Regardless of the method you employ to collect evidence, it is practically worthless unless you can quickly locate it when you need to. This is where the casebook system offers assistance. You identify each item of evidence by serial number. As such, it is filed either in the pages of our casebook or in our supplemental filing system (file boxes or filing cabinet) in either numerical or alphanumerical order, depending on the labeling system you chose.

As you proceed through the investigative section of the casebook, locating discrete items of evidence instantly is a simple task. If you examine a node on the inference model or allegation list that points you to a proposition in the key list, the key list will point you to the serial number of the evidentiary item. Working in reverse order, from evidentiary item to casebook, the serial number of the item corresponds to an entry in the investigative section of the casebook. This entry in turn corresponds to both a witness number/name and key list proposition or allegation number. As you can see, working from either end of the system is a simple task because of its robust cross-reference capability.

Incorporating Your Numbering System into the Casebook

Careful planning and strong organization are important to a successful case conclusion. In the absence of either one, your result will be less than you had hoped. In keeping with this mantra, we have exposed the reader to some powerful concepts for creating an organizational strategy. As we said earlier, what we have introduced and explained are not a series of silver bullets guaranteed to create order from chaos. Instead, they are just what we have purported them to be—concepts. The key ingredient in all the ideas presented here is a reference system and flexibility. Without flexibility you are faced with creating a new system each time the fact pattern you encounter changes slightly from the scenario for which the organizational scheme was designed. Creation is a slow process that is to be avoided unless absolutely necessary. Adaptation is a much better path.

With that in mind, we urge you to think about the ideas that we have offered. You are welcome to borrow, discard, or massage any of them into what will be effective for your particular needs. You may use all, some, or none and we encourage you to think critically about what their strengths are and, more importantly, what their limitations are. By understanding the limitations of the systems, you can navigate around them or mitigate them in the planning stages of your investigation.

At some point between the initiation of the case, and the conclusion of the prosecution, you will have to present your information. Whether the presentation is to a supervisor, a client, a prosecutor, or ultimately, the jury, it will usually take two forms—written and oral.

Written reports will often precede you. Whether you are filing a case, sending an interim update to a supervisor, or briefing a client they will often have the chance to read your written report before you get the chance to explain it. For that reason, your reports must be up to the task. In the next section, we will offer some tips on how to ensure the reporting aspect of your job is successful.

REPORT WRITING

The task of report writing, especially in the area of investigations, is largely controlled by departmental or client policy. While personal preference does play a role, client and superiors' expectations are often more important.

Our experience shows that there are two schools of thought regarding report writing. The first, which we shall refer to as the minimalist school, favors an austere approach advocating sparse detail and brevity—all this, it is supposed, in the name of fewer attack points for the lawyers.

The second approach, which we refer to as the kitchen-sink approach, comes at the problem from the opposite angle; here one should include every possible detail, leaving out nothing. The reasoning behind this approach is obviously that fading memories require significant bolstering. Which approach is most reasonable? The truth, as usual, probably lies somewhere in between.

As a practical matter, an investigative report should include as much significant detail as necessary to accurately document the investigator's actions without being overly burdensome. How much is too much? That is a difficult question to answer—especially in the abstract. It is imperative that your investigation report achieve its goal. It must enable third parties to discern what actions have been taken in a case, and it must help in jogging your memory at some future point in time. Often, this future point in time could be years later. After many years of conducting investigations, the facts of dozens of cases often blend in your mind to form a montage of disjointed images. Culling from that montage the facts during strenuous cross-examination could be a difficult task, leaving you looking rather foolish on the stand.

As for the minimalist school of report writing, we think it treads dangerously close to malpractice (if such a thing existed in the investigative context). As the adherents are quick to point out, when there are fewer details in a report a defense attorney will have fewer details to attack during cross-examination. Although the truth of this statement is indisputable, the logic behind it is fallible.

First, having the benefit of years of trial testimony and legal education, we can assure the reader that a sufficiently skilled defense attorney can effectively cross-examine an investigator regardless of the detail contained in the report. Second, the lack of detail in the report hinders, not helps, the investigator at trial time.

As we stated earlier, trials often occur months, or perhaps years, after the investigative action took place. Given the fact that most investigators have difficulty recalling with total accuracy what they had for breakfast two weeks ago, recalling the minutiae of a criminal investigation after years of intervening cases is an exercise in futility rife with inaccuracy. This inaccuracy will come across during testimony as either deception or ineptitude, qualities neither of which juries find particularly endearing in a witness. At best you will appear to be a buffoon, at worst a liar.

We recommend, as you contemplate how detailed you wish to make your report, that you consider two things. First, and foremost, consider the purpose of your job in the big picture. Your task, whether you are a criminal investigator or a civil investigator, is to discover the truth. Sometimes, this duty becomes obscured by the rhetoric of the pursuit of the bad guys. Whether obscured or not, this is job one. Therefore, accuracy should be the goal of every investigative report—regardless of where the facts point you.

Whether your investigation points you in the direction you anticipate (i.e., the suspect is guilty) or in a different direction altogether, the report should reflect exactly what your inquiry revealed. This ensures that, ultimately, the truth regarding the matter will be known.

Second, an often-overlooked caveat for investigators is "do your job." In other words, fulfill your duty in an objective, professional, and thorough manner and you will have nothing major to worry about. Our justice system does not expect absolute perfection. If it did, we would all be in trouble. It expects reasonable perfection. Reasonable perfection sounds like an oxymoron. It is not. It is simply another way of saying that we humans are what we are. We all suffer from the human condition and mistakes are inevitable. Errors and omissions will occur and memories will fail us. It is a fact of life, and defense attorneys will be quick to point out our failings.

In fact, the whole premise behind the adversarial justice system is the notion that defense attorneys must seize upon mistakes and attempt to hammer holes in the small chinks that reveal themselves in the armor of our case. The result, at least in theory, is that investigators should strive to minimize the glaring errors and obvious mistakes that tend to insinuate themselves into any investigation. Defense attorneys keep us on our toes—they force us to do our jobs.

In truth, it is not the investigator's admission of minor mistakes that loses cases; rather, cases are lost when the defense attorney is able to successfully attack the credibility and veracity of the witness. Nothing is more effective in losing a case than catching an investigator in a fabrication. Whether it's an intentional fabrication resulting from some malicious purpose, or an innocent fabrication that is the result of a faulty memory coupled with shoddy reporting, witness fabrication—especially by professional witnesses like investigators—instantly destroys the credibility of the entire prosecution.

A habit of scanty reporting leads an investigator to rely too heavily on fragile recall. These powers will inevitably fail, and when they do, human nature urges us to "fill in the blanks." Sometimes the answer is accurate, but more often it is not. Avoid placing yourself in this situation by recording your actions accurately and completely.

So, in sum, the clash between Spartan and lavish reporting may be answered by following these two principles. (1) As an investigator, do your job to the best of your ability according to standard accepted procedure and with no shortcuts; and (2) report your investigative activities as accurately as possible, regardless of where the findings lead—truth is the objective, not conviction of the suspect.

Within that framework, you should construct the narrative of your investigative report in chronological order, detailing the events of your investigation as they unfold. An investigative report is different from a fact narrative, in that it tells a story. Not just a story of the event, instead it tells the story of your involvement as an investigator.

In addition to your written report, someone will probably ask you to provide an oral summation, or perhaps even sworn testimony about your involvement. While testifying in open court can be intimidating, there are certain things that you can do to help reduce the inevitable stress.

TESTIFYING AS A FINANCIAL EXPERT

Although conducting the investigation is a substantial task in and of itself, it is only part of your responsibility as an investigator. In addition, you must testify to your findings. In many cases, your role as witness will require substantially less time commitment than your role as investigator. In fact, the more time and effort you have expended on creating a strong case, the smaller the probability is that you will end up in court at all.

If you do your job as an investigator well, the opposing side will have a much greater incentive to avoid the uncertainty of litigation altogether and will be inclined to accept, or offer, a suitable settlement. Whether this settlement is in the form of a monetary award or a plea bargain, the result is the same—pre-trial intervention.

From a litigation perspective, the lawyer's job is ultimately to avoid trial. As paradoxical as this might sound in light of customary legal-fee structures, it is in reality the ultimate goal. The reason for this is simple. Regardless of the perceived strength of a case, all lawyers familiar with litigation recognize that, once the case enters the courtroom, the question of win-lose often becomes a game of chance. It was Louis Pasteur who said, "Chance favors the prepared mind." As true as this may be in theory, in practice the element of chance often dictates taking a more predictable course of action.[6]

Largely uncontrollable variables such as individual juror predisposition, judicial bias, and even the skill and acumen of opposing counsel make all trips before the bar of justice a veritable crapshoot. Therefore, given the opportunity to avoid the uncertainty of trial—regardless of personal conviction about the "righteousness of their cause"—most attorneys will opt for pre-trial settlement. The adage about the bird-in-the-hand versus the two-in-the-bush rings true in this context as well.

As an investigator, your role in avoiding the cost and uncertainty of trial cannot be overestimated. After all, it is largely based on your efforts that the attorneys will make their decisions regarding fight or flight. Assuming that you have done a thorough job during the investigation, it is imperative that you follow through and finish strong. Finishing strong includes being a prepared and effective witness.

In this section, we hope to offer some clarification regarding your role as a witness, both expert and otherwise, that will help you, as investigator, prepare for the "big show." In addition, we hope to offer you some tips that you can incorporate into your investigative routine that will make your role as a witness easier.

There are essentially two species of witnesses: the expert and the lay witness. Legally, the distinction between expert and lay witness makes a crucial difference in the role that each may play. Depending on the complexity of your case and the nature of the financial crime, you may find yourself serving as both expert and lay witness. The most significant difference between the two is the nature of the testimony each may render. Generally, a witness's testimony is limited to matters on which he possesses personal knowledge.[7] Generally, people may only testify to what they have deduced based on use of their five senses—what they have witnessed or personally observed. For example, a lay witness would be quite well qualified—assuming she is competent—to testify to the description of a vehicle or the color of the defendant's shirt. The court would not allow her to testify to the defendant's mental state or to give her opinion about his motivation.[8]

By contrast, expert witnesses may testify to matters outside their personal observation. They may testify to their opinion regarding certain matters that will help the jury determine the ultimate fact in issue. The subject matter to which they may testify is limited to the area in which they have some superior skill, education, or ability. For example, a certified public accountant (CPA) would likely be qualified, based on her education and experience, to testify regarding auditing methods that comprise the Generally Accepted Auditing Standards (GAAS). But it is not likely that she would be qualified to testify regarding the mental state of the defendant at the time he made entries into the accounting records.

The role of the lay witness is generally beyond the scope of this book (although a lay witness might learn a lot from reading it).

The Role of the Professional Witness Generally

Neutrality Primarily, the professional witness must testify from a position of neutrality. It is not your job to influence the jury through emotion: Rather, it is your job to influence the jury through facts. Victims and other eyewitnesses may be used strategically to play upon the heartstrings of the jury. You, however, must appear as a disinterested reporter of facts and results.[9] Just as you are responsible for objectivity and truthfulness during the investigation phase, you also have a duty to report, accurately and faithfully, your findings without any personal biases you may have concerning the case at hand.

This task may in fact be more difficult than it sounds. As the person who has become intimately familiar with every detail of the case, it is difficult to remain objective and report your conclusions regarding the guilt or innocence of the defendant in a detached and professional manner. Nonetheless, as hard as it may be, the integrity of the justice system requires it—your own personal integrity requires it as well. How can you accomplish this difficult task? At the risk of oversimplifying, we would like you to internalize one thing above all else: Do not make the outcome of the case personal.

As veterans of both the investigative and testimonial trenches, we recognize that some cases will make this task nearly impossible. After all, there are just some cases where justice must be done, and the path to justice is clear. Admittedly, in financial crime cases these occasions may be rare. The painfully disfigured victims, the conspicuously absent loved ones, and the heinously evil villains are often only present in the more "glamorous") crimes or personal injury torts. However, there will be occasions when you become personally involved during your investigation. Notwithstanding your burning desire to see the defendant behind bars (or lighten his wallet as the case may be), visibly personal concern over the outcome will in the long run damage both your reputation and your ability to offer effective testimony. Leave the zealous advocacy to the attorneys.

Education Disinterested neutrality does not necessarily mean disinterested monotony. Financial crime evidence often tends to be highly technical and somewhat complicated. Add to this the fact that debits and credits are not nearly as "sexy" as eyewitness testimony about a murder, and you have a recipe for boredom. Be that as it may, it is your job, as a professional witness in financial cases, to capture the attention of the jury. If you do not, your message, and probably your case as well, will be lost.

Therefore, it is important to approach your role as a professional witness in financially focused cases as that of a teacher. As such, you must educate the jury about not only the facts of the case, but often the underlying principles behind the investigative analysis. Juries are invariably an admixture of laypersons with varying experiences and skill levels in terms of financial matters. It is not only possible, but also likely, that the level of financial knowledge among the jurors will range from bookkeepers and accountants to those among us who can barely balance a checkbook. For this reason, as you approach your job of testifying, you should be constantly aware of the diversity of your audience.

As you prepare and deliver your presentation to the jurors, keep in mind the characteristics of most successful teachers. Keeping those characteristics in mind, you will find not only that your message is well received, but also that you will establish a rapport with your audience. Aside from the practical aspect of preventing boredom and keeping their attention, rapport building offers you the chance to subliminally develop credibility. And, as we all know, credibility is the key to persuasive testimony.

Communication As we have said, learning is the product of a teacher's knowledge of the subject matter combined with his ability to communicate his message.

Knowledge can be broken down further into two additional components: subject matter knowledge and practical application. You will gain subject matter knowledge by studying the principles and concepts in this text as well as further exploration on your own. Practical application, however, is entirely dependent on your efforts as an investigator. We can offer you a solid foundation in both the principles of accounting as they apply to financial crime investigation and some techniques for effectively pursuing such investigations. We cannot give you facility in your individual case.

Practical application is entirely about knowing your individual case. Doctorate-level knowledge of accounting will not help you testify if you do not have a working knowledge of the facts of your case. For that reason, preparation is the key to effectively educating the jury. You must know your case inside and out. Failure to know the intimate details will end up costing you credibility in front of the jury and will ultimately detract from your message. Assuming that you have developed both subject matter knowledge and practical knowledge about the case, we will move on to how you communicate that knowledge to the jury.

An effective professional witness is in reality very similar to a professional educator—both must convey an often complicated and dull subject to a somewhat captive audience. In order to achieve this goal, both must have knowledge of their subject as well as the capacity to translate this subject matter knowledge into learning. As a professional witness, you may find it helpful to recall an educator with whom you are familiar that possesses both traits. If you can visualize how this model of education would convey the subject about which you are speaking, perhaps the process of jury education will become more natural.

The Specific Role of the Financial Expert

Generally financial experts play two roles in the litigation process. You may find yourself fulfilling one or both of these roles depending on the individual case with which you are involved. These roles are the testimonial and nontestimonial expert.

The expert witness plays an important role in many stages of the litigation process. It is helpful when thinking about the role of the expert to view the lawyers and everyone who assists them as members of a litigation team. As the captain of the team, the lawyer generally plans and carries out the offensive (or defensive) strategy in order to reach the goal. But, as with any team, his job is made easier by recruiting other individuals that possess skills in areas of team weakness. No lawyer can be expected to be an expert in all areas. In fact, the only area in which a lawyer may be expected to possess superior knowledge or skill is in the area of litigation. For all other areas, the lawyer must call on outside experts for assistance.

The assistance can come in many forms, the most visible being that of a trial witness. However, the expert can play a number of other, nontestimonial roles during the course of a complex case.

The Role of the Nontestimonial Expert

CASE EVALUATION AND STRATEGY Prior to filing the actual complaint, it may be beneficial for the attorney to consult with an expert in the field to assess both the potential for success and the nature of the complaint.[10] Even though the lawyer is the expert in case strategy, his knowledge of the field in which the case falls may limit his ability to plan the course of litigation. An expert's valuable experience in a specialized field such as accounting and fraud can help the lawyer overcome these limitations. Experts assist the lawyer in predicting outcomes, shaping complaints, and testing hypotheses about causation. In addition, the expert's specialized skills can aid in selecting additional helpful witnesses.[11]

Even though an expert is qualified in a particular area, she may not be qualified within a subspecialty of that area. For example, a financial expert in the area of business loss valuation may not necessarily be competent in the area of stock manipulations or Securities and Exchange Commission (SEC) regulations. As a member of a "fraternity of experts," you will be able to guide the lawyer in the process of selecting additional witnesses for the litigation team and preparing other expert witnesses for trial.

EDUCATION Lawyers need to know a little bit about everything, but the depth of their knowledge in specific technical areas is usually limited. Often, they can discover a great deal about a case, or the potential for a case, by consulting with an expert in a tutorial capacity. In this capacity, the expert witness is still an educator. But instead of educating the jury, she is educating the attorney. The expert witness can provide the attorney with a strong working knowledge about the subject matter of the case. In the financial case, lawyers often consult with experts regarding items such as the standard of care for accountants, whether the tenets of generally accepted accounting practice (GAAP) have been followed, and other specific technical issues in the area of finance.

EXHIBITS When dealing with complicated issues or large amounts of evidence, it may be helpful to create demonstrative exhibits. These exhibits are merely visual aids that the lawyer can use to help witnesses educate the jury about their version of the case. Graphic summaries of transactions, or visual representations of the flow of money, help the jury grasp the often-convoluted processes or schemes used by the defendant to conceal a theft. The expert can be of great assistance in preparing these exhibits. Regardless of who will be using them to testify, the expert can facilitate their creation by lending her specialized knowledge of the subject matter.

Generally, as a nontestimonial expert, a lawyer will call on you to do some of the following:

- Prepare interrogatories.
- Identify witnesses and help in preparation of witness lists.
- Help identify Brady and Jencks material.[12]
- Help prepare witnesses.

- Help formulate and revise questions/prepare strategy for attack of opposing witness.
- Create/prepare demonstrative exhibits.

The Role of the Testimonial Expert As we intimated earlier, the role of testimonial expert is often the most visible and so is probably the one most people are familiar with. When lawyers speak of a case being "a battle of the experts," they are referring to the fact that both parties will present expert testimony of opposing opinion regarding a pivotal aspect of the case. Some battles focus on causation issues, while others might center solely on damage issues. Either way, a battle of the experts boils down to which party's expert offers the more compelling explanation of the facts. Although we do not wish to downplay the importance of expert assistance in the preparatory area, we will be focusing for the remainder of this chapter on your role as a testimonial expert—a role that may be broken down into the subcategories of pre-trial testimony and trial testimony.

PRE-TRIAL In every trial, the pre-trial process proceeds through what is referred to as a discovery phase—the part of the case where both sides endeavor to learn as much about the opponent's case as possible. To the layperson, the process of discovery is both confusing and a bit intimidating. It is confusing in the sense that providing your opponent with your game plan ahead of time seems to run counter to the notion of adversarial combat. It is intimidating in the sense that many times the opposition uses the discovery process to probe for weaknesses and gauge the most likely spot for an attack. This probing maneuver is usually aggressive and often seems overbearing to the uninitiated witness.

As an expert witness, it is important that you understand the need for, and the reasons behind, the process. If you understand it, you may be less intimidated, and as a result you will be a more confident and effective witness. Hopefully, we can dispel any concerns you may have regarding your role and participation in the discovery process.

Even though the trial process is basically an adversarial one, the underlying goal is to determine the truth. Therefore, our system of dispute resolution tries to make the battle as even as possible. Our rules are in place to try and ensure that the winner is the winner because he made the best case for his version of the truth—not because he was better at keeping his battle plan a secret. If it were any other way, the attorney more practiced in the art of surprise and ambush would usually win whether or not his case was stronger. For the most part, this is what our modern rules of pre-trial discovery seek to reach. Full disclosure by each side is believed to promote fairness of adjudication on the merits.[13]

As for the intimidating nature of the discovery process, this is an adversarial system. By definition, one side must win by weakening the opponent. Discovery—especially deposition practice—is usually the first shot at locating weaknesses and gauging an opponent's overall strategy. Once a weakness has been found, resources can be marshaled to exploit it. Because the lawyer is probing for weakness, the deposition often becomes a very stressful event. This is essentially a chance for opposing counsel to test your mettle and find out if you will be a viable target while on the stand.[14]

Ultimately, the deposition process is a discovery process. Consequently, the scope of the questions and the manner in which the lawyer may ask them are wildly different from what is seen in the courtroom. There are very few questions that an opposing lawyer cannot ask in the deposition. Even if certain evidence is irrelevant to trial, witnesses in deposition must answer them.[15] This greatly expands the scope of the deposition.

This is not to say that a deposition is a chaotic situation; it is not. In fact, all state courts and the federal courts have very specific rules governing allowable conduct in the discovery process. These rules cover such issues as when opposing counsel must produce information about their case, what must be produced, when and by whom depositions may be taken—and retaken in some cases—and penalties for slow or uncooperative behavior. Although each state's rules of procedure differ slightly, most are patterned after the Federal Rules of Civil Procedure.

There are also rules governing pre-trial discovery in the criminal system. Although they are similar and seek to achieve the same goal, the different nature of the criminal process makes discovery rules in that area slightly different from those in the civil arena.

Once the pre-trial discovery process concludes and the lawyers have made the decision to go to trial, your role as the testimonial expert shifts to center stage. However, before you can even get to the witness stand, you must pass a few tests.

You must overcome two hurdles when trying to qualify as a testimonial expert; the first centers on the actual field in which the expert wishes to qualify, and the second involves the individual qualifications of the witness.

TRIAL: QUALIFYING AS AN EXPERT WITNESS

Field Qualification In overcoming the first hurdle, an expert witness may face an attack on the field in which she practices. These challenges to the legitimacy of the field of study, called Daubert challenges after the Supreme Court decision of *Daubert v. Merrill Dow Pharmaceuticals, Inc.*, 509 U.S. 579 (1993),[16] scrutinize the underlying basis for the scientific principles on which the expert's opinion is based. Daubert challenges are often more difficult than individual qualification. They are an attack on the credibility of the field in which the expert intends to testify. Some have called it a battle between real science and junk science, but the focus is usually on the methods and procedures used in the particular field of endeavor.[17]

Although rules 702 and 703 of the Federal Rules of Evidence do not explicitly require that the field of endeavor fall within a traditional scientific or technical venue, it is easier to qualify as an expert in those fields (provided the individual qualifications are attained).[18] For example, courts universally accept medicine, psychology, and engineering as fields of endeavor from which you can testify as an expert testimony. Conversely, other areas, or highly specialized areas within each recognized area, are open for challenges that are more vigorous. Opposing counsel will often strongly attack areas such as "new age" medicine and other holistic forms of treatment through the mechanisms of Daubert because of their less conventional origin and methodologies.[19]

In general, since the rendition of the Supreme Court's decision in Daubert, the test for admissibility under Rule 702 focuses on the concept of "scientific knowledge." Although the Court refused to elucidate a definitive checklist or test, it did discuss several factors it considered relevant to determining when an area of endeavor was reliable enough to warrant introduction into evidence. The Court intimated that the following factors were pertinent to the inquiry:

- Whether the theories and techniques employed have been tested
- Whether the theories have been subjected to peer review and publication
- Whether the techniques employed have a known error rate
- Whether they are subject to standards governing their application
- Whether the theories and techniques enjoy widespread acceptance

Further, the Court made it clear that, far from a checklist, the procedure must be a flexible one that focuses "solely" on principles and methodology, not on the conclusions that are generated.[20]

This definition clearly narrows the field from which expert testimony may derive. However, this should not prove cumbersome for the expert in the area of financial crimes unless the techniques you employ are so far outside the scope of GAAP or GAAS that they are not within the taxonomy of the science.

For a substantial period following Daubert, there was some confusion regarding its application.[21] Some practitioners believed that the application of the Supreme Court's Daubert opinion was limited to decidedly scientific pursuits such as medicine or engineering or accounting, while others argued that all expert testimony was subject to the Daubert challenge.

The Court finally answered this question in 1999. In *Kumho Tire Co v. Carmichael* 526 U.S. 137 (1999), the Supreme Court examined the question of whether a tire expert who based his opinion solely on technical skill and experience, not scientific methodology, was subject to the Daubert challenge.[22]

The Eleventh Circuit ruled that the Supreme Court's holding applied only to scientific principles and not to other specialized knowledge. However, the Supreme Court granted certiorari and held that Daubert is a doctrine of flexibility that applies to assist the trial court in its gatekeeping function of admitting only relevant evidence in cases of both scientific and technical knowledge as well as areas of other specialized knowledge. Finally, the Supreme Court's position was clear—all areas of specialized knowledge are subject to attack under the Daubert principles.[23]

As we stated, for the expert witness seeking to testify in conventional areas in the financial crime arena, Daubert should be little inconvenience. However, it is important that you remain aware of the burdens that the attorney for whom you work will face when attempting to get you onto the stand. These considerations should help guide your choice of methods and procedures as you go about the task of evaluating or investigating the case at hand. If they do not, your efforts may never see the inside of a courtroom.

After surmounting the challenge of field qualification, you must then turn your attention to the process of establishing your individual expert qualification within that field.

Individual Qualification A witness may qualify as an expert in a particular field when her knowledge, skill, experience, training, or education, or a combination thereof gives her special knowledge above and beyond that possessed by ordinary members of the public.[24] There are no fixed rules regulating how much or what type of experience and education qualifies a witness as an expert. Judges will evaluate each individual case on its own merits, and make the determination of whether the witness qualifies as an expert.[25] Usually, expert qualification is based on one or more of the following criteria:

- Advanced education: bachelor's, master's, or doctorate degree
- Advanced independent study, including documentation of books read, research conducted, and journals read
- Extensive personal experience such as derived from years in a specialized field like:
  - Law enforcement
  - Fire science
- Authorship in refereed or respected books and journals
- Recognition within a particular industry
- Professional certification or designation:
  - CPA
  - CFE[26]

As an expert, or potential expert witness, it is incumbent upon you to maintain an accurate and thorough resume. Your resume should reflect both professional accomplishments and independent learning pursuits in the area for which you wish to be qualified. In addition, you must maintain both a listing and a copy of all articles, books, and papers that you have written, both published and unpublished. In particular, you should also remain aware of any papers or articles that you have written that might advocate a position adverse to that which you anticipate rendering in court.[27]

It is imperative that you maintain currency in all areas related to your area of expertise. You can accomplish this by frequently reading the most relevant journals and scholarly publications in your field. For the financial witness, this includes such publications as *The Journal of Forensic Accounting, The CPA Journal, Practical Accountant, The Journal of Accounting, The Journal of Accountancy,* and many others. Maintaining currency will help to ensure that your opinion (once you are qualified to render it) is not easily discredited by more current research in the field. Not only is testifying to outdated information a serious blow to credibility, but it is a personally embarrassing situation.

The Art of Testifying

Experts often present highly technical information to nontechnical individuals. It is your job, besides testifying truthfully, to help the attorney explain things to the jurors and the judge.

General Points   There is an overabundance of literature dedicated to the topic of "how to testify," so we will not add to the glut of information by adding our own list of the "top ten" keys to testifying. In addition, we will not overburden the reader any more than necessary with discussions of how to behave or how not to react. More eloquent texts are currently available that do far more justice to that area of discussion than we could hope to in a single chapter.

Instead, we would like to offer a set of principles as guidance. These principles fall generally into three categories—demeanor, appearance, and performance—and are really what amounts to common sense. Moreover, as most of us have discovered through years of real-life experiences, common sense is anything but. That is why we will concentrate on effective witness testimony.

DEMEANOR   Demeanor refers to how you relate to the jury. Along with aspects such as presenting a professional approach and conveying a sense of an appropriate seriousness regarding the situation, demeanor includes treating the jury with respect.

Although your education and experience in the subject matter is likely superior to that of the jury, it is imperative that you avoid conveying a sense of superiority. This advice may sound very basic, but it is startling how easily professional witnesses forget to treat the jury as equals. If you talk down to the jury, or treat them as though the concepts that you are discussing are well beyond their comprehension, you risk alienating them. No one likes to feel alienated, and doing so will prevent you from being as effective a witness as you have the potential to be.

Even though the subject you are discussing, whether it is net worth analysis or link matrix analysis, may be somewhat complex, the concepts are obviously of great importance to the success of your case. Therefore, it is imperative that you temper your explanations with respect. You must strike a balance between talking down to the jury and talking over their heads. Such a balance is neither easy to find nor always in the same place. As you move through your career, again, try and keep in mind the definition of the educator who was most influential in your life and strive to filter your explanations through that prism.

APPEARANCE Appearance is an area where once again common sense is the key. Dressing appropriately is such a simple goal, yet many professional witnesses misapprehend the bigger purpose behind this rule. Continuing the comparison of your role as a professional witness with that of an educator, we see that the underlying importance of appearance once again makes sense.

Persuasive authority derives not only from explicit badges of authority but from conduct that implies authority. This is evidenced in the admonition that police officer witnesses should always wear their uniform during court appearances. For nonuniformed officers and those professional witnesses in the private sector, the choice of attire is often more complex.

Generally speaking, conservative business attire is appropriate. A conservative suit with a single-colored shirt, set off with a simple-print tie, should be standard issue in any professional witness's clothing arsenal. Choices in gray, blue, and black all work well for professional witnesses in the financial arena. Either single-breasted or double-breasted, given the individual's build, is a fine choice, as are choices between two- or three-button jackets. At the bare minimum, a professional witness should wear a conservative blazer.

You should avoid loud shirts with wild or busy prints. Regardless of your own personal fashion sense, these shirts tend to be distracting and mar the overall impression made by the witness.

Your choice of tie is often a much more personal one. Here, unlike the suit, there is probably a little more room for leeway, but do not overdo it. Ties commonly referred to as "power ties"—usually red, burgundy, or diagonally striped red and blue—are good choices, as are ties with a simple design or conservative polka dots.

Lest you mistake our point here, let me emphasize that these recommendations have nothing to do with "fashion." What we want to do is point out that your appearance will create an impression on the jury. This impression can be a powerful subliminal motivator and, to the extent that you are aware of it, you can control its impact.

The courtroom, and more importantly the witness box, is not a place to make a fashion statement. A good rule-of-thumb is this: If you feel you look too conservative, you are probably dressed just right. Conservativeness is an inextricably intertwined element of credibility—especially in the area of financial matters. If you doubt the truth of this statement, we suggest you look no further than Wall Street or your local large CPA firm. Most people's mental image of a financial professional conforms to the stereotype of the gray or blue suit, perhaps pinstripe, with a starched white shirt and wingtip shoes.

Anything else connotes an irresponsibility that most people would rather not associate with someone to whom they entrust their fortunes. It is inarguably both an antiquated and an inaccurate stereotype. However, as a professional witness your responsibility is not to change people's stereotypical perceptions. Rather, it is to recognize where they exist, negotiate around them, and persuade people that you are a credible expert. In this case, conservative is as conservative does.

In other fields of expertise, such emphasis on attire might not be nearly as important. For example, if we were discussing a dress code for an accident reconstructionist, there would probably be very little emphasis on attire beyond an exhortation to dress in a professional manner. Their role in the courtroom drama is different, however, from that of the financial expert.

Your role in the eyes of the jury is that of an expert in the area of financial matters, whether you are an actual CPA or merely a highly trained and experienced investigator. The jury must see you as a consummate professional whose opinion is to be given the highest regard. As a practical matter, you can rest assured that the financial professional that the opposition will hire will conform to the jury's stereotypical expectations of a financial professional—even if you don't.

Hand-in-hand with attire goes grooming; our personal grooming habits are a large component of how others perceive us. To that end, a professional witness would do well to visit the barber regularly and maintain a neat and business-like appearance. As with clothing choice, hairstyles are a very personal matter. While we do not propose to tell the reader how to select a hairstyle, we will offer you a few words of advice for choosing from among your options. Outlandish hairstyles suggest unorthodoxy. This in turn detracts from witness credibility in a conservative area such as financial matters.

Similarly, unwashed (or infrequently washed) hair suggests a lack of discipline and poor attention to detail—neither of which you want the jury to infer from your appearance. Undoubtedly, some jurors will perceive a witness groomed in such a manner as being eccentric and perhaps even avant-garde—after all, it worked for Einstein. Whether this is true is immaterial. The truth of the matter is that a courtroom battle between experts is won and lost based solely on the jury's perception of their credibility.

Because credibility and stereotypes play an unavoidable role in the outcome of the case, you must acknowledge them and work within them if you want to win, even if you do not agree with the stereotypes. It is as true inside the walls of the courtroom as it is in life that "you don't get a second chance to make a first impression." The difference is that in life someone's freedom rarely hangs in the balance of your first impression.

Performance as a Component of Testifying Some would argue that performance is an inappropriate topic in courtroom considerations. We disagree, as do many lawyers who have enrolled in college courses and workshops in theater and performance. While the idea of the lawyer as actor seems inherently unethical, you cannot escape the fact that a trial is largely a performance.[28]

In this sense, lawyers are both the directors and actors within this intricate three-act play performed for a captive audience of jurors. Highly successful lawyers try and choreograph the entire process down to the exact phrasing of their closing arguments. From choice of costume to arrangement of witnesses, every litigation-professional stages an elaborate production with one goal in mind—to tell a compelling story. In the end, the critics of this little microdrama are the jurors who offer their "two thumbs up" in the form of a guilty or not-guilty verdict.[29]

Obviously, dishonesty and distortion of the truth are inappropriate within this "theater." The appropriateness of showmanship and staging, however, do not appear to be as clear. Story and theme represent a powerful tool in legal case preparation; why then should the natural extension of this principle not be equally powerful? In short, it is.

As you are preparing your case, you are ultimately scripting a story. Although your involvement in scripting this minidrama ends with presentation to the prosecuting attorney, your role in its production and staging does not.

Once you have completed the investigation and the attorneys take over, you have merely shifted from playwright to actor. The implication of this transition is often lost not only on investigators but also on the attorneys who are running the show. We suggest you remain cognizant of the role that performance plays in presenting the case to the jury.

We should note that performance in no way implies embellishment. In fact, there is very little room for improvisation in the legal arena. Therefore, lest the reader think we advocate playing fast and loose with the facts of the case, we should reiterate that truth, honesty, and integrity are the most important principles in the legal process. To the extent that you can be unwaveringly faithful to them, you should think of how your performance will influence the audience. Although we do not necessarily think a professional witness should take acting lessons, we do think you can benefit from adhering to some of the principles common to great performances. The first and foremost is rehearsal.

REHEARSAL A great actor would never think of stepping on stage without knowing his lines. You should feel the same way. Although memorizing a speech word for word is ill advised, knowing exactly what you are going to say will give you a level of comfort and familiarity with your own words that will convey confidence and credibility to the jury.

A witness's performance consists of essentially two stages: direct examination and cross-examination. There is no reason why a professional witness in an important case cannot be fully prepared for the questions that you will need to answer on direct examination. For that matter, even those questions that you will face on cross-examination are relatively predictable.

BODY LANGUAGE If you appear fidgety, unfocused, and unconvincing, your value as a witness will be negligible. Your tone of voice, choice of words, and extemporaneous movements all feed into the message that you convey. If your body posture or body language overshadows your words, the audience will naturally gravitate toward the more compelling of the two. Distracting movements or poor posture convey a subliminal message to your audience. Which message the audience receives is up to you.

Similarly, eye contact, or lack of it, makes a very real statement about honesty and can either enhance or obscure the importance of your message. As a witness, you should constantly maintain eye contact with the jury. As a cautionary note, there is a vast difference between maintaining nonthreatening eye contact and staring in an obsessive stalker-like manner. Finding a balance between the two comes through practice and experience.

In evaluating and modifying your body language, the first tenet of presentation proves invaluable. As you are rehearsing what you are going to say, you should also rehearse how you are going to say it. This includes not only the body mechanics of your delivery, but also the other nonverbal communications channels such as diction, volume, and emphasis.

Although the words convey the message, how you deliver them injects meaning and shapes their impact. Dry, monotonous delivery is boring, and the jury will soon tune you out. On the other hand, an enthusiastic, inflected delivery with emotion (not overemotion or advocacy) will entrance and capture the jury's imagination and will leave them wanting more. There is no better way to step down from the witness box than feeling as though the jury had lost track of time. In the same way that storytellers strive for a suspension of disbelief, the professional witness should try to suspend time while he is on the stand. The last thing you want a juror to think about is the time. Instead, capture their attention through your delivery. If you do that, they will receive your entire message, and your time on the stand, besides being highly productive, will have a powerful, persuasive effect on them.

In sum, paying close attention to how you testify in addition to content will enhance your value as a professional witness. You can greatly increase your effectiveness as a persuader by paying particular attention to your demeanor, appearance, and performance while on the stand. As we have said, a trial is really a form of performance. As such, how well you play your part influences the critic's opinion of the production. In this case, the critics—the jurors—will weigh in by casting a vote for your version of the performance or that of the opposition. You can tip the scales in favor of your side by knowing your lines, carefully rehearsing your part, and remaining cognizant of the overall impact your part has on the "bigger picture."

CONCLUSION

The investigative efforts you inject into a particular case, though immeasurably important, are of little significance if you cannot put them in front of the jury effectively. This idea of "putting the evidence before the jury" is more than simply taking the stand and reciting a litany of investigative activity. Instead, it is a complex process of capturing both the attention and imagination of the jury and selling them a compelling story.

The process is a complicated tapestry of threads requiring a coordinated effort by the lawyer, the investigator, and all the support staff at both their disposals. As an investigator, it is paramount that you remain aware of your role, of how it intertwines with the role of the lawyer for whom you work and with the other members of the litigation team. Remember that testimony—credible testimony—is the end goal. In order to get there, many technical hurdles must be overcome, only some of which are beyond your control. Once you are there, the impact your testimony has on the jury is entirely within your control. You can influence the outcome significantly by applying common sense coupled with what you have gained from this chapter and this book.

SUGGESTED READINGS

Brinig, B.P., and E. Gladson. *Developing and Managing a Litigation Services Practice*. New York: Harcourt Professional Publishing, 2000.

Bronstein, D.A. *Law for the Expert Witness*. Boca Raton, FL: CRC Press, 1999.

Dessem, R.L. *Pretrial Litigation: Law, Policy and Practice*, 3rd ed. St. Paul, MN: West Publishing, 2001.

Frye v. United States (1923) 293 F. 1013 (D.C. Cir.).

General Electric Co. v. Joiner (1997) 522 U.S. 136.

Graham, M.H. "The Expert Witness Predicament: Determining 'Reliable' under the Gatekeeping Test of Daubert, Kumho, and Proposed Amended Rule 702 of the Federal Rules of Evidence." *University of Miami Law Review*, 54, no. 2 (2000): 317–400.

Haydock, R.S., and D.F. Herr. *Fundamentals of Pretrial Litigation*. Saint Paul, MN: West, 1985.

Mauet, T.A. *Pretrial*. New York: Aspen Law & Business, 2002.

Rodgers, P.A., R.R. Gaughan, and M.J. Trout. *Expert Economic Testimony: Reference Guide for Judges and Attorneys*. New York: Lawyers & Judges Publishing Co., 1998.

Schum, D.A. "Probability and the Processes of Discovery, Proof, and Choice." *Boston Univ. Law Review*, 66 (1986): 825–876.

Yeschke, C.L. *The Art of Investigative Interviewing: A Human Approach to Testimonial Evidence*. Boston, MA: Butterworth-Heinman, 2003.

NOTES

1. T. Anderson and W. Twining, *Analysis of Evidence: How to Do Things with Facts Based on Wigmore's Science of Judicial Proof* (Evanston, IL: Northwestern University Press, 1991), pp. 266–267.

2. Although in reality the terms *casebook* and *trial book* are often used interchangeably, we will reserve the use of the term trial book for those times when we are referring to its use by lawyers. The term casebook will be reserved for those times when we are referring to its application to investigations.

3. The authors claim neither to have invented the notion of the casebook nor to have revolutionized it as a method of organization. Our sole contribution to the field is in applying it to the area of the investigative art.

4. J. Samaha, *Criminal Law*, 8th ed. (Belmont, CA: Thomson Wadsworth, 2005), pp. 283–284.

5. We would like to point out that an entry in the book must appear for the suspect and the victim. In our case, both JoAnn and Frank would be listed in the investigative section with all pertinent information surrounding their involvement.

6. A. Partington, ed., *The Oxford Dictionary of Quotations* (New York: Oxford University Press, 1992), p. 509.

7. C.W. Gerdts III and C.E. Dixon, "The Federal Law Governing Expert Witness Testimony" in R.L. Weil, M.J. Wagner, and P.B. Frank, eds., *Litigation Services Handbook: The Role of the Financial Expert*, 3rd ed. (New York: John Wiley & Sons, 2001), pp. 1–6.

8. Ibid.

9. R. A Gardner, *Testifying in Court* (Cresskill, NJ: Creative Therapeutics, 1995), pp. 111–112.

10. Z. Telpner and M. Mostek, *Expert Witnessing in Forensic Accounting: A Handbook for Lawyers and Accountants* (Boca Raton, FL: CRC Press, 2003), pp. 1–6.

11. Ibid., p. 3.

12. According the case of Brady v. Maryland, 373 U.S. 83 (1967) the prosecution in a criminal case must turn over to the defense all evidence that is either exculpatory or may be valuable for impeachment and is relevant and material to the case. The Jencks Act, requires the prosecution to disclose and turn over any prior statement of a witness relating to the subject matter of that witnesses testimony. Evidence under these two types of evidence are referred to as Brady and Jencks material respectively.

13. R.L. Weil, M.J. Wagner, and P.B. Frank, "The Role of the Financial Expert in Litigation Services," in R.L. Weil, M.J. Wagner, and P.B. Frank, eds. *Litigation Services Handbook*, pp. 9–14.

14. Ibid.

15. Relevance in the context of a deposition has a much broader meaning than at trial. Generally speaking, a question is allowable in a deposition, unless it deals with attorney–client privilege or attorney work product, as long as it is reasonably expected to result in uncovering new information about the case.

16. *Daubert v. Merrill Dow Pharmaceuticals, Inc.*, 509 U.S. 579 (1993); see also C.P. Nemeth, *Law and Evidence: A Primer for Criminal Justice, Criminology, Law and Legal Studies* (Upper Saddle River, NJ: Prentice Hall, 2001), pp. 177–179.

17. Weil, Wagner, and Frank, "The Role of the Financial Expert in Litigation Services," pp. 20–21.

18. See generally, Fed. R. Evid. Sec. 702; see also Nemeth, *Law and Evidence*, p. 181.

19. Weil, Wagner, and Frank, "The Role of the Financial Expert." See also *Daubert v. Merrill Dow Pharmaceuticals, Inc.*

20. *Daubert v. Merrill Dow.*
21. Nemeth, *Law and Evidence*, p. 179.
22. *Kumho Tire Company, Ltd., et al., v. Carmichael, etc., et al.* (1999) 526 U.S. 137; see also Nemeth, *Law and Evidence*, pp. 179–180.
23. Ibid.
24. Nemeth, *Law and Evidence*, pp. 185–189.
25. Telpner and Mostek, "Expert Witnessing in Forensic Accounting," pp. 22–26.
26. Nemeth, *Law and Evidence*, p. 185.
27. Telpner and Mostek, "Expert Witnessing in Forensic Accounting," pp. 7–14.
28. "Learning Acting Techniques for a Real-life Courtroom Drama," *The Washington Post*, July 22, 1991.
29. "Bringing Drama to the Courtroom," *The Christian Science Monitor*, September 20, 1991.

INDEX